Evelyn Everett-Green

A Clerk of Oxford

And his Adventures in the Baron's War

Evelyn Everett-Green

A Clerk of Oxford
And his Adventures in the Baron's War

ISBN/EAN: 9783337341459

Printed in Europe, USA, Canada, Australia, Japan

Cover: Foto ©ninafisch / pixelio.de

More available books at **www.hansebooks.com**

and

His Adventures in the Barons' War

By

E. EVERETT-GREEN

Author of "Shut In," "In Taunton Town," "The Sign of the Red Cross,"
"In the Days of Chivalry," "The Lost Treasure of Trevlyn,"
&c.   &c.

T. NELSON AND SONS

London, Edinburgh, and New York

1898

CONTENTS.

A CLERK OF OXFORD.

CHAPTER I.

THE DIE CAST.

"MY son," spoke a gentle voice from behind the low, moss-grown wall, "we must not mourn and weep for those taken from us, as if we had no hope."

Face downwards upon the newly-made mound of earth lay a youth of some fifteen or sixteen summers. His slight frame was convulsed by the paroxysm of his grief; from time to time a strangled sob broke from his lips. The kindly-faced monk from the Priory hard by had been watching him for some time before he thus addressed him. Probably he now saw that the violence of the outburst was spent.

The youth started upon hearing himself addressed, and as he sprang to his feet he revealed a singularly attractive face. The brow was broad and massive, indicating intellectual power. The blue eyes beneath the pencilled arch of the delicate eyebrows looked out upon the world with a singular directness and purity of expression. The features were finely cut, and there were strength and sweetness both in the curved, thoughtful lips, and in the square outline of the jaw. The fair hair clustered in curling luxuriance about his head, and fell in sunny waves to his shoulders. His hands were long and white, and looked rather as though they had wielded pen than weapon or tool of craftsman. Yet the lad's habit was that of one occupying a humble rank in life, and the shoes on his feet were worn and patched, as though by his own apprentice hands. Beside him lay a wallet and staff, upon which the glance of the monk rested questioningly. The youth appeared to note the glance, yet it was the words addressed to him that he answered.

"I think it is rather for myself I weep, my father. I know that they who die in faith rest in peace and are blessed. But for those who are left—left quite alone—the world is a hard place for them."

Father Ambrose looked with kindly solicitude at the lad. He noted his pale face, his sunken eyes, the look of weary depression that seemed to weigh him down, and he asked gently,—

"What ails thee, Leofric, my son?"

"Everything," answered the youth, with sudden passion in his tones. "I have lost everything in the world that I prized. My father is dead. I have no home. I have no fortune. All that we had is swallowed up in paying for such things as were needful for him while he lay ill. Even that which he saved for masses for his soul had to go at the last. See here, my father, I have but these few silver pieces left in all the world. Take them, and say one mass for him, and let me kneel at the door of the chapel the while. Then will I go forth into the wide world alone, and whether I live or die matters nothing. I have no one in the wide world who will know or care."

But the monk gently put back the extended hand, and laid his own kindly upon the head of the youth.

"Keep thy money, my son. The mass shall be said— ay, and more than one—for the repose of thy father's soul. He was a good man and true, and I loved him well. That pious office I will willingly perform in memory of our friendship. But now, as to thyself. Whither goest thou, and what wilt thou do? I had thought that thou wouldst have come to me ere thou didst sally forth into the wide world alone."

There was a faint accent of reproach in the monk's voice, and Leofric's sensitive face coloured instantly.

"Think it not ingratitude on my part, my father," he said quickly. "I was coming to say good-bye. But that seems now the only word left to me to speak in this world."

"Wherefore so, my son? why this haste to depart? The old life has indeed closed for thee; but there may be bright days in store for thee yet. Whither art thou going in such hot haste?"

"I must e'en go where I can earn a living," answered Leofric, "and that must be by the work of mine own hands. I shall find my way to some town, and seek to apprentice myself to some craft. These hands must learn

to wield axe or hammer or mallet. There is nothing else
left for the son of a poor scholar, who could scarce earn
enough himself to feed the pair of us."

Father Ambrose looked at the lad's white fingers, and
he slightly shook his head.

"Methinks thou couldst do better with those hands,
Leofric. Hast never thought of what I have sometimes
spoken to thee, when thou hast been aiding me with the
care of the parchments?"

The lad's face flushed again quickly; but his eyes met
the gaze fastened upon his with the fearless openness
which was one of their characteristics.

"My father, I could not be a monk," he said. "I have
no call—no vocation."

"Yet thou dost love a quiet life of meditation? Thou
dost love learning, and hast no small store for thy years.
It is a beautiful and peaceful life for those who would
fain flee from the trials and temptations of the world.
And the Prior here thinks well of thee; he has never
grudged the time I have spent upon thee. I shall miss
thee when thou art gone, Leofric; life here is something
too calm and same."

There was a touch of wistful regret in the father's tones
which brought back the ready tears to Leofric's eyes.
After his own father, he owed most to this kindly old
monk, though it had never for a moment struck him that
the teaching and training of a bright young lad had been
one of the main interests in that monotonous existence.

"That is what I have felt myself," he answered quickly.

"I love the calm and the quiet, the books and the parch-ments. I shall bless you every day of my life for all your goodness to me. But I would fain see the great world too. I have heard my father and others speak of things I would fain see with mine own eyes. It breaks my heart to go, yet I cannot choose but do so. I dare not ask to come to you, my kindest friend, my second father. I could not be a monk. I should but deceive and disappoint you were I to seek an asylum with you now."

Father Ambrose sighed slightly as he shook his head; but he made no attempt to influence the youth. Perhaps he loved him too well to press him to enter upon a life which had so many limitations and drawbacks.

Yet he would not let him go forth upon his travels with so small a notion of what lay before him. He led him into the refectory, where strangers were entertained, and had food brought and set before him. The lad was hungry, for he had of late undergone a very consider-able mental strain, and had had little enough time or thought to spare for creature comforts. The long illness of his father, a man gently born, but of very narrow means, had completely worn him out in body and mind; and now, when thrown penniless upon the world, there had seemed nothing before him but to wander forth with wallet and staff, and seek some craftsman who would give him food and shelter whilst he served a long and perhaps hard apprenticeship to whatever trade he chanced upon.

He spoke again of this as he sat in the refectory, and again Father Ambrose shook his head.

"Thou art not of the stuff for an apprentice to some harsh master; thou hast done but little hard work. And think of thy skill with brush and pen, and thy knowledge of Latin and the Holy Scriptures; thy sweet voice, and thy skill upon the lute. What will all these serve thee, if thou dost waste thy years of manhood's prime at carpenter's bench or blacksmith's forge?"

Leofric sighed, and asked wistfully, —

"Yet what else can I do, my father?"

"Hast ever thought of Oxford?" asked Father Ambrose, rubbing his chin reflectively. "There be lads as poor as thou that beg their way thither and live there as clerks, being helped thereto by the gifts of pious benefactors. They say that the King's Majesty greatly favours students and clerks, and that a lad who can sing a roundelay or turn an epigram can earn for himself enough to keep him whilst he wins his way to some honourable post. Hast ever thought of the University, lad? that were a better place for thee than a craftsman's shop."

Leofric's eyes brightened slowly whilst the monk spoke. Such an idea as this had never crossed his mind heretofore. Living far away from Oxford, and hearing nothing of the life there, he had never once thought of that as a possible asylum for himself; but in a moment it seemed to him that this was just the chance he had been longing for. He could not bring his mind to the thought of the life of the cloister; yet he loved learning and the fine arts with a passionate love, and had received just enough training to make him ardently desire more.

" Would such a thing as that be possible for such as I, my father ? " he asked with bated breath, seeming to hang upon the monk's lips as he waited for the answer.

" More than possible—advisable, reasonable," answered another voice from the shadows of the room. Leofric started to his feet and bent the knee instinctively; for, unseen to both himself and Father Ambrose, the Prior had entered, and had plainly heard the last words which had passed between the pair.

The Prior was a tall, venerable man, with eagle eye and an air of extreme dignity; but he was kindly disposed towards Leofric, and greeted him gently and tenderly, speaking for a few minutes of his recent heavy loss, and then resuming the former subject.

" Oxford is the place where lads such as thou do congregate together in its many schools and buildings, and learn from the lips of the instructed and wise the lore of the ancients and the wisdom of the sages. There be many masters and doctors there who began life as poor clerks, begging alms as they went. What one man has done another may attempt. Thou mayest yet be a worthy clerk, and rise to fame and learning."

" Without money ? " asked Leofric, whose eyes began to sparkle and glow.

" Yes, even without money," answered the Prior : " for at Oxford there are monasteries and abbeys to each of which is attached a Domus Dei ; and there are gathered together poor clerks and other indigent persons, to whom an allowance of daily food is made from the monks' table; whilst, through the liberality of benefactors, a habit is supplied to them yearly, together with such things as be absolutely needful for their support. Once was I the guest of the Abbot of Osney, and I remember visiting the Domus Dei, and seeing the portions of meat sent thither from the refectory. I will give thee a letter of recommendation to him, good lad. It may be that this will serve thee in some sort upon thy arrival."

Leofric bent the knee once more in token of the gratitude his faltering lips could scarce pronounce. The thought of a life of study, in lieu of that of an apprentice, was like nectar to him. Prior and Father alike smiled at his boyish but genuine rapture.

"Yet think not, my son, that the life will be free from many a hardship, to a poor clerk without means and without friends. There be many wild and turbulent spirits pent within the walls of Oxford. Men have lost life and limb ere now in those brawls which so often arise 'twixt townsmen and clerks. The Chancellor doth all he can to protect the lives of scholars and clerks; yet, do as he will, troubles ofttime arise, and men have ere this been forced to leave the place by hundreds till the turbulent citizens can be brought to reason and submission."

But Leofric was in nowise daunted by this aspect of the case. Trained up hardily, albeit of studious habits, the fear of hardships did not daunt him.

"So long as I have food to eat and raiment to wear, I

care for no hardship, so as I may become a scholar," he
said. "And can I, reverend Father, rise to the dignity of
a master, if I do not likewise take the vows of the Church
upon me?"

"Ay, truly thou canst," was the reply. "There are the
scholastic *Trivium* of grammar, logic, rhetoric, and the
mathematical *Quadrivium* of arithmetic, geometry, astronomy, and music. These form the magic circle of the arts,
of which thou mayest become a master without taking any
vow to Holy Church. Yet methinks thou wouldest do well
to wear the tonsure and the gown, that thou mayest in all
quarrels or troubles have the right to claim the benefit of
clergy, and so escape from the secular arm if it were
stretched out against thee. This is the usual custom of
clerks at Oxford and Cambridge. But it commits thee to
nought, if thou art not willing to join thyself to any of our
brotherhoods."

The Prior eyed him kindly, but Father Ambrose sighed,
and Leofric himself felt a qualm of shame at his own dis-
taste for the life of the cloister.

"The wish, the call, may come perchance," he answered
humbly, glancing from one to the other; "but methinks I
am not fit for the life of holy meditation, or surely the
kindness I have here received would have inclined mine
heart that way."

"Thou art still too young to take such vows upon thyself," said the Prior. "It is men who come to us aweary
of the evils and strife of the world that know the blessed-
ness of the cloistered life. Thou mayest learn that lesson

in time; or thou mayest link thy lot with that of these wandering friars, who teach men that they have found the more acceptable way. For myself, I have found the place of rest, and I desire to end my days here in peace."

"And how may I journey from here to Oxford?" asked Leofric with some timidity, after a short silence. "Surely the way is long; and I have never fared farther than Coventry, which place I thought to make my home, if I could but find a master who would receive me as apprentice."

The Prior pondered awhile before replying.

"There be two ways of journeying—by land and by water," he replied; "if by land, thou wouldest have to beg thy way from place to place. At some hostel they would give thee bed and board, most like, if thou wouldest make them merry by a song; or at some great house, if thou couldst recite a ballad or speak a Latin grace. At the Monasteries thou wouldest receive food and bed, and mayhap an alms to help thee on thy way. Many a clerk begs his way to Oxford year by year, and is well received of all. Yet the perils of the way are many and great through the forests which lie betwixt thee and thy goal. It might be that the water way would be the better."

"I love the water," said Leofric eagerly; "and my little canoe lies beneath the bank under the alder clump. I have made many a miniature voyage in her before. Methinks she would carry me safely did I but know the way."

"And the way thou canst not miss," answered the Prior.

"This little stream which flows past our walls joins itself, as thou dost know, to the wider Avon, which presently flows into a river men call the Cherwell, and in its turn that doth make junction with the Isis, whereon the town of Oxford is situate. This junction is hard by the town itself; when thou dost reach that, thy journey will have an end."

Leofric listened eagerly. He had heard, indeed, of these things, but hitherto they had been but names to him. Now it seemed as though the great unknown world, lying without the circle of his daily life, were about to open before him.

"I would fain try the water way," he said. "I am skilful with the paddle; and I can carry my little craft upon my back whenever rocks and rapids impede my progress. The season is favourable for the journey. The ice and snow are gone. There is a good depth of water in all the streams, and yet the weed and slime of summer and autumn have not begun to appear; nor will the overarching boughs from the trees hinder progress as they do when clad in their summer bravery. I love the river in the early spring, and if I do but follow the course of the stream I cannot miss my way, as I might well do upon the road in the great forest tracks."

"Yes, that is very true. Methinks thou wilt be safer so, if thou canst find sustenance upon the way. But thou canst carry with thee some provision of bread, and there be several godly houses beside the river where thou wilt be welcomed by the brothers, who will supply thy needs.

Take, too, thy bow and arrows; thou wilt doubtless thus secure some game by the way. But have a care in the King's forests around Oxford how thou dost let fly thy shafts. Many a man has lost his life ere now for piercing the side of some fat buck."

Leofric's heart was now all on fire for the journey which lay before him. He could scarcely believe that but one short hour ago he had believed himself hopelessly doomed to a life of uncongenial toil. He had never thought of this student life—he hardly knew of its existence; but the Prior of the Monastery and some of the monks, who had known and befriended both Leofric and his father, had themselves discussed several times the question of dispatching the youth to Oxford for tuition; and the rather unexpected death of the father, after a lingering illness, seemed to open the way for the furtherance of this design.

Leofric had been the pet of the Monastery from his childhood. Always of a studious turn, and eager for information, it had been the favourite relaxation of several of the monks to instruct him in the Latin tongue, to teach him the art of penmanship, and even to initiate him into some of the mysteries of that wonderful illumination of parchments which was the secret of the monks in the Middle Ages.

Leofric profited by every opportunity afforded him. Already he could both speak and understand Latin easily. He had a very fair knowledge of certain portions of the Scriptures, and possessed a breviary of his own, which he

regarded as his greatest treasure. For the age in which
he lived these were accomplishments of no mean order, and
it would have seemed to the ecclesiastics little short of a
disgrace to them had they permitted their pupil to lose
his scholarship in some craftsman's shop. They had frequently spoken of sending him as a clerk to Oxford, unless
he could see his way to becoming one of themselves. This,
however, was not to be. The boy, though reverent and
devout, had no leanings after the life of the cloister, and
the Prior was too wise a man to put pressure upon him.
But he was willing to forward, by such means as he could,
any project which should secure to Leofric the advantages
of a liberal education.

So the lad was bidden to remain a guest of the Monastery for the few days necessary to his simple preparations.
The Prior wished him to be provided with a habit suitable
to his condition of clerk. This habit was made of a strong
sort of cloth, and reached to the knees, being confined at
the waist by a leather girdle. He was also provided with
a change of under-raiment, with strong leggings and shoes,
and with a supply of coarse bread and salted meat sufficient for several days. The Prior wrote a letter to the
Abbot of Osney, recommending the lad to his favourable
notice, and asking for him a place in the Domus Dei,
should no better lodging be obtainable.

Leofric himself spent his time in the mending of his
canoe, which had been somewhat battered by the winter
storms. He had made the little craft out of the bark of
trees, and had covered it with pitch to make it waterproof.

Some story he had heard about wild men in unknown lands had given him the idea of constructing this little boat, and now it seemed as though it would be of real service to him in his new career.

Father Ambrose would sit beside him on the river bank, and talk to him as he prosecuted this task. There was a strong bond of affection between the old monk and the young lad.

"Thou wilt come back some day and see us, Leofric," he said once, as the task drew near to its accomplishment; "I would fain look again upon thy face before I die."

"Indeed I will, father. I too shall always love this place, and shall never forget the kindness I have received, nor how these many days masses have been said for my father, and never a penny paid by me, albeit I would gladly give my all."

"Nay, nay, boy, it is a labour of love; and we know that thou wilt some day, when thou art rich and famous, give of thine abundance to our shrine here. Thou wilt see strange things in the great world, my son. Thou wilt see the great ones of the earth rising up against their anointed King, and that King taking vows upon his lips which he has neither the wish nor the intention to fulfil. The world is full of terrible things, and thou wilt quickly see many of them. Yet keep through all a pure heart and clean hands, so will God love thee, be thy path what it will."

Leofric looked up quickly.

"I have heard somewhat from time to time of the feud

betwixt the King and the Barons; but to me such tales
are but as idle words. I know not what men mean."

"Thou wilt know more anon," answered the monk
gravely. "We have heard from those who pass to and
fro that times are dangerous, and men's minds full of
doubt and fear. I know not what may betide this land,
but there be those who say that the sword will ere long
be unsheathed, and that brother will war against brother
as it hath not been seen for many a long day. God forbid that such things should be!"

"And will such strife come nigh to Oxford?" asked
Leofric. "Shall we hear ought there of the battle and the
turmoil?"

"I trow well that ye will. Knowest thou not that the
King hath a palace close by the walls of the city, and
another but a few leagues away? Methinks that in yon
city there will be much strife of tongues anent these burning questions of which we scarce hear a whisper. Thou
must seek to be guided aright, my son; for youth is ever
hot-headed, and like to be carried away by rash counsels.
It is a grievous thing for a nation to rise against its
anointed head; and yet, even as Saul was set aside by
God, and another put in his place, we may not always say
that a King can do no wrong—albeit we must be very
slow to judge and condemn him."

Leofric listened eagerly. Every day of late he had heard
words which roused within him the knowledge that beyond
the peaceful circle of his past life lay a seething world
into which he was shortly to plunge. The thought filled

him with eager longings and desires. He wanted to shoot forth in his tiny craft and see this world for himself. And, behold, to-day his task was finished, and the Prior had ordained that at dawn upon the morrow he should go.

His habit and provision were already packed and stowed away. He had received his letter and messages, and had listened in meek silence to the admonitions and instructions of the Prior. He had slept his last night beneath the hospitable Monastery roof, and had heard mass for the last time in the grey dawning.

Now he stood with one foot in his little craft, pressing the hand of Father Ambrose, and looking round at the familiar faces and buildings with smiles and tears struggling for mastery in his face.

Then the canoe shot out into the midst of the stream.

His voyage was begun.

CHAPTER II.

A RIVER JOURNEY.

IT was no light task that Leofric had set himself. The river wound in and out through forest tracts hardly ever traversed. Trees blown down in winter storms lay right athwart the stream. *Débris* brought down from above was often packed tight against such obstructions; and then there was no way of proceeding save by dragging up the canoe out of the water and launching it again lower down. As the forest was often very thick and tangled along the banks of the river, this was no light matter, and had Leofric not been gifted with a strong will and a very resolute purpose, he might well have given up in despair.

As it was, he found travelling a great deal slower work than he had anticipated, and already his store of provision was greatly diminished, although he could not flatter himself that he had travelled any very great distance. He was sometimes disposed to doubt whether, after all, he had been wise in choosing the waterway in preference to the road.

Night was falling, and it looked as though rain was likely to come on at moonrise. The clouds were sullen and lowering; the wind moaned and whistled through the trees, and lashed the water into angry little wavelets. Leofric was feeling weary and a little depressed by the intense loneliness of his voyage, when suddenly he heard himself hailed by a friendly voice from somewhere out of the thicket.

"Whither away, good friend, and why art thou afloat and alone at this hour of the evening? What dost thou in yon frail craft out on the darkling river?"

Leofric looked eagerly about him, and espied, not far away, a ruddy-faced youth of about his own age, sitting beside the water fishing, with a basket at his side that showed he had not thus sat in vain. With a few strokes of his paddle he brought himself alongside the bank. The sound of a human voice was as music to his ears after the long silence of the forest.

"Good-even, good comrade," he answered, stepping lightly ashore; "and welcome indeed is thy friendly voice. For four days have I been alone upon this river, and the sight of a kindly face is like a draught of new wine."

"But what dost thou alone upon the river?"

"Marry, that is soon told. I am a poor lad who would fain become a clerk, and I am on my way to Oxford, there to seek to maintain myself whilst I study the arts and win my way to a livelihood—"

Hardly had he got out these words before the other youth sprang to his feet with a whoop of joy, and to Leofric's astonishment flung his arms about his neck, and fairly danced in the exuberance of his delight.

"Now, what ails thee?" he asked, half amused, half bewildered. "Hast thou taken leave of thy senses, good friend?"

"Thou mayest well ask—methinks it must even seem so; but listen, fair youth, and soon shalt thou understand. I am the son of a farmer, but I, too, have a great longing after letters. I have heard of this same city of learning, and I have begged and prayed of my father, who has many other sons, to let me fare forth and find my way thither, and climb the tree of learning. At first he listened not, but laughed aloud, as did my brothers. But my mother took my part, and I learned to read last winter at the Monastery, and the kindly fathers spoke well of my progress. Through these winter days I have gone daily thither, taking an offering of fish, and receiving instruction from them—"

"That is how I obtained such learning as I possess," interposed Leofric eagerly; "and my father taught me too, for he was a scholar of no mean attainments. But it is the monks who possess the books and parchments."

"Yea, verily; and these last weeks I have mastered in some poor sort the art of penmanship. And now my father has almost consented to letting me go. Only he has said that I must wait until chance shall send me a companion for the way. From time to time there pass by clerks and scholars returning to Oxford after an absence, or making their way thither, even as thou art doing; and my father has promised that I may join myself to the next of these who shall pass by. Now thou dost understand why I did so embrace thee. For if thou wilt have me for a travelling companion, we may e'en start forth to-morrow, and find ourselves in Oxford ere another week be passed."

No proposition could have been more welcome to Leofric. He had had enough of loneliness, and this sturdy farmer's son would be the best possible comrade for him. He was delighted at the notion. His canoe would carry the double burden, and the fatigues of navigation would be greatly lessened when shared between two.

"Come up to the farm with me," cried his new friend, "and there will be bed and board and a hearty welcome for thee; thou shalt find there a better lodging than in some hollow tree by the river-banks; and my mother will give us provision enow ere we start forth upon our voyage to-morrow."

Leofric was grateful indeed for this invitation. He made fast his canoe, saw that his few possessions were safely protected from a possible wetting, and followed his new friend along the narrow winding track which led from the river-side to the clearing round the farmstead.

On the way he learned that his companion's name was John Dugdale—commonly called Jack. The farm where he had lived all his life was situated not more than five miles from the town of Banbury. Jack had plainly heard more of the news of the world than had reached Leofric in his quiet home on the upper river. Something of the stir and strife that was agitating the kingdom had penetrated even to this lonely farm.

The great Earl of Leicester, Simon de Montfort, had

passed through Banbury on his way from Kenilworth to London, not long ago. There was a great stir amongst the people, Jack told Leofric, and men spoke of the Earl as a saviour and deliverer, and he was received with something very like royal honours when he appeared. Leofric asked what it was from which he was to deliver the people, and Jack was not altogether clear as to this; but it had something to do with the exactions of the King and the Pope; and he was almost certain that the clergy themselves were as angry with the King as the Barons could be. He had heard it said that half the revenue of the realm was being taken to enrich the coffers of the Pope, or to aid him in his wars. More than that Jack could not say, rumours of so many kinds being afloat.

"But let us once get to Oxford, good comrade, and we shall soon learn all this, and many another thing besides. I want to know what the world is saying and thinking. I am weary of being stranded here like a leaf that has floated into some backwater and cannot find the channel again. I want to know these things; and if there be stirring times to come for this land, as many men say there will, I would be in the forefront of it all. I would wield the sword as well as the pen."

This was a new idea to Leofric, who had contented himself hitherto with dreams of scholastic distinction, without considering those other matters which were exercising the ruling spirits of his day. Jack's words, however, brought home to him the consciousness that there would be other matters of interest to engross him, once let him enter upon the life of a rising city. Oxford could not but be a centre of vitality for the whole kingdom. Once let him win his way within those walls, and a new world would open before his eyes.

Talking eagerly together, the lads pursued their way through the forest path, and suddenly emerged upon the clearing where the farmhouse stood. Lights shone hospitably from door and window; a barking of dogs gave a welcome to the son of the house; and Leofric speedily found himself pushed within a great raftered kitchen, lighted by the blaze of a goodly fire of logs, where he was quickly surrounded by friendly faces, and welcomed heartily, even before Jack had told all his tale and explained who the stranger was.

The Dugdales were honest farmer folks, always glad to welcome a passing stranger, and to hear any item of news he might come furnished with. Leofric had little enough of this commodity; but the fact that he was making his way to Oxford as a prospective clerk there was a matter of much interest to this household. Farmer Dugdale was a man of his word. He had promised Jack to let him go so soon as he should find a companion to travel with. He would have preferred as companion one who had had previous experience of University life: but he would not go back on his word on that account. Leofric's handsome and open face and winning manner gained him the goodwill of all at the farm: they pressed him to remain their guest for a few days, whilst Jack's mother made her simple preparations for sending out her boy into the world for an indefinite time, and the two companions learned to know each other better.

Leofric was willing enough to do this. He was very happy amongst these hearty, homely people, and became attached to all of them, especially to Jack. Together they strengthened the canoe, made a locker in which to stow away sufficient provision for the journey, and a second paddle for Jack to wield, which he quickly learned to do with skill and address.

Jack's mother took Leofric to her motherly heart at once, and she made sundry additions to his scanty stock of clothing, seeing that his equipment equalled that of her own son. It was little enough when all was said and done; for times were simple, and luxuries unknown and undreamed of, save in the houses of great nobles. The boys felt rich indeed as they beheld their outfits made ready for them, and there was quite a feast held in their honour upon the last evening ere they launched forth upon their long journey.

Happy as Leofric had been at the farm, he was still conscious of a thrill of pleasure when he and Jack dipped their paddles and set forth upon their journey together. The Dugdale family, assembled on the banks, gave them a hearty cheer. They answered by an eager hurrah, and then, shooting round a bend in the stream, they found themselves alone on the sparkling waterway.

To Leofric this voyage was very different from the last. There were the same obstacles and difficulties to be overcome, but these seemed small now that they were shared between

two. Jack was strong, patient, and merry. He made light
of troubles and laughed at mishaps. They fared sumptu-
ously from the well-stocked larder of the farm, and the
weather was warm and sunny. To make a bed of leaves
in some hollow tree, and bathe in the clear, cold river on
awaking, was no hardship to either lad. They declared
they did not mind how long the journey lasted, save for
the natural impatience of youth to arrive at a given destination.

"And I should like an adventure," quoth Jack, "ere we
sight the walls and towers of Oxford Castle. Men talk of
the perils of travel; but, certes, we have seen nothing of
them. I've had more adventure tackling a great pike in
the stream at home sometimes than we have seen so far."

Nevertheless Jack was to have his wish, and the travellers were to meet with an adventure before they reached
their journey's end.

It came about in this wise.

They knew that they must be drawing near their
journey's end. They had been told by a woodman, whose
hut had given them shelter upon the last night, that the
forest and palace of Woodstock were near at hand. They
wanted to get a view of that royal residence. So upon
the day following they halted soon after mid-day, and
leaving their canoe securely hidden in some drooping alder
bushes, they struck away along a forest track described to
them by the woodman, which would, if rightly followed,
conduct them to a hill from whence a view could be
obtained of the palace.

Walking was tedious and difficult, and they often lost their way in the intricacies of the forest; but still they persevered, and were rewarded at last by a partial view of the place, which was a finer building than either of the lads had ever seen before. But the sun was getting low in the sky by this time, and they had still to make their way back to their boat, unless they were to sleep supperless in the forest; so they did not linger long upon the brow of the hill, but quickly retraced their steps through the forest, trying to keep at least in the right direction, even though they might miss the actual path by which they had come.

Suddenly they became aware of a tumult going on in a thicket not very far away. They heard the sound of blows, of cries and shouts—then of oaths and more blows. Plainly there was a fight going on somewhere close at hand, and equally plain was it that travellers were being robbed and maltreated by some forest ruffians, of whom there were always a number in all the royal forests, where fat bucks might chance to be shot, undetected by the king's hunstmen.

The lads had both cut themselves stout staffs to beat down the obstructions in the path. Now they grasped their cudgels tightly in their hands and looked at each other.

"Let us to the rescue!" quoth Jack, between his clenched teeth. "I can never hear the sound of blows without longing to be in the thick of the fray. Like enough in the gathering shades the assailants will think we be a larger party, and will make off. Be that as it may, let us lend our aid whilst it may serve those in distress."

Leofric nodded, grasping his staff firmly in his hand. He had all the courage of a highly-strung nature, even if he lacked Jack's physical vigour.

Springing through the leafy glades of the forest, they soon came upon the scene of the encounter, and easy was it to see that robbery and spoliation was the object of the attack.

Four stalwart young men, wild and dishevelled of aspect, armed with stout cudgels and bows and arrows, had set upon two travellers, whose clothes denoted them to be men of substance. They had been overpowered by their assailants, though plainly not till a severe struggle had taken place. Both were now lying upon the ground, overmastered each by a pair of strong knaves; and in spite of their cries and struggles, it was plain that these sturdy robbers were rifling them of such valuables as they possessed.

Jack took in the situation at a glance. With a yell of defiance he sprang upon the nearest rogue, and hurled him backwards with such right good will that he reeled heavily against a tree trunk, and fell prostrate, half stunned. In a second the traveller had wrenched himself free from the other assailant, and had dealt him such a sounding blow across the pate (he having laid aside his stick in order the better to plunder) that he measured his length upon the turf, and lay motionless; whilst the other pair of bandits, who had been belaboured by Leofric, seeing that they were now overpowered and in no small danger of capture, flung down their booty and made off to the woods, dragging their helpless comrade with them.

It was no part of the travellers' plan to take into custody these knaves, and they made no attempt to detain them, glad enough to see them make off in the darkening forest. But they turned to their preservers with words of warm gratitude, and showed how narrowly they had escaped being mulcted of rather large sums of money; for one had a belt into which many broad gold pieces had been sewn, and the purse of the other was heavy and well plenished.

"We are travelling to Oxford," said he of the belt. "We joined for a time the convoy of one of the 'fetchers,' conveying young lads and poor clerks thither. But as we neared the place we grew impatient at the thought of another night's halt, and thought we would strike across the forest ourselves, and reach our goal soon after sundown. But we missed our way, and these fellows set upon us. It is a trade with some lewd fellows calling themselves clerks, and often pleading benefit of clergy if caught, to infest these woods, and fall upon scholars returning to the University, and rob them of such moneys as they bear upon their persons."

Leofric's eyes were wide with amaze.

"Surely those fellows were not clerks from Oxford?"

"Like enow they were. There be a strange medley of folks calling themselves by that name that frequent the streets and lanes of the city, or congregate without the walls in hovels and booths. Some of these, having neither

means to live nor such characters as render them fit subjects to be helped from any of the chests, take to the woods
for a livelihood, shooting the King's bucks or falling un-
awares upon travellers. Some clerks run to the woods for
refuge after some wild outbreak of lawlessness. There be
many wild, lawless knaves habited in the gown of the clerk
and wearing the tonsure. Are ye twain from Oxford yourselves, or bound thither, since ye seem little acquaint with
the ways of the place?"

Explanations were quickly made, and the two elder
youths, who might have been eighteen and nineteen years
old perhaps, suggested that they should finish the journey
together on foot, lading themselves with the contents of the
canoe, but leaving it behind in the alders, to be fetched
away some other time if wanted. They were near to the
river by this time, and the lads quickly fetched their goods,
glad enough to travel into the city in company with
two comrades who plainly knew the place and the life
right well.

They were very open about themselves. The name of
one was Hugh le Barbier, and he was the son of an esquire
who held a post in the house of one of the retainers of
the Earl of Leicester—"the great De Montfort," as the
youth proudly dubbed him. His companion was Gilbert
Barbeck, son of a rich merchant. His home was in the
south of England, but he had been travelling with Hugh,
during an interlude in their studies. In those days regular
vacations were unknown. Men might stay for years at the
University, hearing lectures all the time through; or they

might betake themselves elsewhere, and return again and resume their studies, without reproof. The collegiate system was as yet unknown, though its infancy dates from a period only a little later. But there was a Chancellor of the University (if such it could be called), and learned men from all lands had congregated there; lectures in Arts and also in the sciences were regularly given, and degrees could be taken by those who could satisfy the authorities that they had been through the appointed courses of lectures, and were competent in their turn to teach.

The religious houses had been the pioneers in this movement, but now there was a reaction in favour of more secular teaching. The monks had some ado to hold their own, and obtain as many privileges as were accorded to others; and friction was constantly arising.

Moreover the recent migration of friars to Oxford had struck another blow at the older monastic system. The personal sanctity of many of these men, their self-denying life, their powers of preaching, the strictness with which they kept their vows, all served to produce a deep impression upon the minds of those who had grown weary of the arrogance of the Priors and Abbots.

The Grey Friars in particular, followers of St. Francis, were universally beloved and esteemed. They went about barefoot; they would scarce receive alms in money; their buildings were of the poorest and roughest, and were situated in the lowest parts of the town. They busied themselves amongst the sick and destitute; they lived lives of self-denial and toil. The favour of princes had not corrupted them, and the highest powers of the land spoke well of them.

Hugh told all this to his comrades as they walked through the darkening forest. He was plainly a youth of good parts and gentle blood, and he seemed taken by Leofric's refined appearance and thoughtful face.

"I would not go to Osney, or live in the Domus Dei there," he said. "Thou hast saved me the loss of all my wealth; it would go hard if thou wouldst not accept the loan of a few gold pieces, enough to establish thyself in some modest lodging in the town, or even in one of the empty niches upon the walls, where clerks have made shift to dwell ere now. Out beyond the walls, shut up on the island of Osney, away from all the bustle and roistering and tumult of the town, it scarce seems life at all; and methinks the monks will get hold of thee, and win thee to be one of themselves. Better, far better, be one of us in the town. Then wilt thou see all that is to be seen, and learn far more, too, than thou wilt in the schools of the monks."

Leofric listened eagerly to this advice.

"Is Osney then without the walls?"

"Ay verily, on one of the many islands that the river makes in its windings. Oxford itself is little more than an island, for that matter, since the city ditch has been dug on the north side of it. But within the city there is life and stir and stress, and all the Halls where the students lodge are there, and the lodgings amongst the townsfolks which some prefer. Come and belong to us, not to the monks.

So wilt thou learn the more, and enjoy life as thou couldst not do cooped up on yon damp island in the Domus Dei."

"I would fain do so," answered Leofric readily. "I have no desire for a monkish life. I would see what life is like without the cloister wall. But I have little money; I love not debts—"

"Tush! be not over scrupulous. Thou hast done me one good turn; I claim right to do thee another. Now no more of that. Let us put our best foot forward; for it will be dark ere we reach our destination. Perchance we may yet have to camp once more in the woods; for if the city gates be locked, we may have some trouble in getting admitted. The townsmen, albeit they live and thrive by them, love not the clerks. They will do us a bad turn an they can; yet methinks we are even with them, take one thing with another!"

Hugh showed his teeth in a flashing smile, and Gilbert laughed aloud. Then the party strode on through the darkness, till they paused by common consent to light a fire and camp for the night in company—it being plain by this time that they could not enter Oxford that night.

CHAPTER III.

OLD OXFORD.

WITH glowing cheeks and beating hearts, Leofric Wyvill and Jack Dugdale beheld the walls of Oxford towering above them in the clear morning sunlight.

For many long hours during the previous night had the four travellers sat over their camp fire, listening and telling of the life of the mediaeval University city. Already Leofric and Jack felt a thrill of pride in the thought that they were to be numbered amongst its sons; already they had well-nigh made up their minds that they would set up together in some nook or turret in the city walls, make a sort of eyry there for themselves, and live frugally upon the small sum of money they possessed, until they were able to earn something towards their own maintenance, or could borrow from one of the " chests" provided for the benefit of poor students.

Hugh had carried his point, and Leofric's purse now held a few gold pieces as well as his own small store of silver. By the exercise of economy the two friends would be able to live in modest comfort for a considerable time, and Leofric, at least, hoped before long to earn money by his penmanship and talent in illuminating parchments.

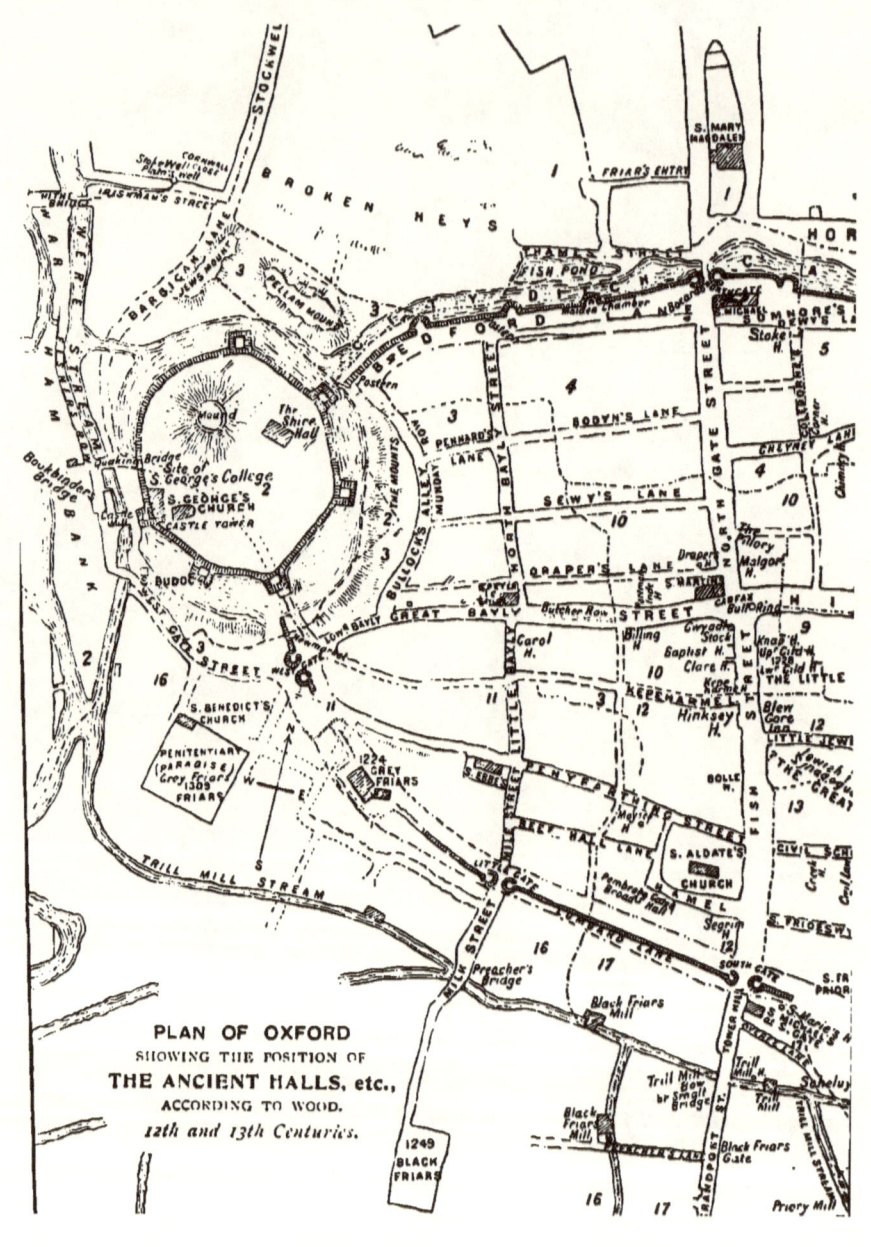

PLAN OF OXFORD
SHOWING THE POSITION OF
THE ANCIENT HALLS, etc.,
ACCORDING TO WOOD.
12th and 13th Centuries.

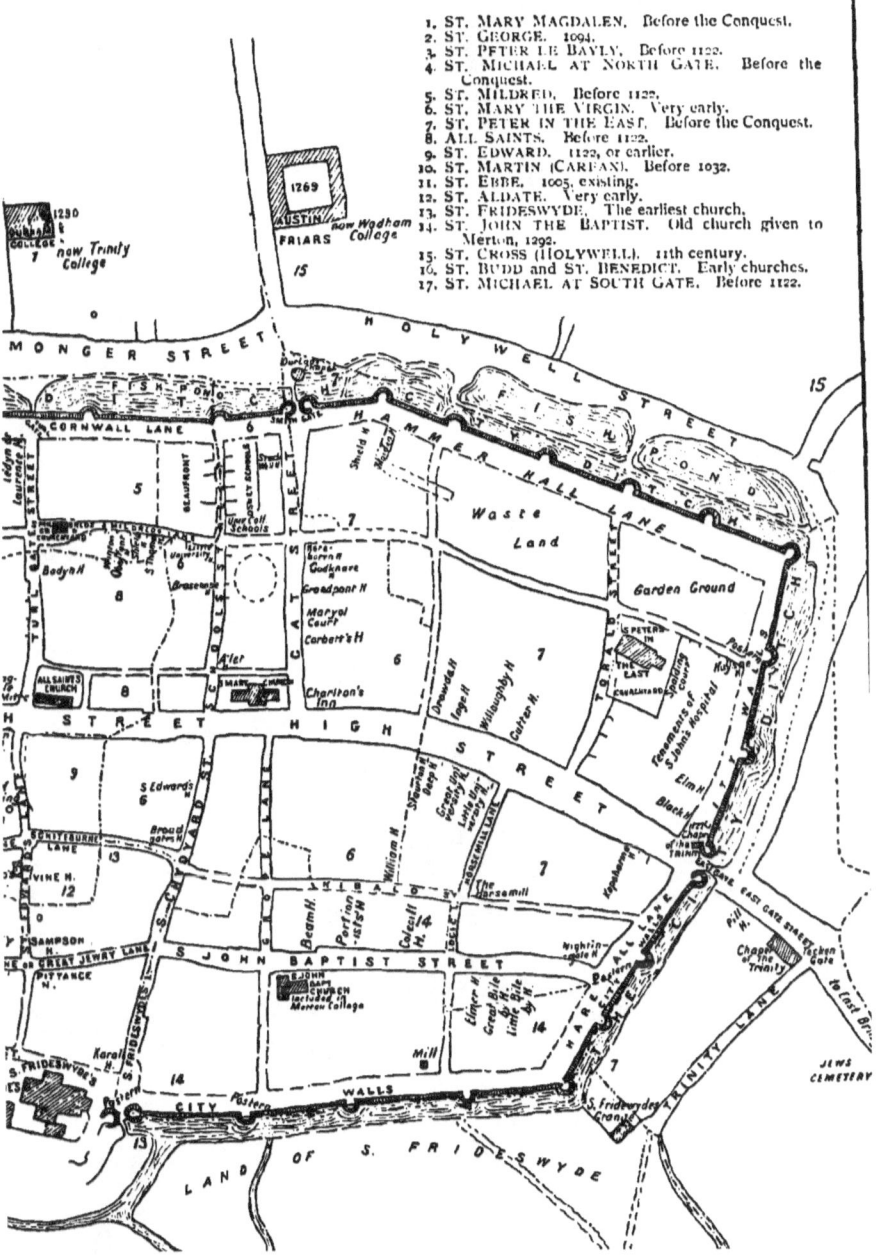

PARISHES.

1. ST. MARY MAGDALEN. Before the Conquest.
2. ST. GEORGE. 1094.
3. ST. PETER LE BAYLY. Before 1122.
4. ST. MICHAEL AT NORTH GATE. Before the Conquest.
5. ST. MILDRED. Before 1122.
6. ST. MARY THE VIRGIN. Very early.
7. ST. PETER IN THE EAST. Before the Conquest.
8. ALL SAINTS. Before 1122.
9. ST. EDWARD. 1122, or earlier.
10. ST. MARTIN (CARFAX). Before 1032.
11. ST. EBBE. 1005, existing.
12. ST. ALDATE. Very early.
13. ST. FRIDESWYDE. The earliest church.
14. ST. JOHN THE BAPTIST. Old church given to Merton, 1292.
15. ST. CROSS (HOLYWELL). 11th century.
16. ST. BUDD and ST. BENEDICT. Early churches.
17. ST. MICHAEL AT SOUTH GATE. Before 1122.

They knew by this time where their new comrades lived. Gilbert had a lodging with an honest citizen of the name of Seaton, who kept a shop hard by Carfax, and sold provisions of all sorts to clerks and others. He was one of the burgher class, who contrived to keep on good terms both with the scholars and his fellow-citizens, and in the frequent collisions between "town and gown"—to borrow the modern phrase—he stood good-humouredly aloof, and would not take sides in any dispute.

Hugh lived in one of the many Halls which had sprung up within the city walls. These were not collegiate institutions, but were merely places of abode, hired perhaps by a number of clerks collectively, perhaps by some master, who received inmates as boarders. They lived in these houses, and took their meals there—everything being of the roughest and simplest description—and attended lectures in the different schools according to their own fancy. Some of the richer students enlisted the services of a tutor; but many lived a free and lawless existence, learning almost nothing, frequenting lecture just for the fashion of the thing, but making no progress in scholarship, and spending the best part of the day in amusement or fighting.

In the schools attached to the religious houses there was more order, more comfort, and more decency of life than in these self-constituted Halls; but amongst such clerks as had no leaning towards the religious life there was a strong feeling of preference for simply secular abodes; and there were difficulties between the monks and the University authorities with reference to the course in Arts which hold back many from attaching themselves to the monastic schools.

All this Leofric and Jack had been told with more or less of detail, and already Leofric was resolved against settling himself upon Osney Island, in the Domus Dei there. He would present his letter to the Abbot, but not until he had made a nook for himself somewhere else. Gilbert declared that he knew of a little turret in the city wall, not far from Smith Gate, in which two students had lived for a considerable time. If it were empty, they could take possession of it, and by the expenditure of a little money and ingenuity could transform it into quite a respectable living-chamber for themselves. Many a poor clerk had inhabited a chamber of that sort before, and Jack and Leofric secretly thought that they should prefer the quiet life on the wall to the noise and confusion which plainly too often reigned in the various Halls.

"We will go in by Smith Gate, and see if the turret be empty," said Gilbert; "if so, these lads can take possession forthwith, and we will show them where they can provide themselves with such things as be needful for them."

They were nearing the city by now. Already there had spread beyond the walls a certain number of Halls and other buildings. The Church of St. Mary Magdalene and the colony of the Austin Friars were without the wall on the northern side, and a few Halls had sprung up along Horsemonger Street, as it was then called, which was on the north side of the city ditch, where Broad Street now runs.

The Austin Friars were only just beginning to appear
in Oxford; but the Black, White, and Grey Friars had
already obtained a footing in the city. As the travellers
approached the gate, they saw the cowled figures flitting
about, some with black habits over their long white
under-dress, some with a simple gown of grey or brown,
bound with a cord at the waist. These latter, who all
(save the old and infirm) went barefoot, were the Franciscans or Minorites—the Grey Friars of whom the lads had
heard; and they regarded them with curiosity and venera-
tion, believing them to be full of sanctity and virtue.

Out through the gate, just as the youths approached it,
came a couple of Masters in their gowns and hoods. Leofric
and Jack scanned them curiously, and eagerly inquired of
their companions who they were.

"Nay, I know not the names of all the Masters in the
city," answered Hugh, laughing; "there be too many for
that. Belike they have been 'lecturing in School Street
this forenoon, and are going back to their Halls. Some of
these same Masters will like enough come and invite you
twain to attend their lectures; but give not too ready an
answer to the first who asks. Rather visit several and
pick out those who please you most. It is oft the poorest
and least learned who are most eager for listeners, the
better sort having always their lecture-rooms full."

And now they were actually within the city precincts.
Smith Gate being so close to School Street, the eager eyes
of the two new-comers were immediately gratified by the
sight of many hurrying figures of clerks and Bachelors

and Masters, some going this way and some the other, talking earnestly together, disputing with some warmth and eloquence, or singing snatches of songs, like boys released from school.

It was not easy for unaccustomed eyes to distinguish the rank of the various passers-by; for academic dress was still in its infancy, and there were few, if any, statutory rules respecting it. The habit of the clerk was very much what he wore at home, and the black cappa of Bachelor or Master was often the same, though Masters were beginning to wear the square, tufted cap, and had the right to the miniver hood of the nobles and beneficed ecclesiastics. The scarlet gown of the Doctor had just come into use, but was at present seldom seen, as many were unable to purchase so costly a robe. The most common garment for every person in the University was the " tabard" with the girdle, and these tabards might be either red, black, or green; but black was the commonest colour, as being the most serviceable in daily wear.

Fain would the lads have lingered to watch the shifting throng of clerks and their preceptors, as they streamed out from the lecture-rooms for the mid-day meal; but Hugh and Gilbert laughed at their eager curiosity, and drew them along to the left down Hammer Hall Lane, pausing suddenly upon reaching a small turret in the wall, which once had been open to the street, but was now closed in by a few mouldering boards.

"Good!" cried Gilbert, as he pulled aside one of the boards; "the place has not been taken. Now look well

at it, you two, and see if you think you can make shift to
live here till a better place offers."

Pushing their way within the circular recess, the lads saw
that a rude stairway led up to some sort of chamber overhead. Mounting the rickety steps with care—for they had
become loose and rotten—they found themselves in a small
and not unpleasing little chamber, lighted by several long,
narrow loopholes, and roofed in securely from the weather
overhead.

The flooring was rather decayed, and there was a
mouldering smell pervading the place; but its former
occupants had done various things to render habitation
possible. A fireplace and chimney had been contrived in
one corner, and some rude shutters had been affixed to
keep out the cold air at night, or in inclement weather.
A rickety shelf that would serve as a table still hung drooping from its nail. Plainly the place had been lived in
before, and might well be again. Leofric and Jack looked
round it, and smiled at one another.

" We could live here like princes, if there be nothing to
hinder," said the latter. " Can we come and fix our
abode here without making payment to any one ? "

" Marry yes, since nobody uses the place. There be
many such nooks along the walls, and poor clerks have
settled themselves there again and again, no man saying
them nay. In times of war they might post archers or
marksmen at these loopholes; but short of a siege, I trow
none will disturb you. And from without ye can climb
easily upon the wall, and enjoy the air and watch what

goes on beneath. Also there be the Fish Ponds just below, and I warrant ye will catch many a good supper from thence when ye be in need of a good meal."

Jack laughed, for he had no small skill as a fisherman; but just now he was all agog to see Oxford and settle into these new quarters.

"Had I but a few tools and some boards, I would fix us up bench and table, mend the stairs and the floor, and make the place as comfortable as heart could wish," he cried.

"And I would gather rushes for the floor, and wood for the fire, and we should feast right royally on the last of the provisions we laid up for the way," added Leofric.

"Then come away to Carfax, where ye can lay in such stores as ye need," cried Gilbert. "I will take you to honest Master Seaton, where I have always lodged. He will tell you where to go for all ye need, and the right price to pay: for there be dealers in the city who seek to mulct clerks and scholars, and charge them more than the fair price for goods; and the Chancellor, and even his Majesty the King, have had to interpose."

"What is Carfax?" asked Leofric, as, after depositing their goods carefully in the turret, they replaced the boards and sallied forth once more.

"Why, the meeting of the four great streets of the town—Quatrevois some folks call it—where High Street, Great Bayly Street, Fish Street, and North Gate Street all meet. St. Martin's Church is there with its great bell, and whenever there be strife 'twixt citizens and clerks, that bell booms out to gather the citizens together; whilst our rallying - point is St. Mary's, whose bell rings to warn us that they are rising against us. At other times Carfax is the chief mart of the city, and the bull-ring stands in the centre. But come, and thou shalt see for thyself; and good Master Seaton will give us all some dinner, I trow."

Gilbert led the way, and the rest followed him willingly. The streets had thinned considerably, the noontide hour having driven in clerks and masters alike to their dinner. Gilbert strode down Cat Street, and pointed out to his comrades several Halls situated there, and sounds of laughter and loud talking and jesting broke upon the ears of the passers-by, plainly indicating the proximity of considerable numbers of inhabitants.

"That was the Hall where I lived last," observed Hugh, as he pointed to a house, somewhat better than the rest, on the left-hand side as they walked down Cat Street. "Corbett's Hall it was then called; and the Master was an excellent man. I heard he was about to go elsewhere; probably I shall find a new head by now. But I will not pause there now; I will wait till the fetcher has brought in my goods and chattels. I will come with you to Carfax, and pay my respects to good Master Seaton first."

So on went the four, the pair who had never before seen a town gazing with wonder at the quaint-timbered houses on either side the street, whose projecting upper floors seemed almost to meet overhead. There was no

footpath or paving of any sort; the roadway was but
a track, deep in mud in winter, and in dust in summer.
St. Mark's Church at the corner, where they turned into
High Street, brought Leofric to a standstill, for such edifices
were new to him; but his companions laughed and hurried
him on, telling him he could drink his fill of churches in
Oxford any day he chose, but that Master Seaton's dinner
would not wait for his leisure.

On they went along this wider thoroughfare, not pausing to examine anything in detail, but taking in the
general effect of a populated city, which was immensely
wonderful to the two lads from the country, till Gilbert
pointed to a tall tower standing out against the sunny
sky, and said,—

"Yon is St. Martin's Church, and this is Carfax."

It was, as he had said before, just a meeting of the
ways, but such a sight as it presented Leofric and Jack
had never dreamed of. The open place seemed full of
people: there were stalls on which merchandise of all sorts
was being vended; loud-voiced salesmen were crying their
wares, or chaffering over bargains with customers. There
were shops, with signs swinging over them, that displayed
a better sort of ware; and lads of all ages, from thirteen
upwards, in the tabard of clerks, were strolling about,
buying or examining goods, or exchanging a rough sort of
banter with the townsmen. A few Masters or Bachelors
would be seen threading their way through the crowd, but
they did not often linger to speak to any; it was the
clerks who seemed to have all the leisure, and some of

these were playing games or throwing dice, whilst others looked on, encouraging or jibing the players.

"Heed not that rabble rout," said Gilbert, forcing his way towards a rather fine-timbered house at the corner, where Fish and High Streets joined; "come to Master Seaton's house, and let us hear all the news."

Gilbert led the way into a shop, where he was greeted somewhat boisterously by a merry-looking youth behind the counter. He nodded a reply, and pushed open a door which gave access to a steep and narrow staircase, and after ascending this he opened another door, and instantly a number of voices were raised in welcome and greeting.

Gilbert and Hugh pushed into the room from whence these sounds issued, whilst Leofric and Jack stood together just on the threshold, gazing about them with curious eyes.

They saw before them a quaint, pleasant room, rush-strewn, and plainly furnished with table and benches, in which a party of six was gathered, seated round the board, which was hospitably spread with solid viands.

The master of the house was easily distinguished by his air of authority and his general appearance. His wife was a comely dame, ruddy of face and kindly of aspect. On either side of her sat a pretty maiden, one of sixteen, another of fourteen summers; and the good-looking, strapping youth, who was now greeting Gilbert and Hugh right eagerly, was very plainly the son of the house. An apprentice looked on wide-eyed and silent at the apparition of four strangers; yet it was plain that neither Gilbert nor Hugh were so regarded in the Seaton household.

Not only were they joyfully received themselves, but their two comrades quickly shared in the hospitable welcome. They were placed at the table, their trenchers were heaped with good food, and the story of the encounter in the forest was eagerly listened to by all.

"There be many poor rogues who have taken to the forest in these times of scarcity," said Hal Seaton, the son. "The harvests have been bad, and prices have been raised; and the idle and prodigal have had much ado to keep body and soul together. Sometimes they take to theft and pillage, and then flee to the forest for safety; and some go thither in the hope of killing a fine buck unseen by the huntsmen, or to rob unwary travellers, especially those that be coming with full purses to pursue their studies here."

"Ay, and there be some that think there will be fighting ere long 'twixt his Majesty the King and the Barons," added Seaton himself gravely. "Heaven send such a thing come not to pass! It is ill work when brother takes up arms against brother, and city against city."

The youths would willingly have asked more of the state of parties at this stirring season, but just now personal matters were of more pressing importance. So they left politics for another time, and told about the turret hard by Smith Gate, where Leofric and Jack were about to ensconce themselves; and Hal begged a half-holiday from his duties in the shop, that he might take his tools, and some odds and ends of planks lying about in the workshop behind, and help the lads to settle themselves in.

This was willingly accorded, and Master Seaton and his wife both showed great kindness to the would-be clerks. The former unearthed from his stores some strong sacking fashioned into huge bags, that, stuffed with straw or dead leaves, did excellently for bedding; and the latter put up in a basket a liberal supply of food from her well-stocked larder, for her motherly heart went out towards the two lonely lads, coming to settle in a strange city, knowing nothing of the life before them. Leofric's blue eyes and gentle manners won her affections from the first, and no one could help liking honest Jack, who was so merry and so full of hope and courage.

Laden with a number of useful odds and ends, the little party made their way back to the turret chamber; and soon the sound of hammer, chisel, and saw spoke of rapid advance in the necessary work.

Leofric crossed the river again to gather dead leaves and bracken for bedding, wood for firing, and rushes for the floor. By the time he had collected and brought in sufficient stores, the work overhead had rapidly progressed, and he uttered an exclamation of delighted astonishment as he beheld the result of the afternoon's toil.

The stairs and flooring were mended, rudely, to be sure, but strongly. Something like a fastening had been contrived to the lower entrance, so that they could use the basement of the turret as a storehouse for wood and other odds and ends. Up above, the little chamber began to look quite comfortable. The holes in the masonry had been filled up with mortar or patched by boards. The window shutters had been mended, and could now be used for keeping out inclement wind. One of the loopholes had actually been glazed by Hal's deft fingers, and he promised to keep his eyes open for any chance of picking up some more glass, so that the others might be served in the same way. To be sure, the glass of those days was none too translucent, and save in very cold weather, it was pleasanter to have the loopholes open to the light of day; but if heavy rain or bitter cold should drive the occupants to close their shutters, it was certainly advantageous if one or two of the narrow slits could be glazed, so that they would not be left in total darkness.

The shelf table against the wall had been mended, and two stools of a suitable height contrived. When the fire was lighted on the hearth, and the smoke had been coaxed to make its way up the chimney, the place wore a really cosy and homelike aspect, which was greatly enhanced after the floor was strewn with rushes, and the two mattresses stuffed and laid side by side in a little recess. The spare habits of the boys were hung against the wall on pegs. and their few worldly possessions laid in order upon the shelf which had been fixed up to receive them.

"I vow," cried Hugh, as he looked around him, "that I would almost sooner have such a lodging as this than spend my days in a Hall. There be Halls where fires are scarce known save in the coldest weather, and where the rushes lie on the floor till they rot, and become charged with so much filth that the stench drives the luckless clerks out into the streets. It hath not been so where I have lodged, 'tis true; but there be Halls wherein I would not set foot for the noisome state they are in."

Leofric and Jack were charmed with their quarters, and when their guests had bid them good-bye, and they had fastened themselves in for the night, they looked at each other with a sense of triumph and joy. Here they were, established as a pair of clerks in a lodging of their own in Oxford, where none was likely to molest them. They had money in their purses enough to last them a considerable time. They had made kind friends who would help them through the difficulties and perplexities of their first days; and surely before long they would find themselves at home in this strange city, and would enter into its busy life (of which they had caught glimpses to-day) with the zeal and energy of true students.

As they sat at their table, partaking with good appetite, though frugally, of the provisions left from the journey, seasoned by some of Mistress Seaton's dainties, they spoke together of their plans for the morrow.

"Methinks I should go to Osney, and present my letter. But I shall have no need to ask for shelter in the Domus Dei, seeing how well we be sheltered here."

"And I would fain see something of the good Grey Friars, of whom so much good is spoken in the town," answered Jack; "and we must seek out such Masters as we would learn from, and find out what fee we must pay to attend their lectures. It is not much, methinks, that each clerk gives, but we must be careful how we part with our money, for we may not find it easy to put silver in our purse when our store has melted away."

"I shall ask the Abbot of Osney if he will give me vellum or parchment to illuminate, for I have some skill that way," said Leofric; "I used to help the monks of St. Michael. I might e'en do the same here; and, perchance, I might teach thee too, good Jack."

Jack looked at his rough, red hands, and shook his head.

"I can make shift to read and write, but I never could do such work as that," he answered. "I will fish in the ponds, and snare rabbits in the woods, and make bread of mystelton for us to eat. My care shall be the larder, and thou shalt have leisure for work if thou canst get it. So will we live right royally in our nook, and learn all that Oxford can teach us!"

CHAPTER IV.

THE FIRST DAY.

THE lads slept soundly in their new quarters, but awoke with the first light of day, eager to enter upon the strange life of the city. Making their way first to the top of the wall, they had a good look round them over the still sleeping town; and then finding a place where, by the exercise of a little activity, they could clamber down on the outer side, they refreshed themselves by a plunge in the Fish Ponds, by way of ablutions, and returned through the gate to their lodging.

They had a great curiosity to go forth together and see the city, but they did not intend immediately to decide upon the preceptor they should follow. Just at starting they felt almost too excited to settle to regular study, and the visit to the Abbot of Osney was the first business of the day.

Putting on their better habits, and making themselves as trim and neat as circumstances permitted, the boys sallied forth, and took the way to Carfax as before. They knew that Osney lay to the west of the city wall, beyond the Castle, and they had a great wish to see that building at close quarters; so they pursued their way along Great Bayly Street, till they reached the mound itself, crowned with its frowning walls and battlements.

As they passed along they saw not only numbers of clerks sallying forth to their daily lectures, but great numbers of the Black Friars, who appeared to be exercising considerable activity. Some were wheeling little trucks or carts which held loads of what appeared to be goods and chattels, and they appeared to be very busy, passing to and fro with their loads or their empty trucks, like a colony of industrious ants.

"What are they doing?" asked Jack of a bystander.

"Removing themselves from the Jewry to the new House that the King's Majesty has bestowed upon them without the city walls through Little Gate and down Milk Street," was the answer. "They came and settled in the Jews' quarter, hoping to convert the Hebrew dogs to the true faith; but methinks they have but a sorry record of converts. Anyhow they are going thence, and their new house is all but ready. A few may linger on in the Jewry, but the most part will fare forth to the more commodious building yonder."

Having thus satisfied their curiosity on that score, the boys passed onwards to the Castle, and just as they approached the West Gate, they were in time to prevent something of a catastrophe. As they drew near, they perceived that a young lady, mounted on a fair palfrey, was approaching from the outer side. She was quite young, perhaps fifteen or sixteen, and was very fair to look upon.

Her hair was a dusky chestnut colour, and was loosened by the exercise of riding, so that it framed her face like a soft cloud. Her eyes were bright and soft and dark, and her figure was as light and graceful as that of a sylph. As the two lads passed under the gateway, marking her approach, they bared their heads, and glanced at her with honest admiration in their eyes.

The little lady noticed their salutation, and returned it with a gentle dignity of manner; but just at that moment a piece of rag lying in the gutter was suddenly whirled round and up by a gust of wind, right against the face of the spirited little barb she was riding.

The creature suddenly took fright, reared up on its hind legs, and then made a sudden swerve, dashing off along West Gate Street at a headlong pace.

But luckily the girl rider was not borne away too in this reckless fashion. When the creature started and reared so violently, she had been almost unseated; and Leofric, seeing this, had with one quick movement thrown his arm about her; and as soon as the palfrey swerved and made off, the lady was simply lifted from her seat and gently set down by the strong arms of both lads—for Jack had rushed up to give assistance.

She stood now in the roadway, dazed, but safe, looking from one of her preservers to the other, and faltering out broken words of thanks.

Then the servant who had been behind, and who had in vain striven to stop the runaway horse, rode up, lifted the little lady to his saddle, and carried her away, before she had sufficiently recovered her breath to do more than wave her hand to her two deliverers.

The sentry at the gate, who had now come up, looked after them with a laugh.

"Old Ralph is a grim guardian. He will never let his young mistress have speech of any. But I doubt not when it comes to the ears of the Constable, he will seek you out to reward you; for fair Mistress Alys is as the apple of his eye."

"Who was the lady?" asked Jack eagerly.

"Mistress Alys de Kynaston, only daughter of the Constable of the Castle, Sir Humphrey de Kynaston. They say she is the very light of the house, and I can well believe it."

After a little more talk about the Castle and its Custodian, the sentry directed the lads how to find Osney Abbey; and after crossing Bookbinders' Bridge and passing the Almshouses, they quickly approached the gate by which access was had to the Abbey itself.

It was a fine building, inhabited by the Canons Regular of St. Augustine. There were the Chapel, dedicated to St. Nicholas, the fine cloistered refectory, the Dormitory, the Abbot's Lodging, to say nothing of the fine kitchens, and the Domus Dei of which mention has been made.

The present Abbot was Richard de Appelton, and when Leofric presented his letter and asked speech of him, he was ushered into the presence of the great man with very little delay.

Strangers, even youthful strangers, were always received

hospitably at the religious houses, and the Abbot, after reading the letter of his friend, spoke kindly to the boys, asking them whether they desired the shelter of the Domus Dei.

Leofric explained what had befallen him since that letter was penned, and how he had met with kind friends, and had already found a lodging within the walls of the town. The Abbot stroked his shaven chin, and looked from Jack to Leofric, letting his eyes rest somewhat longer upon the face of the latter as he said,—

"So thou art not as yet disposed to the religious life? Yet thou hast the face of a godly youth."

"I trust we may yet be godly without the cloister wall," answered Leofric modestly. "It is not for roistering and revelry that we have chosen to live within the town, but we would fain have some small spot that we may call our own, and I had thought that perchance I might turn such skill as I have in penmanship to account, so that I might earn fees for—"

"Ah yes, I know what thou wouldst say. Perchance we can give thee some work of that kind from time to time. But there be other ways of winning money too, open to poor clerks. Thou canst say a prayer or a grace at some rich man's table, or the Chancellor will give thee a licence to beg for thy maintenance. A likely youth, with a face like thine, will not find living hard. And if thou art ever in any trouble, thou canst always come to me. The Domus Dei is open to such as thou, and any son who comes from my good friend the Prior of St. Michael will be welcome for his sake."

Leofric thanked the Abbot gratefully, and received from him a small present in money, and two or three squares of vellum, such as were used in the making of breviaries. This was a very great acquisition for Leofric, as he could now begin some illuminating or transcribing work in his leisure hours, and by the sale of this add to their scanty store of money, and obtain the material for fresh work of a like kind.

This he preferred greatly to begging, notwithstanding that mendicancy had been made respectable, if not honourable, by the friars, and that to give alms to a poor clerk, or reward him for singing a "Salve Regina," or saying a prayer or grace, was one of the regular and esteemed forms of charity.

"And remember, good lads, that there are homes in the city open to such as ye," said the Abbot, as he bid them adieu. "There is Glasson Hall in the High Street, which pious John Pilet gave to Osney Abbey not long since. We might find room for the pair of you there, if you were disturbed in your nest. There is Spalding Court in Cat Street, which the burgesses of the town have bought for the use of poor clerks; and there be Halls where the poorer clerks serve the wealthier, and earn a pittance thus. Ye will find many ways of living; and pray Heaven we have a good harvest this year, so that the present scarcity may cease."

And with a nod and a word of blessing the Abbot dismissed his young guests.

"Let us take a prowl round the town," said Jack, as they

turned their backs upon the stately buildings of the Abbey, "there is so much to see at every turn, and I would fain know the streets and lanes of the city by heart. We must enter by the West Gate that we left, but we will wander round the walls and see what lies in the south ward of the city."

Leofric willingly agreed, and they retraced their steps as far as the gate, where they were at once hailed by the same sentry as had spoken to them before.

"Fortune favours you, honest lads," he said. "The Constable of the Castle has just sent down this purse, to be given to the two clerks who saved the Mistress Alys from hurt when her palfrey took fright," and he put into the hands of Jack a small leathern satchel, in which were a goodly number of silver pieces.

"Now this is luck indeed!" cried the youth, as they took their way onward. "We meet with success at every turn. Methinks that either thou or I must have been born beneath a lucky star."

But they had little time for discussing their good luck, for almost immediately they found themselves in the heart of the Grey Friars' colony, which lay close to the West Gate, just where there was a gap in the city wall, probably owing to the proximity of a marshy tract which rendered the protection of the wall of comparatively little use. Trill Mill Stream wound round the little colony, and formed its southern limit. The parish was that of St. Ebbs, perhaps the poorest in Oxford. This was doubtless why the Minorites, or Grey Friars, had made of it their headquarters. To dwell among the poor, and to live as poorly as any of them, was their principle and practice; and down in these low-lying, swampy districts, fever, ague, even leprosy abounded, and the Friars toiled with might and main amongst the sick.

The boys saw them going forth by twos and threes, or passing in and out of their low, poverty-stricken buildings. It was against the desires of their founder that they should ever possess property or aspire to learning; but the practical inconvenience of the one prohibition, and the thirst for knowledge which was growing up in the hearts of men at this time, militated against the strict code of St. Francis.

The Franciscans made their houses as simple and unpretentious as possible. They lived the most self-denying of lives; but they were beginning to frequent the schools, and to teach in schools of their own, and although there were often drawbacks and difficulties placed in the way of their advancement, they had already many great and notable scholars in their ranks.

The main difficulty was that by statute no one might begin in theology who had not first taken a degree in Arts, whilst the vows and rules of the monks and friars debarred them in many cases from any sort of secular studies. They were so well qualified to lecture in theology that it was often difficult to refuse their plea; and yet the statutes stood in the way.

As the boys reached the corner of Milk Street, they observed a Franciscan Friar of venerable aspect coming towards them, and instinctively Leofric bent the knee as if to ask a blessing.

The old man stood still, and smiled benignly. It was one of the characteristics of the Grey Friars that, in spite of the self-denial and austerity of their lives, they were more uniformly cheerful, kindly, and even merry in their talk and ways than any other of the religious orders. For this reason, perhaps, they were beloved above others; and the great ones of the world, as well as the poor, came to love and venerate them.

"Peace be with you, my children," said the Friar. "Come you as strangers to this city? Methinks you have the air of the country clinging to you yet."

"We did but arrive yesterday," answered Leofric; "and we have scarce the right to call ourselves clerks. But that is what we hope to be soon, so as we can make up our minds where we shall gain the best learning for such fee as our purse will enable us to give."

"You must needs first study the *Trivium* and *Quadrivium* of Arts," said the Friar, when he had questioned them a little more as to their intended manner of life; "but since I hold that no learning is complete that doth not embrace the study of the Word of God, come ye both, if it please you and ye have time, to the school of our order, where I strive to impart a few crumbs of knowledge to our clerks and younger brethren. Many lads like ye twain come without fee, and glad shall I be if any poor words of mine can give help or comfort."

The boys would have stammered out some words of thanks, but the Friar put them aside with a smile.

"Nay, nay, lads, we are sent here not for our own

but for others' good. Ask for the School of the Franciscans, and for Brother Angelus. Most mornings from nine till eleven I am to be found there. You will be welcome. Go in peace."

"We will of a surety go," said Leofric, as they pursued their way. "He had the face of a saint. I trow that this is a right godly place. We get kindness from all we meet."

"Methinks it is thy face that wins it for us," quoth Jack, with a laugh; "thou hast somewhat the face of a saint thyself."

There was some shrewd truth in this remark. Leofric's was a countenance that could not but attract; and at that time there were such numbers of rude, rough, ill-mannered and ill-living clerks in the place, that favourable notice was often bestowed upon such as appeared of gentler nature and manners. All the religious brotherhoods were more or less on the look-out for likely pupils, and though the more enlightened of their members would not put pressure upon lads to make too early a choice of the cloister life, or of that of the friars, they gladly recruited their ranks from such promising students and clerks as they succeeded in drawing beneath their influence.

As the boys stood looking down Milk Street, they continued to see the Black Friars flitting busily to and fro, fetching and carrying their simple goods and chattels; and prompted by curiosity, they turned into the Jewry, and were soon gazing with the greatest interest at the Jewish denizens of that quarter.

The Jews had had a footing in Oxford from the very early days; they had a synagogue in Fish Street, nearly opposite to St. Aldate's Church. (It may be noted that the old Fish Street is the present St. Aldate's.) They were, of course, the most moneyed class in the city, and they had their own code and manner of life, were exempt from the operation of the common law, and were treated as serfs of the King. Had it not been that the Kings protected them from pillage by their neighbours, in order to plunder them themselves, the Jews would scarcely have continued to exist. The people hated and feared them, even whilst they borrowed from them at a rate of usury limited by statute. But they were too valuable to the Crown to be exterminated, and the Black Friars had settled amongst them in the hope of effecting their conversion.

For many years they had considerable success, so much so that the King established a house called the Guild Hall for the reception of the baptized Hebrews. It was not really their lack of success (although fewer conversions had taken place of late) but lack of room which occasioned the flitting of the Black Friars from the Jewry. They were not all of them leaving immediately, even now; but their new building was almost complete, and a number of the brothers were about to take their departure, hence the excitement prevailing in the locality of the Jewry.

When the lads had gazed their fill at the strange dress and dark faces of the Jews, and had listened to their talk, and their covert jests as they secretly derided the Christian brothers who had dwelt so long amongst them, they turned southward down Fish Street, and then by St. Frideswyde's Street to the great group of beautiful and ancient buildings comprising St. Frideswyde's Church and Abbey—the oldest in Oxford—occupying the site where Christ Church now stands.

Grave, stately looking men walked with slow, meditative steps about the enclosure in which stood those buildings. They were habited in a long white coat of cloth down to the heels, girt about with a leather girdle; over this was a short surplice of linen, and over that again a short black cape that reached to the elbows. On their shaven heads they wore a black square steepled cap. These were the Canons Regular of St. Augustine—the same order as those of Osney.

Here again the walls were broken down, and had crumbled to decay, groves and meadows and fish ponds extending southward to Trill Mill Stream. The boys looked about them in silent wonder, but nobody addressed them; and though they would have liked to steal into the church and see St. Frideswyde's shrine, they did not venture to do so, fearing that they would be regarded as intruders in that sacred place.

"Hugh le Barbier was telling me of notable miracles done at yon shrine," said Leofric, as they turned away at length up St. Frideswyde's Lane. "St. Frideswyde was a daughter of an ancient king, and she built a nunnery here, and was herself a nun. Afterwards it became a place for monks, and now it is an Abbey; but the shrine of St. Frideswyde still remains, and great wonders are wrought there."

" Hark ! " suddenly cried Jack, whose ears had been more
attentive to some sound in the distance than to his companion's words, " I hear the noise of a tumult. There is
something stirring not far off. Let us e'en run and see
what it be. Methinks I hear the sound of blows and
shouts."

Leofric heard the same sound which had attracted Jack's
attention. It seemed to proceed from a short distance off,
and they hurried along till they reached the corner of
Great Jewry Lane where it joins Shydyard Street (now
Oriel Street), where the shouting began to take more
articulate form, and the boys heard the words, " North,
North !—South, South ! " bawled and yelled from scores
of throats.

" It is some fray betwixt the clerks," said Jack, who
had not listened for naught to Gilbert's tales during the
night they camped by the fire in the forest.• " Did he not
tell us that they were banded into two or more great
bodies, North and South, and that they were ofttimes
coming to blows together ? Haply we had better stand
close in this doorway, and let the rout go by. Clerks are
killed by their fellows in the open streets every year, if
what we hear be true, for nothing worse than belonging
to the adverse faction."

Leofric, who though no coward was by nature placable,
and adverse to blows, was ready enough to take this
counsel, and set his back against the door in the little
porch which offered shelter to the pair. The fight seemed
to be coming their way, and presently a few clerks scudded

by, yelling, laughing, cursing; brandishing their clubs and
hurling all manner of foul and derisive epithets at those
behind them, from whom, however, they evidently thought
it well to flee. Others followed, some having cut heads
or bleeding noses, dishevelled, out of breath, angry, yet
inclined to make game of themselves and others all the
while.

"North! North! North!" they shouted, interlarding
their words with many an oath and epithet that need not
be transcribed. "Ye coward Southerners, ye only dare to
attack when ye be ten to one. We will give you back as
good as ye gave! North! North!"

Plainly the pursuers were close behind the flying feet of
the last fugitive, when suddenly the rout was brought up
short by the appearance of a tall man in a long gown, with
a weapon at his side, who came round the corner at a quick
pace, and confronted the rioters with stern glances.

"How dare you disturb the peace again, you good-for-
nothing brawlers?" he cried in ringing accents. "Let me
have such another scene within the week, and I will have
some of you to answer for it in the Chancellor's Court.
As if it were not enough that you must be fighting the
burgesses, fighting the citizens, fighting the Jews, but ye
must be fighting one another too, and that in broad daylight, when you should be at your studies. To your Halls
and lodgings, every man of you; and if I hear of such
another brawl as ye come from lecture, I will deal differently with some of you."

The clerks, who had pulled up suddenly at sight of this

stalwart functionary, now began to slink away this way and that. Many of them were mere lads, led on by the boyish instinct of fighting ; a few were evilly-disposed rogues, who were always to be found in the streets, ready for any brawl ; others, again, were scholars who had followed in the wake of the crowd, with an idle interest in anything that savoured of a fight rather than with any particular desire to take part in it.

These sorts of frays were of almost daily occurrence in old Oxford, and only when they became too numerous or too severe was any particular notice taken of them. The students for the most part lived and brawled, studied and played, very much as it pleased them, and a fight, with many or with few, was part of the day's work.

Jack espied Gilbert at the edge of the crowd, and made for him quickly.

"What is the matter? and who is he that stayed the fight?" he asked, with eager curiosity ; and Gilbert answered, laughing,—

"There is naught the matter ; the fight was but a bit of play as the men came out from lecture. We have such almost every day, and they seldom come to more than a few cracked crowns. Yon man of the gown is the Proctor of the South. There be two such in the University, one for the North and one for the South ; and I trow they have their hands full to keep order sometimes ! But come along, let us to dinner, and ye shall tell your news."

CHAPTER V.

THE NEW LIFE.

BEFORE a week had passed away, Leofric and Jack felt as though they had been months at Oxford, so many new experiences had been crowded into that short space.

The more they saw of the strange life of the place, the more glad were they of the chance which had given to them this little private shelter of their own, instead of casting them amongst a number of strange clerks in one of the poorer Halls or lodgings of the city.

For in the days of its infancy the University had enough to do in protecting its own liberties from outside attack. It was therefore unable to exercise individual authority over its heterogeneous members. It provided instruction for them, it guarded their persons jealously from assaults from without, and fought their battle right lustily when jealous townsmen or papal emissaries sought to interfere with liberty or life. But for the rest, the clerks and scholars lived in a state of glorious and almost barbaric liberty, and all that Chancellor or Proctors could hope to attempt was to restrain any serious outbreaks of violence, either between clerks and citizens, or between the various sections of the clerks themselves.

Open rioting in the streets was checked as far as possible ; but an immense amount of roistering and disorder could and did prevail without let or hindrance, and there was no certainty from day to day that some bloody collision might not occur in the city which might have a serious termination.

Stories were told of clerks who had been set upon and killed by angry citizens, of citizens who had been slain by clerks, of Masters even who had met with injuries too often fatal in their effects, sometimes from the hands of citizens, sometimes from those of scholars inflamed by passion or drink.

There had been times when the King had had to interfere in order to calm the strife between the contending parties. There had also been times when the Masters and scholars had deserted Oxford by hundreds, if not thousands, and had threatened to establish themselves in other localities. This had been done when the citizens had put upon them some marked indignity and affront, and had generally resulted in the submission and humiliation of the town. For, as was pointed out to the burgesses, the importance and prosperity of Oxford mainly depended upon the presence there of this school of learning, and if they drove away the scholars by their ill-judged enmity, they were signing the death-warrant of their own city.

It was often to these quarrels and their adjudication that the endowments (if such a word can be employed) of the University were owed. The citizens would submit, and agree to pay so many marks a year in token of their penitence, and these moneys were called " chests," and formed a fund from which poor scholars might borrow without interest, leaving a pledge behind ; and private individuals would sometimes start a similiar chest, from which system gradually developed the scholarships and exhibitions of our own days.

But the life of the infant University was a very strange one as compared with the collegiate system which gradually grew out of it. Thirteen or fourteen was a common age for a youth to commence life as a clerk, and even at that tender age very little supervision was given him.

Originally the University copied to a certain extent the guilds of a city corporation, and as a seven years' apprentice-ship was imposed upon lads entering trade guilds, so a seven years' course was expected of a student between the date of his entry as a clerk and the time at which he might take his M.A. degree. In the previous century there were regular University guilds, and as the University was inter-national, and men from all countries came thither, these guilds naturally partook of a national character, men of the same language consorting together, so that different Halls became associated with the names of different nationalities.

Even amongst the inhabitants of the British Isles there were distinctions and race divisions. The Welsh formed a colony of their own, whilst North and South were the two main factions in the place in the thirteenth century, and these brawled terribly at times between themselves.

Even when no actual brawling was going on, the streets of Oxford after dusk were places where it was needful to walk warily. By day studies and games occupied the clerks the best part of their time; but with the setting of the sun a stop was put to these occupations. Candles were dear, firing was often scanty, and the close, ill-smelling Halls, where the rush-strewn floors were often not cleaned for weeks together, became almost intolerable when shut up. Naturally enough, the clerks preferred to sally forth into the streets, some to drink or sing songs at the taverns, others to parade the streets, shouting and joking, and playing any pranks that entered their heads. When it is remembered that almost every person in those days carried arms of some sort, and that the most trifling quarrel provoked blows, it may well be understood that the evening hours in the city were anything but peaceful, and some sympathy can be felt with the citizens in their enmity towards the gownsmen, even though these were a source of profit to them.

Evening by evening Leofric and Jack heard hideous sounds of drunken revelry proceeding from the various streets in the vicinity, and if ever they had the curiosity to parade the town after dark, they were amazed at the disorder and violence which seemed to prevail.

"I had thought," said Leofric, "that Oxford would be full of grave and reverend doctors, whose presence would impose order and gravity upon all. But methinks it is full of wantonness and revelling and fighting. Right glad am I, good Jack, that we have our own little nest on the walls. I should be loth indeed to belong to yonder herd."

Jack was not quite so particular, and a frolic in the streets, so long as things did not go too far, was rather agreeable to him than otherwise. Sometimes he would steal out, whilst Leofric was poring over his illuminating work, and enjoy a stroll with some of the clerks of the better sort with whom he had made acquaintance, and as he grew used to the strange ways of the city, he found much to amuse and interest him.

Leofric had purchased, with the money given him by the Abbot of Osney, some materials to enable him to work at the illumination of his vellum leaves, and was doing some fine and beautiful illumination which was certain to fetch him a good sum at some wealthy man's house. Jack looked on in amaze at his skill, but sometimes felt the time hang a little heavy. On such occasions he would sally forth to do the necessary marketings, or to collect fuel, and so forth; and often Hugh le Barbier would drop in to watch Leofric at his toil and exchange ideas with him on many subjects.

Hugh was of a studious turn, and he had the same sort of refined instinct as Leofric, and shrank from the tumult and rowdiness of the streets. He had not yet succeeded in finding a Hall quite to his mind, and was lodging at present at "Dagville's Inn" (now the Mitre), which belonged in those days to one Philip Pady, a burgess, who had rented it to an Italian of the name of Pedro Balzani, who had lived long in the city, and made an excellent innkeeper, having great skill in culinary matters, and a good English wife who understood the likings of her countrymen.

"Thou must come and sup with me one of these days," said Hugh one day, as he sat with Leofric after Jack had sauntered forth. "I have a comfortable chamber enow, though somewhat chilly when the wind is riotous; but I have found favour in the eyes of mine host, and I take my meals with him and his family. This is not a grace he accords to all who come, nor even to all who stay long in his house, as I am doing. And, in truth, he does right to be cautious; for he has a pair of wonderfully beauteous daughters, twin sisters, and so much alike that it was long before I knew one from the other."

Leofric looked up with a gleam of interest in his eyes.

"Beautiful, thou sayest? I was wondering if perchance I could find in this place a beautiful face; for see thou here, I would fain on this square of vellum portray an angel with a roll in his hands, upon which I shall inscribe, in fine penmanship, certain prayers. I have some small skill in drawing faces. I used to amuse the monks of St. Michael by taking likenesses of them, and they said I did it well. But it is not easy to find a face for an angel, though there are some pretty lads here and there walking the streets. I wonder if I could find an inspiration in the face of your twin sisters."

"Thou shalt come and see," quoth Hugh eagerly; "methinks it would please them well to be thus portrayed. For my part, I think that Linda's face would be the better;

it is ofttimes full of a sweet seriousness and repose, whereas Lotta is all sparkle and fire; and it is by these two expressions that I begin to know them the one from the other, though, should Lotta be pensive and Linda merry, I am at fault again!"

"I should like to see them," said Leofric. "I have heard of such things—sisters so alike that none may distinguish between them—but I have never seen such. It must be something strange."

"Thou shalt come and see; thou and Jack shall sup with me to-morrow. I have spoken to Balzani about you both before now. Thou hast a quick eye and a keen understanding, and I would ask what thou dost think of Tito Balzani, the son of mine host. For my part I like him not, and methinks he has no love for me. He consorts with one Roger de Horn, one of the biggest braggarts and bullies of the place. He calls himself a clerk, but it is little of learning that will ever get into that pate of his. He, too, comes to table with mine host and his family, and methinks he is vexed and jealous because the same grace is accorded to me. He speaks insolent words anent upstarts and fine-gentlemen fops; and it is plain that he seeks a quarrel with me, or else to drive me to other quarters."

Leofric was interested in all that concerned his friend, for he had a sincere liking for Hugh, who had been kind to him in a variety of ways. He gladly promised to visit him on the morrow, and take supper with him, being interested in the thought of seeing these Balzanis.

" I suspect there is some love-jealousy at the bottom of this fellow's dislike for Hugh," remarked Jack, when he heard Leofric's account of the matter ; "there be some fellows who must always have a sweetheart, and perchance this bully thinks that the fair ladies will think more of Hugh's open face and gentle bearing than of his own. We will go and see for ourselves ; for I would be sorry that any hurt should come to good Hugh. He is a very proper fellow ; but in such a city as this any evil-disposed person might seek a quarrel with his rival, and do him a deadly mischief without fear of anything worse than the Chancellor's prison. Benefit of clergy may be source of safety to some, but it can be a source of peril too, when the vilest of the land claim it as a cloak for their worst sins."

The new clerks were beginning to learn many lessons as to the working of the prevailing system, and they heard many things from Brother Angelus, whose lecture-room they sought whenever they could, and who seemed to take a special interest in these two lads. Once they had accompanied him in a round of visits amongst the poor in the parish of St. Ebbs, and had longed to emulate his skill and tenderness with the sick. It seemed strange to them to see one who was so learned in saintly lore, and who was so revered in his own school by the pupils of St. Francis, humbling himself here to perform the most menial office for the poorest person, without a thought for his own dignity or position. But it was alike the theory and the practice of the friars to humble themselves to tend their brethren ; nor did they think it shame to ask alms at the doors of the rich, for they might possess nothing of their own, and must needs beg sustenance for themselves and for those whom they desired to help.

Leofric and Jack had by this time settled what lectures to attend and what masters to follow. They had been perplexed for a while at the choice before them, and by the solicitations of their superiors for a hearing in their particular schools. They had visited a considerable number before finally deciding, and were now deeply interested in the daily lectures they heard upon a variety of subjects. Jack declared he had never had such a hard time in his life, and he wanted a good deal of help from Leofric in taking in what he heard. But both lads had sharp wits and a great thirst for information, and they soon attracted the notice of their instructors by their regular attendance, and by the attention they bestowed upon the lecture.

So far they had not made a great many acquaintances amongst their fellow-clerks, the number of whom was quite confusing at the outset. Some amongst them were too rough and uncouth to attract them, whilst others, more gently born, were superior to them in station, and they feared a rebuff should they attempt to make advances. Life was simpler in its conditions in those days, and friendships easily grow up when the young are thrown together; but pride of race is nowhere absent, and both Leofric and Jack had a great dislike to putting themselves forward in any way.

There was a great deal of talk in the city at that time, and indeed all over the country, as to the condition of

affairs betwixt the King and the Barons. Leofric and
Jack were only gradually beginning to take any interest
in political matters, being sufficiently engrossed just now in
their own affairs; but Hugh talked often to Leofric about
the great Earl of Leicester, who had married the King's
sister, and who was now the head and champion of the
Barons' party. He spoke of him with the ardent enthusiasm of youth, called him the greatest and noblest man of
the day, would tell long stories of his prowess in Gascony
and other places, and of the ill-treatment he had ofttimes
received at the hands of the capricious and unstable
monarch.

"The King never knows his own mind two days
together!" the young man had scornfully declared, "and
he makes promises only to break them. He is the tool
and dupe of the Pope, and is bleeding his country to death,
sending all its wealth across the seas for objects with which
we have no concern. And then he breaks every promise
whereby he has attained these moneys, and our charters
and liberties are trampled underfoot, even when he has
most solemnly promised to observe and respect them."

Hugh was an ardent supporter of that party in the
kingdom which began to be called the Barons' party, and
Leofric and Jack drank in his spirit eagerly. It was, in
fact, the prevailing one amongst the members of the
University of all grades. The friars, too, were far more
in sympathy with the champions of the liberties and rights
of the people and the constitution, than with the aggres-
sions and tyrannies of a Pope-ridden monarch. So that

Oxford, although divided in some measure upon the burning questions of the day, inclined on the whole very much in favour of that party of which Simon de Montfort, Earl of Leicester, was now the acknowledged head.

When Hugh escorted his two friends through the streets to Dagville's Inn, where they were to sup with him as arranged, he was considerably excited by a rumour which had just reached the city, and which was causing no small stir there.

It was said that Oxford had been chosen as the place where in a short time, perhaps two months hence, a Parliament was to be assembled in which the burning questions of the day were to be discussed, and some settlement of a definite nature arrived at between the King and his nobles. The very idea of this great assembly sent a thrill of excitement through the place. The streets were crowded with knots of clerks and citizens, for once all gathered amicably together, discussing the news which had been brought from London, and wondering whether it were true.

Dagville's Inn presented a lively appearance. Its porch and bar were crowded with guests, and a dark-faced man, who spoke with the accent of a foreigner, was busy serving the guests, as was also a youth with a tousle of frizzy hair and a pair of shifty black eyes, who bore a strong resemblance to mine host, but looked a great deal more crafty and cruel.

Leofric observed his face as he passed in, and noted that he gave an ugly scowl at sight of them. It seemed plain that he had no liking for Hugh, although what was the cause of the grudge he bore him it was less easy to decide.

Hugh pushed his way through the lower room, his guests following; and after mounting to the upper floor, they found themselves in a pleasant room, not unlike that in which they had seen the Seaton family assembled on their first arrival at the city. Its window, which was large and latticed, though the lattice stood wide open to the mild evening air, looked upon the High Street; and upon the window seat lay a lute, and a piece of fine embroidery work such as was seldom seen save in the nunneries or in the houses of fine ladies.

A table in the centre of the room was set for supper, but the apartment itself was empty, and Leofric took up the lute gently, and fingered it with loving touches. But the next moment he put it hastily down, for the door opened, and a pleasant-looking motherly woman came in bearing a smoking dish, and she was followed by two maidens, each with a dish in her hands.

Hugh stepped forward to relieve one daughter of her load, and Jack did the same by the second. Leofric, who was more shy by nature, stood where he was in the window, looking in a sort of amaze from one girl to the other. Both were dressed exactly alike, in a semi-Italian fashion which he thought most bewitching; but it was the beauty of the two faces, and their extraordinary similarity, which confused and bewildered him. No wonder Hugh had said it was hard to tell one sister from the other; he marvelled that any should learn to know them apart. To his eyes the faces seemed identical, the same rich colouring, the same dark velvet-soft eyes, the same flashing smile and finely-pencilled brows.

Hugh made him known to the sisters, who were girls of about his own age, albeit their southern blood made them appear older than their age. He called one Lotta and one Linda, and asked Leofric if he thought they would do as models for him.

The young artist blushed to the roots of his hair, and knew not what to say; but one of the maidens laughed merrily, and looked archly into his face.

"Methinks if he wants an angel-model, he had best take his own portrait," she said, in clear musical tones; whilst the other sister added in a voice of precisely the same character,—

"Or seek to get a glimpse of lovely Mistress Alys at the Castle. Methinks she has the fairest face of any maid in the city."

Whilst the young people were talking together in the window, and drawing out Leofric to tell them of his art, and even to show them what he could do by means of a bit of charcoal upon a piece of wood, a tall, burly, dark-browed young fellow lounged into the room, and looked across at the group round Leofric with a scowl in his deep-set eyes.

Jack was the only one who noticed his entrance, and he knew the intruder to be Roger de Horn, who had a certain notoriety in the place as being one of its most turbulent spirits.

"Supper, supper, good folks," called the mistress from

the head of the table, where she had seated herself before
another smoking dish which she had been to fetch. " If the
father and Tito are busy for the moment, we must not let
the supper spoil. Doubtless they will join us when they
smell the viands.—Come, young sir, and let us see if thou
canst wield a knife as well as a pen, for I believe not in
your starveling clerks. Good victuals make good scholars,
as I always say."

The hostess was a cheerful soul, and her calling in life
had given her easy, pleasant manners that won her good-will
from all. She looked little enough like the mother of the
crafty Tito, or even of these beautiful girls. Tito, in truth,
was not her son ; for Balzani had been married twice, and
his first wife had been of his own nationality. Tito was
several years older than the twin sisters, and no very great
likeness existed between them. Yet the daughters looked
far more Italian than English, although they spoke their
mother's tongue with perfect fluency, and without any sort
of accent. They were both very charming girls. Leofric
could not on that occasion decide in the least which was
the more charming, for he could not tell them apart.
Sometimes he thought he was beginning to know them,
but again found himself completely at fault. But he was
delighted with the permission accorded to him of drawing
their portraits, and the girls' eagerness over this matter
amused and gratified him not a little.

Roger seemed in a very ill temper all the while, as Jack
was not slow to notice. He sat silent and sullen at the
board. nor did it soothe him to observe that nobody seemed

to miss him or take note of his ill-humour. All were occupied with Hugh and his guests, chattering and laughing
gaily. Nobody appeared to have a word or a look for him,
unless it were the hostess, who pressed him sometimes
to partake of one or another of the dishes on the table,
but always returned to join the chatter of the young folks,
which plainly interested her much more than the morose
responses of Roger.

When Balzani and his son appeared, they were full of
the news which was exciting the place. The innkeeper
was pleased with the thought of all the fine company that
this meeting would bring to the town. He did not profess
to know or to care very much about the rights of the case;
he was still too much the foreigner to enter keenly into
English politics. But the local excitement he thoroughly
appreciated, and when he got a chance he questioned Hugh
closely about the great Earl of Leicester and his household
and retinue, wondering whether so great a man would con-
descend to lodge in his house, and if so, what gain such
a thing would bring to him.

When Jack and Leofric took their leave, promising
another visit soon, Hugh walked with them part of the
way, asking their opinion of his quarters and his friends.

"I'd have a care if I were thee," said Jack, with one of
his shrewd glances; "for that braggart Roger de Horn is
no friend of thine, and methinks Tito and he are fast
friends. In this city it behoves men to walk warily if
they have foes abroad. I would have a care if I were
thee."

CHAPTER VI.

A "MAD" PARLIAMENT.

"'TWILL be a mad Parliament, gentlemen, a mad Parliament," said one reverend doctor, as the news was definitely made known in Oxford that that place had been selected by King and Barons as a neutral spot where the adjourned Parliament should meet.

Great excitement reigned throughout the city and University. Nothing was talked of but the political situation, the weakness of the King, the resolution of the Barons to enforce the terms of the Great Charter upon the tyrannical monarch, and the possibility (only too well grounded) that the Sovereign, advised by his foreign favourites, would seek to call in aid from abroad, and overrun the fair realm of England with foreign mercenaries.

"But hireling foreigners must be paid," remarked one citizen grimly, as this danger was mooted, "and until the nation gets its rights and liberties, no more money will his Majesty wring from it. The sinews of war are in our pockets, and there they shall stay unless the King chooses to hear reason."

"Ay, and more than that," cried Gilbert, hurrying up to

join the eager crowd; "I have had good news from my
father in the south. He tells me that the Barons have
garrisoned the Cinque Ports, so that no foreigners may
land on our coasts. As the truce with France has just
expired, they have good reason for this step, without doing
any disloyalty to his Majesty; but all the world knows
with what special object it has been done at this moment.
Methinks we shall be free from fear of foreign invasion,
and that we shall obtain our liberties without bloodshed."

"Heaven grant we may!" cried the older and graver
amongst the townsfolks, some of whom remembered, and
others had heard from their fathers, the tales of the
terrible struggle in John's time, which had led to the
granting of the Great Charter. They wanted no re-
petition of such scenes as those; albeit some of the
younger and more ardent spirits, and the lawless and
violent ones, would not have been displeased had some
open collision occurred which should cause the whole
country to fly to arms.

Even as it was, great impetus had been given to the
joustings and practices of wars in the meadows around the
city. Both clerks and citizens went out afoot or on horseback during the long evenings of summer, and often such a
tumult arose, and such a din of arms, that one might well
suppose some real battle was going on rather than an
imitation of it.

June had come, and all the world was clothed in verdure.
Oxford was looking her best and brightest at this season.
As the day for the assembling of this Parliament drew

near, the excitement became intense. Lectures in some cases were suspended, and discipline of any kind became enforced only with difficulty.

As usual, there were two parties in the city. The very fact that the scholars sided almost to a man with the Barons' party disposed some of the citizens to throw in their sympathies with the King. Henry was no special favourite, but he was personally beloved by those who had at any time had access to his presence. He was not vicious, and he was devout; his defenders could always say many things in his favour. He was not a monarch to inspire respect or personal enthusiasm; but then neither was he one who roused against himself any great outbreak of popular rage. Had he lived in less critical days, or been better advised, he might have passed through life comfortably and easily, and have been regarded as a good and well-meaning monarch.

" We must needs see some of these great sights!" cried Jack excitedly to Leofric, after coming back from a prowl round the city one evening. "They say that to-morrow the Barons will march into the city; and upon the day following the King will arrive at Beaumont Palace. We must go forth to see these brave sights. Marry, what a time it will be for Oxford! Right glad am I to be here at such a season! Think of it—I might have been following the plough behind my father's horses, knowing naught of the great things that be doing in the world!"

A few minutes later and Hugh burst in, quivering with excitement.

"The great Earl of Leicester with his train comes to-morrow," he cried, "and many others of the Barons as well. Some will lodge here, and some there; but the great De Montfort and his sons will come to Dagville's Inn, and for the nonce all who are there must make way. So I come to beg a lodging with you, my friends; and if fortune favours us, I will seek to get speech with my old play-mates, Guy and Amalric, and will present ye both to them."

"Are they the sons of the great Earl?" asked Leofric eagerly.

"Ay; and time was once when I went as a page with my father to Kenilworth, and we played together, we boys. Guy and Amalric are the two youngest sons. The elder pair have won knighthood for themselves beyond the seas. But these be yet lads still, albeit, if report says true, very proper and noble lads. Right well do I hope that they will accompany their father on the morrow. Me-thinks they will not have forgotten me. Amalric was very friendly in those past days, and we vowed to love each other always."

There was little sleep for the trio in the turret that night. Jack and Leofric made Hugh tell them everything he could remember of the De Montfort family at Kenil-worth, when he had been there as page.

They wanted to know, too, the names of the other Barons who would support the Earl of Leicester; and although parties changed with somewhat confusing rapi-dity, as private jealousies or conflicting interests made the friend of to-day the enemy of to-morrow, yet Hugh knew pretty well who were likely to range themselves upon the side of the liberties of the nation, and could give bits of information to his companions about the great nobles of the day.

The Earls of Gloucester, Hereford, and Norfolk were, he thought, certain to support the Earl of Leicester, and also Hugh le Bigod and Hugh le Despenser, whose names were pretty well known at that time. The King was more likely to be backed by Bishops and Archbishops, especially such as still held themselves subservient to the Pope. Then he was almost certain to be attended by some of the De Lusignans, his half-brothers, and by numbers of other foreign favourites, whose constant presence at Court was such an offence to the nation.

"They eat up everything before them, like so many locusts!" cried Hugh hotly. "So soon as any place becomes vacant, the King, instead of promoting some honest English gentleman to it, who may have served him faithfully for years, throws it to one of his foreign favourites, who may have a dozen such offices already. They drain the life-blood from the country, and we, its sons, are left to take what pickings we can get!"

It was easy to understand how bitterly the English nobles and gentlemen were beginning to resent this kind of thing; and when it was combined with a constant infringement of their liberties, and an equally constant imposition of new and illegal exactions, anger became exasperation, and the sense of a coming crisis was in the very air.

The short night was soon over, and with the first of the sunlight the three lads awoke from their light slumbers.

There was no lingering abed for any that day. Hardly had they returned from their plunge in the pool, and arrayed themselves in their best habits, before sounds in the streets warned them that all the city was up and doing.

Hurrying forth, they saw that the citizens had begun to deck their houses as if for a festival: flags were flying from windows, and bands of clerks paraded up and down the streets, singing songs, cracking jokes, and sometimes striving to make speeches in imitation of those which would be made when the conference should have assembled.

Mummers were pouring into the town, as they always did on any holiday, and at the street corners they were to be seen going through their rough representations or practising some rude sort of jugglery. It was plain that there would be no lectures that day. The clerks were far too excited to attend, and the masters little less so.

But many hours must of necessity pass before the Barons would be likely to arrive at the city gates. These hours had to be got rid of somehow, and Leofric suggested that they should go and see if Brother Angelus were lecturing in the school of the Friars, since perhaps the excitement had not spread so much into the religious establishments as into the Halls and lodging-houses.

Friar Angelus truly was there, and so were the pupils of his own school, but very few outsiders came in that day; and the lecturer did not keep his hearers very long, dismissing them with a smile, and cautioning them not to get into any mischief or trouble in their excitement.

He looked pleased to see Leofric and Jack, and spoke to them as he passed out. They asked him rather eagerly which side he took—that of the King or that of the Barons. He answered, with one of his thoughtful smiles, that these matters were not given to him to judge of—that he meddled but little in the strife of nations; but if he had to judge of any question, he sought always to discover the teachings of Holy Scripture, and to judge according to the mind of Christ.

By this time messengers had come to report that the Earl of Leicester, together with the Earl of Gloucester, had reached Abingdon, where they had halted to dine, and that they might be expected to arrive at the Grandpont by three o'clock in the afternoon.

All the city seemed in motion towards the South Gate, which led towards the Grandpont (as Folly Bridge was then called), and Gilbert rushing up joined himself to the other three, and urged them to come and see all that was to be seen.

The narrow street was quite blocked with foot passengers—clerks, citizens, masters and doctors all mingling together in one moving mass. It was a good-natured crowd, and there was much laughing and jesting as they had to squeeze through the gateway, and again across the bridge, until in the meadow beyond they had breathing room, and could spread themselves out more at ease. Here, dotted about in picturesque groups, were knots of

persons who had come from the surrounding districts—
farmers on their stout nags, with wife or daughter perched
on a pillion behind; and there, too, were groups of squires
and gentlemen from the neighbouring houses or castles,
many of these having brought their women folk to watch
the procession pass.

One group attracted attention from the fine trappings of
the horses, and from the general air of importance it wore.
There were two ladies, several horsemen in fine garments,
and one tall, commanding personage, who was evidently
an official of some sort. He was surrounded by several
soldiers, who observed an attitude of watchful attention;
and Gilbert said to his comrades in a quick whisper,—

"Yon is the Constable of the Castle. They say he is
very favourable to the cause of the Barons, though he calls
himself the servant of the King. He is a good man, and
well beliked in Oxford, albeit he and the Chancellor sometimes come to loggerheads anent the limits of their jurisdiction; yet they be good friends for all that. There goes
the Chancellor to speak with him and join his party."

Leofric looked rather eagerly towards the little group
around the Constable, and truly enough there sat Mistress
Alys upon her palfrey, her golden hair hanging like a cloud
about her face, her eyes gazing round her full of curiosity.
Suddenly she met the gaze bent upon her, and started a
little. Then a look of recognition flashed into her face.
She glanced at her father, but he was engrossed in conversation, and did not see. Failing in getting his attention, she just raised her hand, and waved it for a moment

towards Leofric and his companion; then blushing a little as if at her boldness, she drew back behind one of the horsemen in the group.

Leofric bared his head and bowed low at the little lady's salute; but he made no further attempt to attract attention, and the friends passed quickly through the crowd lingering at the head of the bridge, and made their way along the road towards Abingdon, where numbers of the citizens were already straying, in hopes of catching sight of the foremost of the Barons' followers.

Presently they came upon a group gathered beneath the shade of some large oak trees, and heard themselves hailed in tones of welcome. This group consisted of the Seaton family, and the beautiful twins, Lotta and Linda. Pedro Balzani, not desiring that his daughters should remain in the inn when it was like to be crowded from garret to basement by fine gallants in the train of the Earl of Leicester, had asked of his neighbours the Seatons house-room for them at this season, Joanna Seaton being the great friend of the twin sisters. The whole party had come forth to picnic under the greenwood trees and watch the show go by. And now, as was but natural, these four comrades, who always consorted more or less together, were invited to share in the remains of the repast, and to join the pleasant party.

Nothing loth, they all sat down, and having been too excited to provide themselves with dinner, were glad enough of some of Dame Seaton's excellent fare. By this time all the party were very well acquainted—laughter and fun were the order of the day. By this time Leofric had come to distinguish as a rule between the twin sisters, although he frequently made a mistake which evoked amusement and banter. Hugh never made any mistake now, and always gravitated towards Linda, the gentler of the two girls. Leofric sometimes wondered whether or not he was beginning to love the maiden. She was certainly very sweet and winning, yet she was but the daughter of an innkeeper, and half a foreigner to boot; whilst Hugh was a gentleman's son, and might hope one day to win his spurs.

The sun overhead shone down hotly, though beneath the trees it was pleasant enough. The afternoon was wearing on, and excitement had become intense.

At last the long-waited-for sounds arose, telling of the approach of a number of riders. Rushing helter-skelter along the dusty road came bands of clerks and others, who had gone on towards Abingdon, and now came pouring back towards the city with the cry on their lips,—

"They come! they come!"

All sprang to their feet. The youths helped the maidens to clamber into good places of observation amid the branches of a gnarled old oak, blasted by lightning, that stood hard by the road. Then they drew themselves up bare-headed beneath, prepared to swell the shout of welcome which arose as soon as the foremost horsemen hove in sight. Leofric strained his eyes to gaze at the on-coming procession, for it was such a sight as his eyes had never looked upon before.

Hugh stood close beside him, his eyes shining with excitement and anticipation. The tramp of horse-hoofs and the ringing sound of armour made itself heard through the still, clear air.

"Come they in arms?" whispered Gilbert with bated breath, for he was not prepared for that. Yet, sure enough, as the first ranks of the horsemen rode up, it was plainly to be seen that they were armed from top to toe—a brave spectacle in truth, yet one that the by-standers had scarcely expected to see.

Row after row, row after row of bravely-trapped horsemen passed by at a gentle trot, and still Hugh made no sign. Then he suddenly grasped the arms of those next him, and exclaimed,—

"There he is! there he is! Is he not a right royal man?"

Leofric's gaze was instantly fastened upon the eagle-like face of a warrior in a richly-chased coat of mail, with a plumed head-piece on his head—a man who sat erect in his saddle, returning the greetings of the by-standers with a grave dignity of demeanour—a man who looked born to command and born to rule, and who, in spite of his own foreign blood, was at this moment the champion of England's liberties, the enemy of those hordes of foreign aliens who were preying upon the land to her destruction.

Close behind him rode in pairs four young men, all of them bearing some sort of likeness to their eagle-faced sire. The faces of the first two did not specially attract Leofric, for there was too much haughtiness in the bearing of the

young men, albeit no trace of that passion was to be seen
in their great father. But the younger pair were far more
attractive, being bright-faced boys, who looked about them
with eager eyes, and flashed a quick smile at Hugh as they
rode by.

"Those be my young lords, Guy and Amalric," cried
Hugh with beaming face, "and they have not forgotten
me. Anon I will seek speech of them. And see—see!
yonder rides mine own father, amongst the retainers bringing up the rear. Ah! I had scarce thought to see him
here. Now, perchance, we shall see something of the
great scene when this Parliament, which men call "mad,"
shall assemble itself. Methinks there will be sound sense
found amongst those who gather together to discuss the
welfare of the nation."

It was hopeless to try to keep up with the riders; the
hot sun and choking dust alike precluded such a thing.
The party returned leisurely to Oxford, to find the city
half mad with excitement. Nor was there any diminution
of excitement possible; for on the morrow there would be
a yet grander sight, when the King himself should arrive,
and when the Barons should ride forth to meet and
welcome him.

This was indeed a very fine spectacle, and Hugh took
care that his friends should share it with him. He had
managed to borrow steeds from some of his father's servants, who had no need to take part in this ceremony, and
upon these horses he mounted his friends and himself. They
posted themselves at a certain spot hard by Beaumont

Palace, where they were told they would obtain an excellent view of the meeting betwixt King and Barons.

To-day Leofric and Jack were able to obtain a far nearer and better view of the Earl of Leicester, and the more they studied his handsome face, the more admiration did they feel for him. He seemed the soul and centre of that noble assembly. The other Barons appeared to regard him as their natural chieftain, and whenever he spoke they hung upon his words, and appeared to give the utmost respect to them. Although he was habited more plainly than any, he was like a king in their midst. His face was lined by anxiety and care, but the fire in his eyes was unquenched and unquenchable. He looked like one born to rule, and his expression seemed to show that, on this occasion at least, he meant to exercise that faculty to the uttermost.

A blare of trumpets suddenly announced the coming of the King, and a thrill seemed to run through the assembled crowd. The Earl drew himself erect in his saddle, and the other nobles fell into rank around him. The trumpet notes drew nearer and nearer, and at last the cry was raised,—

"The King! the King!"

In gorgeous array, surrounded by courtiers dressed in the extreme of foppery, appeared the procession of the monarch. The nobles bared their heads, as did also the crowd, and all faces were turned expectantly towards the oncoming procession.

Everything that pomp and state could do to add dignity to the King's Majesty was present here; and yet there was

so little of true kingly majesty in that weak, handsome
face, and in the shifting expression of the uncertain eyes,
that Leofric, looking from one face to the other, said in
his heart,—

"Is it possible that that is the King and the other the
subject? Surely it should be just the other way about."

It did indeed so appear; for the Earl, whilst showing
every mark of respect to his sovereign, yet wore himself
so lofty and kingly an aspect that Henry seemed unwit-
tingly to shrink before him, but he strove to conceal this
by taking a haughty and rebuking tone.

"How, now, my lord of Leicester! is it in arms that
you come to meet your King?"

"Sire," replied the Earl, speaking for himself and his
companions, "we are on our way to quell the troubles that
have arisen in Wales, and therefore come we armed, as
indeed needs must be if we are to do there your Majesty's
behests. This business once over for which we are met
together, and we must to the West to serve your Highness
there. Let us hope for a speedy settlement of affairs here,
for our presence is needed urgently against the troublers
of the peace of the realm."

As he spoke the Earl swept with his eagle eyes the
ranks of swarthy faces that surrounded the King, and a
murmur went up from the crowd which was sufficiently
significant.

It was almost an open challenge of defiance, and Henry
knew it as such. This could be seen in the flush upon his
face, and in the flash of his eye. Yet he could not meet

the calm gaze of the Earl, and he strove to pass the matter off with a laugh.

"Thou wert always something too ready with thy tongue, Simon," he said; "be careful thou art not some day too ready with thy sword likewise."

"My sword can never be too ready, an it be unsheathed in the service of your Majesty's peace and honour, and for the safety and welfare of the fair realm over which it has pleased God to set you," was the steady response.

The King laughed, and shrugged his shoulders.

"Come and ride with me, and tell me of my sister, thy wife," he said, as though willing to let other matters rest for the present. "Thou art as great a tyrant as ever thou wast, Simon; but beshrew me if I can help from liking thee when we meet face to face. Ride by my side and talk to me. Let the people at least see that we bear each other no ill-will."

So King and subject rode side by side to the palace of Beaumont, and the people made the welkin ring with their acclamations.

"Though whether they be shouting for thee or for me," remarked Henry, with a short laugh, "perhaps it would be well not to inquire too closely."

CHAPTER VII.

THE CONSTABLE'S CHILDREN.

"FAIR Mistress Alys, this is sooth a wondrous city, in the which strange sights are to be seen. Fain would I myself belong to it, and make one of those bands of scholars whom I see passing to and fro through the streets. Fain would I learn more of the life here, and share it for a while. I am aweary of the clash of arms and the strife of tongues. The life of a scholar has more charms for me."

The fair-faced Alys looked up from the frame where was stretched a great piece of tapestry work, upon which her nimble fingers were at work. There was a smile in her eyes as she made reply,—

"And yet, from all I hear and see, there is plenty of strife of tongues and clash of arms even within the walls of this city, and amongst the clerks and scholars themselves. I have not dwelt long enough here to know what it is all about; but methinks those who have the charge of the city have hard work sometimes to keep the peace there."

"That is very true," spoke a second voice, not at all unlike the one which had just ceased, although it belonged to

a lad of seventeen summers, who lay full length upon a
wide settle, over which a great bearskin rug had been
first laid. The face of this youth was thin and hollow, and
his hands were white and wasted. But his hazel eyes were
liquid and full of brightness, and though the broad brow
was often furrowed by pain, the smile which lit up the
thin, well-cut features was frequent and full of brightness.

"Yes; Alys speaks no more than the truth," said the
youth, as Amalric de Montfort turned to look at him. "We
have not been long in this place, as thou dost know.
Until our father had been settled here some time as Constable of the Castle, he would not summon us to be with
him. We remained with our mother's kindred in the
south, and have only been a few short months within these
walls. Yet we have learned many strange things during
this time, and truly do I think that the city of Oxford can
be one of the most turbulent spots upon the face of the
earth. I have heard my father and the Chancellor of the
University taking counsel together how the peace may be
kept, and in sooth it seems no easy matter to decide."

"Ah yes, where many hot-headed youths be pent up together in narrow bounds, there must needs be strife of a
kind," answered Amalric; "but that, after all, is a brotherly
sort of strife, far removed from this other strife of which
I begin to grow strangely weary. If ye twain could know
but the half of what my noble father has endured at the
hands of the King—how he has spent his substance and his
own life-blood away there in Gascony, all to establish the
King's royal authority there; and how for all his faithful

service he has received naught but hard words and humiliations which would have turned many another into a bitter foe! The tyranny and caprice of the weak King (uncle though he be of mine, I will speak the truth of him) has been heartbreaking. It has aged my lady mother, and embittered my father's life. And now, when he is forced to stand forth as the champion of the nation, to hold the King to his promises, there will be nothing before him but one long, strenuous fight. Oh, I begin to weary of it all! If I could help him, I would be ever at his side; but I can do nothing, and my heart grows sick within me. Would that he would leave me behind in this city of learning, that I might join the ranks of scholars, and gain, perchance, by my pen what I scarce think I shall ever do by my sword! Methinks I was not born for such strenuous days as these."

"Would that I might be in the very thickest of the strife!" cried the lad, Edmund de Kynaston, his eyes dilating with a quick flash. "Methinks were I as others are, I would ever seek out the post of greatest peril, and stand in the foremost of the fight! Yet here am I, a useless log, scarce able to put one foot before the other. Such is the caprice of Dame Fortune!"

Alys rose from her frame, and crossed the room with light steps; she bent over her brother and gently smoothed away the hair from his brow.

"But thou art happy here with me, my brother?" she questioned pleadingly; "and when our father has time to see to the matter, we will study together, and grow learned and wise, even if we cannot go forth into the great world of battles without."

Edmund's smile was bright and eager as he imprisoned his sister's fingers in his own.

"Verily, we will do great things together in one fashion or another, sweet sister. I am always happy with thee at my side; yet I would that I could serve and tend thee, instead of receiving all the service at thy hands."

"I love to tend thee, brother mine," whispered Alys, as she bent over him and kissed his brow, and then tripped lightly back to her frame; for idleness was not permitted to the daughter of the Constable, and her mother required a daily portion of work from those skilful fingers.

This conversation took place in a pleasant upper chamber belonging to one of the many solid buildings enclosed within the walls of what was known as the Castle of Oxford.

There were several buildings within these circling walls —the College and Chapel of St. George, the Constable's quarters, and certain strong towers that were often used as prisons for unruly clerks and scholars. The Chancellor himself, although exercising a wide jurisdiction over the liberties of the members of the University, had no place of durance in which to place offenders, so that they were most often brought into the Castle and lodged there.

Sir Humphrey de Kynaston had not occupied the position of Constable very long, and so far he and the Chancellor had been excellent friends. They were both anxious to maintain the peace of the city, and were agreed to act in concert, instead of in rivalry, as had sometimes been the case between former Governors of Castle and University.

Sir Humphrey had only two children, a boy and a girl. Edmund had always been famed for his daring spirit and sunny temperament, and during his boyhood had been the pride and joy of his father's heart. Two years ago, however, he had received what appeared at the time to be a fatal injury during a boar-hunt in the New Forest, where he was staying with his mother's kinsfolks. The boar had turned to bay, and when some daring huntsman, together with Edmund's uncle, approached to try to give the final blow, the maddened creature sprang at them with such fury that both fell before him, and all thought their lives must pay the forfeit. But Edmund had seized a strong spear, and had made so sudden and fierce a rush that the beast was borne back for a moment, giving the two time to gain their feet once again. When they turned to slay their quarry, however, they found that he had inflicted a terrible wound upon Edmund with his great tusks. The boy was carried home in what was thought to be a dying state, and although his fine constitution had enabled him to pull through the long and dangerous illness, he had remained permanently crippled, unable to do more than trail himself painfully from room to room, or occasionally in warm weather to take a little very gentle exercise on the back of a quiet and well-trained horse, which would be content to pace sedately without prancing or curvetting.

Since that day it had been the chiefest happiness of Alys's life to wait upon her brother, soothe his hours of suffering, which were many, and share with him every simple joy and interest in life. Brother and sister had both been greatly pleased to join their father at the Castle here, and were ready to take a keen interest in all that went on at this seat of learning.

Edmund had been fired with the desire to excel now in learning as he had once excelled in feats of skill and strength. Their father had promised to find for them a tutor with whom they might study; and perhaps some youthful clerk to read to them out of such books as were then obtainable, that they might progress the faster in their studies.

But the present excitement occasioned by the Parliament assembled in the city had for the moment driven everything else out of the minds of those dwelling there, and Sir Humphrey had his hands and mind and house alike full.

The Parliament was sitting in the vacated quarters of the Black Friars in the Jewry. The largest of their buildings there had been hastily fitted up as a Council chamber; and the King and Barons met in daily conclave to discuss the situation, and agree upon some definite plan for the future.

The great De Montfort, who had been accustomed to rough it under all sorts of climates and in all sorts of conditions, would have been content to take up his own quarters at the inn in the town, had not Sir Humphrey insisted that he and his sons should be his guests at the Castle, leaving only the retinue at Dagville's Inn.

Thus it came about that, whilst the Earl and his two
elder sons went daily to the meeting-place in the Jewry,
the younger sons, Guy and Amalric, were left pretty much
to their own devices, and spent their time for the most part
either in wandering about the town and learning what
they could as to the life there, or with the fair Alys and
her brother in this pleasant, airy chamber.

The room was itself very attractive, for it was adorned
with tapestry hangings which Alys's skilful fingers had
wrought, and upon the stone floor lay the dressed skins
of many a wild creature of the woods which Edmund
had slain ere he had been laid low. Several stuffed birds
and small beasts were to be seen set upon the brackets
which Edmund carved in his hours of ease; and a tame
falcon upon a perch occupied a little recess, and when
released from his chain would fly about the room or
perch affectionately on the hand of the master he loved.
A great wolf-hound also was generally to be found lying
at full length beside his master's couch. He had been
Edmund's most faithful follower almost from boyhood,
and was now growing old and a little infirm. Therefore
his master's ways were little trouble to him, and save
when he paced backwards and forwards in the courtyard
with his mistress, he seldom cared to move from beside
Edmund's couch.

Both Guy and Amalric de Montfort had grown fond of
this upper chamber and its inhabitants, and came and went
almost at will. Edmund had been keenly interested in all
that these lads could tell him of their father's campaigns,

and of the battle for constitutional liberty which he was
so strenuously fighting now. Edmund knew that his own
father was strongly in sympathy with the action that the
Barons were now taking, and he listened eagerly to any
items of information which he could pick up. But whilst
the Parliament was sitting, little was said as to the course
the deliberations were taking. There were whispers of
stormy scenes, and of outbreaks of fierce and rather im-
potent anger on the part of the King; but for the most
part a discreet silence was observed as to the probable result of the deliberations, though from the King's increasing
irritability and fits of gloom it was surmised that he was
not best pleased at the course things were taking.

The talk between the De Kynastons and Amalric de
Montfort on this particular day was interrupted by the
sudden entrance of Guy, who came in eagerly and joyously.

"I have a plan!" he cried. "I was wandering down
hard by the Grandpont, when I saw a man in a right
comely wherry, and he was pleased to hire it to me for a
few pence. He says that it will carry a party well, and
that if we lift it over the fall by Iffley Church, we can
navigate a great stretch of the river, or if we better like
we can go up against the current. Methought thou
mightest well go with us, Edmund, for thou canst ride
down to the river-bank, and then the boat will carry thee
bravely, and we can take with us that bear's skin and
make a couch for thee along the bottom."

Alys clapped her hands in delight at the thought.
Somehow it had never occurred to them that the river

might open up a new source of amusement for the invalid.

Quickly was the matter settled. Dame Kynaston, though rather a martinet in her household, as a managing housewife in those days had some need to be, was a loving mother also, and was only too glad to forward any plan whereby Edmund might benefit in health or spirits. Very soon the little party was on its way to the wherry lying by the bridge, eagerly planning the day's pleasuring, and finally settling that the navigation of the Cherwell would afford the most amusement and novelty.

"What is yon tower hard by the bridge?" asked Amalric of Alys, by whose side he was walking, a little in advance of the other pair.

"They call it Friar Bacon's study," answered Alys. "You may have heard of Friar Bacon. They say he was a great and a good man, and he joined himself to the Minorite Friars. But he grew too learned in what men call the black arts—in astrology and astronomy; and he built himself yon tower, that he might the better study the stars. So men got frightened at him and his learning, and he was banished the city and the realm. I have heard that he went to Paris, but I know not if that be true. They say that if a greater or more learned man should ever pass beneath the tower, its walls will crumble away, and it will fall to the ground. But it has not fallen yet!"

"I have heard of Friar Bacon and his learning in very truth," answered Amalric. "I call it shame that such a man should be banished the realm. I believe not that any learning hurts the soul of man, so it be gotten in the fear of God and the love of man."

Just at that moment a youth in the dress of a clerk turned a corner, and came face to face with Alys and her companion.

" Hugh !" cried Amalric joyfully. " If I have not been looking for another sight of thy face ever since we first entered the city, and I caught sight of thee in the crowd ! Now this is well met, for we are bent on a day's pleasuring on the water, and I am very sure that fair Mistress Alys will give me leave to ask thee to join our company."

Alys bent her head with ready assent. She was interested in all clerks; and the pleasant, open face of Hugh was attractive, besides the guarantee of his being known to Amalric. Guy also gave him a friendly greeting when the palfrey was led down to the water's edge, and before long the whole party had embarked, and were rowing gently down the stream to the point where the Cherwell made its junction with the Isis.

Hugh was called upon to tell his experiences as a scholar in the city, and was nothing loth to do so. Amalric listened with all his ears, and Edmund likewise. The youngest son of the warlike Earl of Leicester had more of the scholar than the soldier in his composition, and was already deeply bitten by the idea of remaining in Oxford and becoming a scholar there. It was not likely that his father would oppose the wish if strongly urged, and Amalric thus lost no opportunity of obtaining information as to the life there.

Edmund lay along the bottom of the boat, delighted with the easy motion, with the tree-crowned banks between which they were gliding, and the beauty of all they saw in wood and meadow. The waterway was so narrow in places that Alys could hardly believe they could force their way through it at all; but this they always managed to do, and pushed on and on until the sound of falling water told them that they would find an obstruction to further progress.

"Never mind," cried Hugh; "it is but the fall. We must disembark and carry the boat a few yards, and launch it afresh on the upper stream. There we shall have a wider highway and more water. Ha! and here, as happy chance wills it, are two good friends who will lend us a hand."

They had come in sight of the fall now, and also of a little canoe drawn up near to the bank, in which a pair of lads were seated, one diligently fishing in the pool, the other poring over a small volume which he held in his hands; and so intent did this latter appear over his task, that it was not until hailed in a loud voice by Hugh that he lifted his face.

When he did so, however, Alys gave a little cry, and bending over Edmund, she said eagerly,—

"Brother, yonder is the clerk who saved me when the palfrey went nigh to hurting me that day in the springtide. I am sure it is he; and it was he I saw in the meadows the day when the Barons made their entry into the city. Prithee may I speak to him? he seems to be known to Master Hugh."

"I will speak him first," answered Edmund; and then with a good deal of confusion of tongues the boat was drawn ashore, and all the party disembarked—Alys giving her shoulder to her brother to lean upon whilst the wherry was carried to the upper waters close above the fall.

"May I not help you, sir?" asked Leofric, coming up with a shy smile in his eyes. The other four youths— for Jack had taken his part there—were carrying the boat, and Leofric had been sent back to help Edmund up the narrow path. "I am very strong, and the way is not long. Lean upon me, and I will take you there gently."

"Thanks, good lad," answered Edmund, availing himself of the strong arm extended to him. "I was wanting a word with thee, for my sister here tells me that thou didst do her a good turn one day some while back, when her horse took fright, and might have thrown her from its back."

Leofric blushed and disclaimed, declaring that Jack had done more than himself; but Alys was of another opinion, and both brother and sister fell into conversation with their new acquaintance, whose face, as usual, won him favour at once.

"Thou wert reading when we came up," said Edmund; "art thou a scholar of this place?"

Leofric told of himself, who and what he was, and admitted that he was able to read Latin fairly well and understand it too, and that Brother Angelus had given him several books to study, to help him to a greater proficiency.

"These are the 'Sentences' they think so much of in the schools," said Leofric, drawing the little volume from his pouch; " but Brother Angelus prefers to go straight to the Scriptures themselves for learning, and loves not the Sentences very greatly. But it is well for a clerk to be versed in them. I have begun to study the philosophy of Aristotle too, for all men talk much of him now, though some say that his learning is dangerous to the soul. Howbeit all men are eager to learn it."

"And where dost thou dwell ?" asked Edmund eagerly; "and if thou be poor, as thou sayest, how dost thou live ?"

"Our wants are but few, and we live in a little turret on the walls, where we have made a chamber for ourselves, no man forbidding us. My comrade, Jack Dugdale, fishes, and snares rabbits in the woods; and I gain small sums of money by painting on vellum, which I learned from the good monks of St. Michael. We have enough for our needs, and can pay our fees to the masters we seek after. Your father, sir, gave us money that day of which you spoke. It was very welcome to us then, for we had but come into the city, and scarce knew then how we should live."

By this time the boat was launched again, and the whole party assisted Edmund to regain his former position along the bottom. Guy de Montfort had taken an immense fancy to the canoe he had seen, and nothing would serve him but that Jack should bring it up and give him a lesson in the management of the craft. When he heard

how the two lads had travelled in it from a region not so
very far from his own home of Kenilworth, he was very
much astonished; and getting Leofric to take his place in
the boat, he and Jack set off together up the stream, and
were soon lost to sight of the others.

This left Amalric, Hugh, and Leofric to navigate the
larger boat, and to talk together of those matters which
interested them and Edmund so much. It was natural
that Amalric and Hugh should consort together, having
been friends and comrades in old days. This left Leofric
free to answer the many eager questions put to him by
Edmund, whilst Alys sat by with eager face and shining
eyes, not losing a word of the conversation, and sometimes
taking a share in it herself.

"I can get books," said Edmund, "but they be nearly
all in Latin. I can neither read them easily nor understand what I read. I want to find somebody who will
come and read with me; for soon my eyes grow weary,
and my back aches if I try to hold up the volume myself,
and I am wellnigh ashamed to ask my father for a tutor,
when perchance I might so soon get aweary of his teachings. What I want rather, to begin with, is a tutor for
perhaps a few hours in the week, and for the rest a youth
like myself, himself a clerk, but with more learning than I,
who would come and read to me and with me till I could
get the mastery myself over the Latin tongue."

Leofric's eyes were bright with interest. He was too
modest to speak the words that trembled on his tongue;
but the thought of having access to books was strangely

tempting, and there was something about Edmund and
Alys which attracted him greatly. The gentle refinement
of their manners and speech was in such pleasing contrast
to the *brusquerie* of the bulk of his associates. When
Alys said timidly,—

"Would Leofric Wyvill come to us if our father
approved?" his face burned with gratification and joy
at being thus singled out; and Edmund looked at him,
saying,—

"I had scarce liked to ask, in case thou mightest have
other work more important; but I trow my father
would approve, and would pay thee for thy time and
labour."

"O sir, to have books to read would be payment
enough!" cried Leofric eagerly. "I have longed to see
more, but there be all too few in the city for the needs of
scholars and clerks; and but for the kindness of Brother
Angelus, I should never have aught to study save what I
can write down of the things we hear. I am but a learner
myself; but if I can help you, it will make me glad and
proud to do so. I could at least strive to remember all I
hear, and repeat it to you. That is what I have to do for
Jack, who is not used to learning. He forgets all too soon,
and then we go over each lecture together, and I write
upon the walls such things as we most desire to remember,
and there they are to remind us if we want information
another day."

Before the boat and its occupants made their way back
to the town, Amalric de Montfort had made up his mind

to ask of his father grace to remain behind and enter himself as a clerk in some Hall at Oxford; whilst Edmund had fully resolved to beg his parents to engage Leofric Wyvill to come to him several times in the week, to read with him, and instruct him in brother-like fashion in those things which he was learning for himself.

CHAPTER VIII.

STORMY SCENES.

"HAVE a care how thou dost answer me, Mistress; I am not one who brooks trifling!"

"I have never trifled with thee, Roger de Horn," answered the maiden addressed, speaking firmly though gently. "Methinks thou dost forget thyself in speaking such words to me to-day."

The dark face of Roger was deeply flushed. He looked as though he had been drinking—as indeed was probably the case; at any rate he was very angry, and his words came hissing from between his teeth in a fashion not pleasant to hear.

"Not trifled with me, quotha? Canst thou look me in the face and say that?—whilst the love-token that thou didst give me lies now upon my heart!"

The face of Linda Balzani flushed deeply, partly with anger, partly with maiden modesty. She drew herself away with a gesture full of simple dignity.

"I have given thee no token," she said. "If thou hast received aught, it must be from the hands of my sister. I know nothing of any token."

" What ! " cried the young man, the flush mounting even
to his brow, " wilt thou deny the kiss that thou didst
bestow upon me out in the greenwood on Midsummer Eve,
and the token thou didst give me as proof of thy love ? "

Linda drew away yet a little farther, and glanced round
the room as though seeking some way of exit. The excitement in Roger's manner was unpleasant, and the claim
he was making upon her was revolting. She had always
disliked this braggart, even though treating him with
civility as her brother's friend. Of late she had come to
dislike him more and more, and to shrink from his approach as one shrinks from the proximity of some noisome
reptile. She had fancied that her sister had of late been
seeking the society of Roger with pleasure ; which thing
rather perplexed her, because in private Lotta never
masked her dislike and contempt for the bully and swag-
gerer, and of late had been more severe in her strictures
than ever.

The very thought of what had taken place under the
greenwood trees upon Midsummer Eve brought a flush to
Linda's brow and a throb to her heart. Was it not then
and there that Hugh le Barbier had breathed into her ears
some words so full of music that the echo of them had
never left them since ? She had scarce dared to think
what those words might imply. She was content to
dream rather than to think, and she had lived in dream-
land almost ever since. To be spoken to thus was un-
endurable, and the spirit of the maiden was roused.

" Methinks, sir, that thou hast been drinking, and hast

overheated thy blood," she said, rising as if to leave the room. "I spoke scarce three words to thee upon that Midsummer Eve. I have done nothing and said nothing to warrant the claim thou dost make. Prithee let me go; I have had enough of this."

But Roger planted himself before the door, his sombre eyes glowing with passion.

"Beshrew me if thou be not a false and fickle jade! But I will brook none such answer from thee. See here —behold the token! Wilt thou dare to look upon it and tell me it was never thine?"

Linda looked, and started slightly. It was indeed a little trinket that had belonged to her for years. As a child she used to carry it as a charm about her neck; but latterly she had ceased to do this. She had not even missed it from the box where she kept it together with a few more little keepsakes and girlish treasures. How it had come into the possession of Roger she could not imagine. He saw her start, and his eyes gleamed.

"So!—thou dost not dare to deny the witness of thine eyes!"

"The heart was once mine," answered Linda quietly, "but I have not seen it for many weeks. I never gave it thee. It must have fallen into the hands of another, and so have come to thine. Let me pass, sir; we have had something too much of this already."

"What!" he cried furiously, "thou dost own to the trinket, but dost deny the gift? Thinkest thou that I will endure to be flouted thus?"

"I flout thee not, sir; I do but speak sooth. I gave thee no trinket—I gave thee no kiss. I have never bestowed upon thee aught save that meed of friendship which my brother's friend has a right to look for."

He grasped her slim wrist in his strong hand. He brought his swarthy face and flashing eyes close to her shrinking face.

"Thou didst give me much more than that till *he* came amongst us—the upstart, the fine gentleman, the fop with the smooth speech and dainty dress! Thinkest thou I have not seen it all—how that thou dost seek to play us one against the other? But thou shalt never make a tool of me; I will have all or nothing! And I will wring the neck of any man who shall dare come betwixt me and my love!"

The last words were hissed rather than spoken, and so cruel and fierce was the aspect of the speaker that Linda tore herself suddenly away and uttered a shriek of fear.

The next moment the door was quickly opened from without, and Joanna Seaton appeared, with Lotta a little behind her, the latter wearing rather a strange look upon her handsome, haughty face, whilst her gaze glanced rapidly from one to the other of the occupants of the room.

"Is aught amiss?" asked Joanna quickly; "methought that I heard a call."

Roger turned upon his heel with one sinister glance over his shoulder, and made as if to depart.

"I will finish what I have to say another day," he ob-

served, "when thou art in a better frame for listening, fair
Mistress Linda, and when thou hast something refreshed
thy memory."

"What does he mean?" asked Joanna, as Roger clanked
down the stairs and Linda sank trembling upon a couch.

"He is a bad man—I fear and I hate him!" she cried
in panting breaths.—"Lotta, what hast thou done that he
should say such things to me? It must have been thy
doing! He has the agate heart that once I wore. None
can have given him that but thou. And thou must have
given him other tender tokens too, for he speaks of things
of which I know naught. Sister, thou doest not well to
show treachery to thine own flesh and blood!"

Lotta tossed her handsome head, and a flush crept into
her dusky cheek. Of late the likeness between the sisters
had grown somewhat less. A softness and subtile charm
had crept over Linda, whilst Lotta, though handsome as
ever, had seemed to grow harder and more defiant in her
proud beauty. Mistakes between the pair were of less
frequent occurrence, and although it would be easy for
Lotta to personate her sister of set purpose, the difference
between them was becoming more clearly marked day by
day.

"What now, Linda?" quoth the other; "thou art always
fancying some new thing. I have scant patience with thy
whims. What do I know of thy trinkets, or of thy lovers?
Thou art like a skilful bowman, who has a second string
to his bow ready to hand. But when thou dost find that
such a game has its perils, and that thou art playing with

edge tools, prithee do not seek to drag me in to help thee
out of the slough. It is a paltry trick, and unworthy of
thy name."

"But Lotta—"

"Peace, child! I will hear no more. I am sick to
death of thee and thy lovers! Let me alone. Manage
thine own affairs as thou wilt, but no word shalt thou
have from me. Go, and do as thou dost choose. Play
them one against the other, and see what comes of it. I
will have nothing to do with the matter; it is no concern
of mine."

And Lotta swept out of the room with her whirlwind
air of displeasure, whilst Linda looked in perplexity at
Joanna, and asked piteously,—

"Why is she so changed to me?"

"I fear me it is jealousy," answered Joanna, who had
seen a great deal during the weeks that the twins had
been with them. Joanna had been friendly with both
from childhood, but had always liked Linda best. Now
she began to find that she loved Linda and rather disliked
and feared Lotta. There was something wild and untamed
in her nature, and her conduct towards her sister often
provoked the indignation of the onlooker.

"Jealousy!" repeated Linda, with rising colour.

"Ay, jealousy of what she sees betwixt thee and Hugh
le Barbier," answered Joanna. "Hast thou not seen that
Lotta has gone nigh to lose her heart to yon courtly youth?
I have observed it these many weeks, and once I did think
that he might return her regard; but it seems plain now

that his fancy has been elsewhere fixed, and poor Lotta has to bear the pain of seeing it too."

Linda's cheeks were scarlet; she faltered as she spoke.

"Methought Lotta was pleased by the notice of Roger. I had thought that her fancy went that way."

"Perchance it did—till Hugh appeared. But there can be no comparison betwixt the two, and Lotta has ambition. She would fain link her lot in life with one who could raise her higher in the world. And Hugh has prospects of becoming, if not a knight at least an esquire to some noble lord, in whose service he may rise high. It may be ambition rather than love; but be it what it may, it is bitter to her to see herself passed by for another. I think perhaps it is the more bitter because that other is her sister, and so like to her in outward show that she cannot understand why she holds not an equal place in his heart."

Linda's face was all aglow. It could not but be sweet to feel that others had read the secret of Hugh's attachment to herself; but, again, it pained her that her sister should regard her as a rival, and still more that she should stoop to subterfuge, and seek to embroil her with so dangerous a man as Roger de Horn.

"What can it profit her to behave thus?" she asked of Joanna, when she had told the whole story; "why should she seek to anger him thus against me? It is cruel to me, and also to him, if indeed a creature so full of ferocity has any room in his heart for the gentle passion of love."

"Love is not always a gentle passion with natures such as his," answered Joanna shrewdly; "and methinks I see

what Lotta seeks to accomplish. She knows that thou
hast a timid nature as compared with her own; and she
thinks, possibly, that Roger will terrify thee into com-
pliance with his wishes, or that doubt and distrust may
be awakened in the heart of Hugh by what he hears and
sees; in which case, perchance, he might turn to her
for comfort. Such are the unworthy wiles of a jealous
nature. But it is playing a dangerous game to trifle with
a creature so untamed and savage as Roger. There is no
knowing to what excesses his anger may lead him."

Linda shuddered slightly at the memory of the past scene.

"Pray Heaven he hurt not Hugh!" she murmured. "He
said he would wring the neck of any man that dared to
come betwixt him and his purpose!"

"That is bad," said Joanna, looking grave. "I will speak
to my brother and also to Gilbert Barbeck, and tell them
to give an eye to Hugh should any riot arise in the city,
as is like."

"Why is it like?" asked Linda anxiously.

"Marry, because of all the excitements in the city during the sitting of this 'Mad Parliament,' as the King's
friends have dubbed it. It has been hard work to keep
down rioting all these weeks; and men say they are certain
there will be some great collision ere long—we are never
safe from such in this place, as thou dost know. The
marvel is that none such took place whilst the Parliament
was sitting. Had it not been for the presence within the
walls of so many armed men under discipline, I verily
believe it would have done so."

There was much truth in the words of this citizen maiden. Great had been the excitement ruling in Oxford during the days of the sitting of the Great Council or Parliament, and great was the joy and triumph of the supporters of De Montfort and the Barons at the result thereof.

This is not the place in which to give a history of those Provisions of Oxford of which so much was heard during the following years of Henry's reign. Suffice it to say that by those provisions the Barons obtained for themselves all that they desired, and for the time being the King was little more than a puppet in their hands. They had no desire to make new laws—that had never been a part of their purpose; what they aimed at was to rid themselves of illegal exaction, of feudal service, to obtain justice for themselves and others, and to rid the country of the multitudes of foreign favourites who were eating up the substance of the land, whilst its own sons had perforce to stand by empty-handed. "England for the English" was in effect their cry; and their position having been granted, steps were immediately taken to ensure the carrying out of the measure agreed upon.

Those who desire information will find in every history book how this was done, and will read about the twenty-four nobles and men of high estate chosen in equal numbers by King and Barons—the Council of Fifteen, the Twelve Commissioners of Parliament, and the Twenty-four Commissioners of the Aid.

All this belongs to the region of history rather than to

that of fiction ; but the result of this Parliament was that the King's power and that of his foreign favourites was, for the time being, broken, and a wave of enthusiasm and delight swept over the land, causing an outbreak of excitement and triumph which was quite enough to give anxiety to the authorities in such a turbulent city as that of Oxford.

The great Earl of Leicester was for the moment the idol of the University. Whenever he appeared abroad he was hailed with shouts and cheers. His strong personality and the fascination of his manner won upon the clerks and scholars, till they would have been ready to lay down their lives in his service. He received the adulation of the crowd with a kindly dignity that won all hearts, and when it was found that he was about to leave one of his sons behind him to study the Arts in Oxford, public delight knew no bounds, and Amalric was almost as much lauded and praised as his great father.

But, of course, there was never unanimity in this turbulent body of undisciplined youths. The very fact that the presence of De Montfort aroused in the breasts of many such unbounded enthusiasm, tended, as if from pure contrariety, to inflame others against him—to throw them into the arms of the party who sided with the King, and called De Montfort and his friends sacrilegious usurpers of the power and authority which had been vested by God in His anointed servant.

The monks were for the most part ardent supporters of the monarchy, whilst the friars unhesitatingly declared

that the kingly power could be abused, and that, when
this was the case, God Himself raised up men of right and
might to turn the King's heart from his errors, and to be
champions of truth and freedom. Scripture precedents
could, of course, be quoted on both sides, and controversy
often raged fiercely. In an age and in a place where
disputation and argument was as the elixir of life, and
where a man's fitness for promotion in the University
depended much on his oratorical powers and his ability to
hold his own in some wordy warfare, it was likely enough
that such burning questions as these should be discussed
by high and low alike, with every weapon from the
armoury of logic and rhetoric.

Although by this time the Parliament had broken up, the
Barons had taken themselves away, whilst the King had
retired for a short time to Woodstock, and had then left
that part of the country, controversy and excitement still
ran high. It seemed as if some sort of explosion must
take place ere the atmosphere was cleared, and the authorities were very watchful to try to put down with a strong
hand anything like street rioting or disturbance.

But the spirit of the time was too strong for them.
The students themselves seemed weary of good behaviour.
How it originated none exactly knew, but soon there was
no hiding the fact that a great jousting was to take
place shortly in the meadow of Beaumont, where the
various nationalities should try their prowess in feats of
skill and strength, and hold high revelling there such as
was due to them upon the feast of Holy Trinity; only

that the presence of the King and Barons in Oxford at that date had caused an adjournment of the holiday.

At that time the holidays of the Church were nearly all that students could claim. There was no regular break in the lectures as now, and men remained for years at Oxford without thinking of visiting their homes. But they regarded these Church holidays somewhat jealously, and they, together with the Fair of St. Frideswyde, formed the chief interludes in the monotony of University life.

"Tito," said Roger de Horn, taking his friend by the arm and leading him down a dark alley where none might see or hear them, "I have discovered all too much. Both your sisters love yon upstart Hugh, and Linda will have none of my wooing. I knew how it would be directly he crossed my path. He has been mine enemy from first to last. He will undo us if we undo not him."

Tito's eyes gleamed fiercely in the darkness.

"Methought thou hadst some token from Linda, and that all was well," he said.

"So had I; but now she flouts me, and denies it. She says that Lotta must have given it me. I could have sworn it was Linda; yet in the darkness it is no easy matter to tell one from the other."

"I would not wed Lotta were I in thy place," said Tito, with a short laugh. "She would run a stiletto through thy heart if thou didst anger her, as soon as kiss thee if thou didst please her. She is a veritable shrew when she is angered. Linda is a different sort. A man may lead her anywhere through her affections, or terrify her into submission. It matters little which, so we may win her to our purpose. I had thought that all was going well."

"And so did I, till I spoke with her a week since, and found her as adamant. I thought she was mine own till then; now I know that another has her heart."

Tito gave a short laugh that was somewhat like a snarl.

"We must rid ourselves of that other then."

"So said I," returned Roger promptly. "So told I my pretty fond love—"

"Then thou wert a fool for thy pains," interrupted Tito roughly. "If the man be warned, we shall have trouble with him."

"If the maid be frightened, she may come to her senses," retorted Roger.

Tito shook his head slightly.

"Thou dost not know what our southern women are made of," he answered. "They love with a different love from your cold northerners, and yet the northern blood from their mother has given to both a prudence which may be dangerous to our plan."

Roger muttered something that sounded like a curse.

"We will be a match yet for their prudence and their caution. Men have vanished from Oxford ere now, or have been found dead in the streets, and none have been the wiser for it. The Chancellor shakes his head; the other clerks clamour against the townsfolk, and perhaps a citizen is slain in reprisal; and then the matter is forgotten. What has been before can be again. Her lover dead, and pretty Linda will soon forget her fancy; or, mourning for him, she will be the more easily persuaded—and once we are sure of her, we can commence our plan, and wealth and renown will flow in upon us. We have all in readiness save the high priestess of the mysteries!"

"Hist, hist! have a care what thou dost say!" whispered Tito, in some alarm. "There is peril as well as profit in our plan. The black art finds scant favour in the eyes of the Church. Men have perished at the stake ere now for dabbling even as deeply as we have done. Have a care what thou dost speak in the open streets."

"Tush! none can hear," quoth Roger, with some contempt; "but as to the other matter, we must watch our chance and use it well. Men talk of the joustings which will soon take place if this horrid rain will but cease, which is rotting the corn in the fields, and bringing famine to our doors. When man meets man in full tilt in the jousting-field, it cannot be a very hard matter to run a lance into his eye, or even to pierce his heart. Moreover there be other chances, if eyes are kept open. Leave yon upstart to me, and I will soon find a way of wiping off my score against him. I have played that game before now. I shall play it the more skilfully for the practice I have had."

"Well, well, do as thou wilt; only be cautious, for we want none of the Chancellor's prison, and he watches over the lives and liberties of the clerks with jealous eye. Well enow should I like to see him cleared out of the path. I have no love for him, and he stands in the way of our cherished plan."

"He shall not stand so long," muttered Roger between

his teeth; and then the two men moved away along the dark and unsavoury lane, whilst a head, which had been thrust out awhile ago from an upper window, was now drawn in, and Linda Balzani pressed her two hands to her throbbing brow.

"What devils men can be!" she whispered. "What devilry is this that they are desiring to practise, and in which I am to be their tool? Heaven send me strength and courage to thwart their evil schemes! O Hugh, my love, my love! they shall not hurt thee if I can save thee. Twice warned is thrice armed. I will save thee from their cruel malice, or I will die with thee!"

CHAPTER IX.

A STUDENTS' HOLIDAY.

"WILT thou come to see the joustings in Beaumont meadows to-morrow, fair Mistress Alys?"

Alys raised her eyes from her frame, and saw that Amalric had entered the room with his eager, elastic step. The young De Montfort was no stranger to that upper chamber now. Indeed, scarce a day passed but he found his way thither, to tell the news of the city in the eager ears of Edmund, or to look into the eyes of the fair Alys, and listen whilst she played upon the lute.

A great friendship had sprung up between these three, and the fact that Amalric had entered as a scholar at St. George's College in the Castle gave them the more chance of frequent meetings. Sir Humphrey and his wife were glad that Edmund should be enlivened by the visits of a friend, and in his heart of hearts the Constable was devoted to the cause of the Barons, although his position obliged him to maintain an air of neutrality when political questions were discussed.

A great change had recently come over the lives of brother and sister. Instead of passing their days alone in this upper room, seeing hardly any faces but those of their

parents from one week's end to another, they now enjoyed
a variety of diversions. A master of Arts came twice in the
week to instruct Edmund in some of that lore he was so
eager to make his own, and upon three other days in the
week the young clerk Leofric Wyvill made his appearance,
to read with the invalid, and to assist him with such pre-
paration for his tutor as it was possible to make in those
days. Alys shared these readings with her brother, and
was almost as keenly interested as he. She almost neglected her tapestry frame now for a more congenial task,
but her mother still looked for the daily portion, and she
would return to it and work hard again, whilst Leofric
retailed to them such things as he had heard from those
various masters whose lectures he sedulously attended.

He was sitting beside Edmund's couch now, drawing
mathematical figures and working out the problems attached, when Amalric's voice broke in upon them, and for
the moment thoughts of study were thrown aside.

"They say it will be a brave show," continued young
De Montfort: "North and South will meet together and
tilt and hold joustings. They say the Welsh have joined
the Northerners, and that they will challenge those of the
South to meet them in mock combat. They have chosen
St. Bartholomew's Day, and all men say it will be a goodly
sight.—Art thou to be there, fair mistress?"

"I know not," answered Alys; "methinks my father
little likes these students' holidays. He says there is too
often more of purpose than of jest in their joustings. I
trow he will judge that I am better safe at home."

Leofric looked up with parted lips, as though about to speak ; and Edmund observing him, said,—

" Is that thine opinion also, Leofric ? "

" Perchance it is not for me to speak, seeing that I have but little knowledge to go upon. Yet I have a feeling that to-morrow will not pass without trouble. I have heard ill-whispers in the air. I have a fear that one whom I love right well may be in danger on that day."

This was interesting, and all looked eagerly at Leofric.

" Tell us all," said Edmund quickly ; " it may be that we can help thee."

" I speak of one whom you all know," answered Leofric,—" Hugh le Barbier, who has shown me great kindness since I came hither a poor, raw lad—"

" Hugh le Barbier ! why, I know him well," cried Amalric. " What hast thou to say of him ? If peril threatens, sure we can protect him ! Tell us what is in thy mind."

" He has an enemy," answered Leofric, " one Roger de Horn—"

At that name Edmund interrupted in his turn.

" I have heard my father speak of him. He is a turbulent fellow who has often disturbed the peace of the town, and but for the benefit of clergy, which he claims, would have met with some severe chastisement. What is his cause of quarrel with honest Hugh, our friend ? "

" In sooth I think it is about a maid," answered Leofric. " There be two fair sisters—daughters of the host where both Hugh and Roger dwell. Methinks I have told of them before. It is their faces I have drawn in my idle hours—the two sisters so alike that few may tell them apart. From what I can learn, methinks that Hugh and Roger both love the same maid, and that she returns the affection of Hugh, as any maiden would. Why Roger cannot please himself with the other, who is her very counterpart to look at, I cannot tell," continued Leofric, who knew nothing of the mysteries of love, and was puzzled to know how even Hugh had come to give such deep affection to one sister, whilst showing a calm indifference to the other; "but it seems that they have both set their fancy upon the same. And it is whispered that Roger has vowed vengeance upon his rival, and that he may seize upon his chance of doing him a mischief to-morrow."

"That must be stopped," said Edmund quickly; "I will speak to my father."

But Leofric slightly shook his head.

"I fear me that would do no good. Hugh will certainly not be withheld from joining in the joustings. He is to tilt, with Linda's snood of crimson ribbon fastened to his headpiece. If Roger be his antagonist in the lists, none can well interpose. These joustings are held to be the right of all clerks and citizens upon a holiday. To seek to stop them now would but stir up a riot in the place which might be worse than any mock battle in the fields."

Then we must be there to see that our friend Hugh comes to no unfair mischief at the hands of his rival," said Amalric quickly. "Which side doth Hugh take—North or

South ?   He is a dweller in the middle parts of the country,
and might choose either."

"We have agreed to throw in our lot with the South,"
answered Leofric, "and Roger is of the fierce Northerners.
Some men say that at the last there will be a grand mock
battle, in which all men will join.   For myself, I would
sooner it came not to such a pass.   I fear me there might
be less of mock fighting than true were it so."

Alys looked a little alarmed at the thought, and Amalric
exclaimed,—

"Surely the Chancellor and Proctors, and the Constable
your father, could contrive to keep men from falling upon
each other in such savage fashion ?"

Edmund slightly shook his head.

"I am not sure.   Strange things happen in Oxford
every year.   It is not many years since there was such a
riot betwixt some Irish clerks and some of the Northerners
as made the Chancellor take oaths of the students to keep
the peace for the future.   But new men pour in every
year, and oaths are forgotten all too quickly.   I would
that I could come abroad to-morrow and see the tilting.
I should not take it amiss if there were to be some collision betwixt party and party.   I sicken of this life between high walls.   I long to see life once more."

"And so thou shalt !" cried Amalric eagerly ; "I have
my horses here, and I will borrow a litter from somewhere,
and will take thee and Mistress Alys to the jousting-field.
There shalt thou see all that goes on, and thy father shall
give thee a few trusty fellows for a guard ; so that if there

be any rioting, thou and Mistress Alys can be brought
safely back in haste, by Barbican Lane. The rioters will
give the Castle a wide berth, we may be sure; the tide
of battle—if battle there be—will all set the other
way."

Alys clapped her little hands together; Edmund's eyes
lighted with anticipation. To escape from his prison, to
go abroad in the streets, was the great ambition of his life.
But it was seldom that he had achieved this end, and the
thought of sharing in the gaieties of the morrow was enchanting alike to him and to his sister.

Sir Humphrey was willing to fall in with the plan suggested. He had a great liking for Amalric, and perhaps
had already formed an idea that the youth was attracted
by his young daughter. Both youth and maiden were still
full young, but at least there was no harm in permitting
them some pleasant intercourse if they were disposed to
like one another. The Earl of Leicester was at this juncture perhaps the greatest man in the kingdom, and an
alliance with the noble house might prove of great advantage to the knight in his career. His wife had suggested
this notion to him, and he had listened not unwillingly.
In those days men regarded their daughters somewhat in
the light of chattels, to be disposed of as best promoted
the advancement of their own interests; and the fact that
Sir Humphrey was a tender father, and that Alys was the
light of his eyes, did not detract from the pleasure of the
thought that she might make a grand match, when a few
years had passed over her head, with the scion of a house

as likely to thrive and increase in power and glory as that
of Simon de Montfort.

Upon the next day, therefore, he forwarded all the
arrangements suggested by Amalric, furnished a guard to
his son and daughter, and putting them under the care of
young De Montfort, permitted them to sally forth into the
town to see the gay pageantry of a students' holiday.

The sun shone brightly to-day—the clouds had all rolled
away. The town had assumed a holiday appearance, and
from every door a motley multitude poured forth. Church
bells rang; at every corner were to be met processions
of clerks and scholars, many of whom had just achieved
some scholastic success, and were in consequence crowned
with wreaths of flowers; whilst their friends and supporters
danced around them similarly adorned, some disguised with
masks, others in grotesque garments like mummers—all
alike bent on amusement, and all with their faces set towards Beaumont meadows, in which the jousts and games
and tiltings were to be held.

Conspicuous amongst the gay throng in holiday attire
(for the citizens with their wives and daughters were pouring out to see the fun) was a small group of what some
took to be mummers—tall figures dressed all in black,
with masks upon their faces and weapons in their belts.
There were some six of these in all, and they glided hither
and thither amongst the shifting throng, unknown and
silent, people making way for them as they moved, as if
half afraid of their strange appearance.

Alys and Edmund caught sight of them more than once,

and eagerly asked Amalric who and what they were; but he could give them no reply, and soon they ceased to think of them in the entertainment of watching the gay shifting throng.

A good position for seeing the jousting was fixed upon by the men in charge of the Constable's children, and Edmund's litter was drawn up upon a knoll under a clump of trees, which gave a pleasant shade from the sun's rays; whilst the horse, tethered close at hand, could feed upon the grass.

"I should like to see some of the people we have been told about," said Alys, as she stood beside her brother's couch.—"Prithee, good Leofric, bring to us here thy friends Hugh and Gilbert and Jack, and those two twin sisters Lotta and Linda, and any others of whom thou hast spoken. I would be friends with all the world to-day. Go seek them and bring them hither, and at noon we will feast here together under the greenwood trees, and watch the merry joustings at our ease."

Alys was in unwontedly gay spirits that day, and Leofric hurried off to do her behests. It was easy to persuade his comrades to accept the invitation of the Constable's daughter, and she on her side had a pretty way of putting people at their ease in her company.

The twin sisters interested her greatly, but she did not think them quite so wonderfully alike as she had expected. One of them was pale and pensive, and had an anxious look in her soft eyes; whilst the other was radiant and flushed, talking and laughing gaily with all who approached,

and throwing towards Hugh le Barbier glances of such
witchery and fascination that Alys at first thought she
must be the lady of his choice.

All seemed to be gaiety and good-humour during the
early hours of the day. Games of all sorts, trials of skill
and strength, wrestling, archery, and quoits were entered
into with great zest. The jousting was to take place after
the mid-day meal, and at present the horsemen were comparatively few ; but these few rode hither and thither, and
carried off the ring from the pole with considerable skill.
Alys watched everything, and enjoyed herself mightily,
making herself a very graceful and gracious hostess to
her invited guests.

As the meal proceeded she found herself able to speak
a few words to the pensive twin, whom she now knew to
be Linda, the maiden whom Leofric had said that Hugh
loved. Hugh had been sitting beside her for some little
while, but now he had gone off with Gilbert to look to
their horses for the tilting, and the shadow had fallen
again upon the face of the girl.

"Is aught troubling thee, maiden?" asked Alys, in
a gentle tone. "Methinks that thou art pensive where
others be gay. Tell me what is in thy heart, and I will
seek to comfort thee."

Linda gave a sudden start, and glanced timidly into the
face of the younger girl ; but what she saw there seemed
to inspire her with confidence. She had heard before of
the gentle Alys, and felt that she was not quite a
stranger.

After a quick glance round to be sure that none else could hear her words, she made reply,—

"In sooth, sweet mistress, I scarce know how to answer; and yet my heart is heavy within me, and I fear I know not what. I have one who is near and dear to me, and I trow he is in danger. Yet how to succour him I know not; for he is brave of heart, and smiles at thought of fear; yet I have known terrible things happen in this strange city, and I fear—I fear!"

"What dost thou fear?" asked Alys, drawing a little closer.

"I fear foul play for him," answered Linda; "I have heard things which make my heart heavy as lead within me. Lady, hast thou seen some strange men in the crowd to-day—men all in black, who look to me like devils moving amongst the merry-makers? Hast thou seen them?"

"Ay, verily have I. Methought they were mummers, but none could tell me of them. Who and what are they?"

"I know not for a certainty, and yet I fear them. I saw through the mask-hole of one of them a pair of evil, flashing eyes, and methought it was Roger de Horn who thus gazed at me with malice in his heart. I truly think that my brother is another, and there are more whose names thou wouldest not know. But I fear me there are certain wild spirits bound together to do evil, and that the safety of my lover is to-day threatened amongst them."

Alys sat silent, a sympathetic fear creeping over

her. What could she say to comfort this trembling maiden?

"But how can these men hurt him? he will be mounted, and they are on foot. Dost think that they will join in the tourney too?"

"Nay; I should fear them less did they do so. Hugh would be more than a match for any of them, skilled as he is in knightly exercises, strong, and full of courage. He could unhorse Roger de Horn at one blow, despite his size and strength; and that does yon coward and braggart well know, wherefore he will not meet him in fair fight. What I fear is an ambushment, in which my lover will be carried off by those wicked men. And if he be thus spirited away, Heaven alone knows what fate may await him : for I am very sure that these confederates have sold themselves to the Evil One, and are masters of unholy crafts that we wot not of; and as all men know, when such seize upon a human victim, they do him to death with their black arts in some fearful fashion, seeking to wrest his soul from him ere they let go their hold upon his body!" and Linda trembled in every limb.

Alys shivered also, for these words sounded mysterious and terrible. She did not understand their import, but none the less did they fill her with horror.

But before another word could be said the sound of trumpet blasts smote upon the ears of the crowd, a great shout rent the welkin, and from opposite sides of the field two gallant parties of mounted revellers rode in—banners flying, lances in rest—and made a complete circuit of the meadow, the crowd flying right and left before them, until the field, lately covered with groups of merry-makers, became cleared for the tiltings of the mounted rivals.

It was a gallant show of student prowess, and for a while all went well; the combatants were fairly well matched, and good-humour prevailed over feelings of emulation and rivalry.

The sun slowly sank in the sky, but the revelry and joustings still went on. The crowd had closed in more and more upon the combatants, and now there was to be one great final charge, all the horsemen taking part in it together—a sort of mock battle before the sun should set.

Edmund was growing rather weary, but was still keenly interested; whilst Amalric, who had declined to join in the jousting, and had remained all the while with brother and sister, gazed very intently at the grouping of the crowd, and in particular at the movements of certain black figures, who seemed to be directing in a rather curious fashion the actions of certain knots of clerks and citizens, who were drawing ever nearer and nearer to the scene of action.

" Methinks, Edmund," he said suddenly, " that thou and Alys had better be turning homewards. The sun will soon be gone, and this is the last of the merry-making. It would be well not to get hemmed in by the crowd as it breaks up. I will call up the men, and we will return," and as he spoke he gave Edmund a look which the latter instantly understood.

Alys would fain have lingered, fascinated by the strange

sight presented by the plain, where she could have fancied a real battle was raging. There were such shouting, such clashing of arms, such defiant yells from the combatants, that she almost trembled where she stood; and when she mounted her palfrey, she felt that the creature was trembling also at the unwonted clamour.

Suddenly a girl's voice close at hand broke into a quick wail of horror and fear. Linda, clasping her hands closely together, cried in tones of lament,—

"It has begun! it has begun! They are fighting now. Oh, what will be the end of this?"

"Come, Mistress Alys," spoke Amalric, in tones that unconsciously betrayed anxiety and authority, "we must not linger here. It is too true; they have begun to fight in earnest now."

And so it was. Either the excitement of the moment had been too much for the combatants, or there had been evil influences at work; but whatever the cause, there was no mistaking the result. Yells of execration and defiance, screams of agony from the wounded, threats, menaces, curses, rent the air, and in a moment the scene was changed from one of revelry and sport to one of fury and bloodshed. It was no sight for a maiden's eyes, and Alys was hurried by her attendants through the rough ground of Broken Heys and into the Barbican Lane, where still the shouts of the multitude pursued her, and the din of battle drowned all other sounds.

"Oh, what is happening—what is happening?" she cried, as the party halted at last beneath the gateway. "Oh, do not let Hugh le Barbier fall into the hands of his foes! Cannot some of you rescue him from those wicked men ? "

Her words were not altogether understood, but enough had passed upon the subject to cause Amalric to cry,—

" Now that thou art safe, sweet lady, I will ride back and see what I can do to stop this riot, and save our friend if he be in any peril; " and Leofric sprang to his stirrup and said,—

" Let me run with thee, sir, and strike a blow for my friend, if need be. I know not what is purposed against him, but methinks this fight will not fail to be taken advantage of by his enemy."

Leofric could run like a hare, and had no difficulty in keeping pace with Amalric's steed as they once more crossed the broken ground towards the meadow. The light was fading by this time, but the din of battle was louder than ever, and it seemed as though the whole populace of the town had now joined in one indiscriminate *mêlée*. From within the walls could be heard the clanging of the bells of St. Martin's and St. Mary's—signals that mischief was abroad ; and from the gates of the city the Chancellor and his men were already issuing, the Proctors in attendance, to seek to quell this formidable riot, in which at least half the University clerks were involved.

The Constable of the Castle on his side had come forth with a guard, and at sight of these dignitaries bearing down upon them from either side the combatants paused and wavered. Then the men of the North, who were getting the upper hand, made a sudden dash forward, drove their adversaries before them pell-mell through the open gate from which the Chancellor had lately issued, hewed down numbers of them in their rush, and made for their own Halls and lodgings, barricading themselves into these and hurling defiance at the promoters of law and order, and flinging stones and other offensive missiles at any who sought to dislodge them.

The fight was practically over, the victory, if such it could be called, remaining with the Northern section, who had certainly inflicted much damage upon their adversaries, whilst meeting with many reprisals themselves. Quite a dozen clerks had been killed or mortally wounded, whilst minor injuries had been inflicted upon more victims than could be numbered that night.

Amalric and Leofric, joined later on by Jack (whose head had been broken by a quarter-staff) and by Gilbert (who had received a few bruises and contusions), hunted all over the place for some trace of Hugh. His horse they found grazing quietly in one corner, which excited some alarm for the safety of the rider; but Gilbert declared he had seen Hugh ride safely out of the *melée* when it began to turn into a battle, and that he had called out to him to go home quietly before worse happened. He himself rode off towards the Bocardo gate, and Gilbert lost sight of him in the confusion; but he never guessed that harm had come to him till he found he had not been heard of at the inn, and he started off again in search of him.

From dusk till moonrise did his friends seek for him, exploring every corner of the field and the streets. and asking all whom they knew if they had seen him. Hugh was well known and popular in Oxford, and even the Chancellor and the Proctors gave a passing assistance in the search; but at length the party had to pause and look at each other in blank dismay.

"He has been spirited away!" said Amalric, beneath his breath.

"This is the doing of Roger de Horn," quoth Jack, between his shut teeth.

CHAPTER X.

THE FAIR OF ST. FRIDESWYDE.

"I TELL thee the fault is thine own. Thou couldst have saved him an thou wouldst!"

"Thou art cruel to me, Lotta—cruel, cruel!" wailed Linda. "As though I had not enough to bear without these taunts!"

"Taunts! they are true words every one, and I did warn thee before. If thou hadst given thyself to honest Roger, thou mightest have saved thy lover."

Linda's pale face flushed; she wrung her hands together; her eyes, that were sunken and hollow, flashed suddenly.

"Honest Roger, quotha! and he little better than a common assassin! I hated and feared him long ere I saw Hugh. Wouldst thou have had me betroth myself to a murderer?"

There was an answering flash in Lotta's eyes.

"To save the man I loved from death, *I* would have promised anything," she cried—"ANYTHING!"

"So would not I," answered Linda, drawing a deep sigh. "I dare not sware a falsehood—not even for his sake. Nor would he wish it of me. There are things worse than death."

"Ay, verily there be," answered Lotta significantly; "who knows but what thy dainty lover (as thou dost call him) may even now be suffering some such fate."

Linda started and gazed earnestly at her sister.

"Lotta, what meanest thou? Speak! What dost thou know?"

"I know nothing," was the dogged reply, and a hard gleam shone in Lotta's eyes.

The likeness between the twin sisters was growing less and less every week. Linda had grown pale and drooping of late, and went about heavily, as one in whom the vigour of life is sapped; whilst Lotta was almost as blooming as of old, save that her beauty was harder in character, her laugh more forced, and her speech more reckless. Some thought her more bewitching than ever, but Linda was of a different opinion. She began to fear her sister, and to suspect that Lotta hated her with that cruel sort of hatred which is born of jealousy.

Linda had not realized until the mysterious disappearance of Hugh that Lotta loved him; but the knowledge had been forced upon her during those dreadful days following the fight in Beaumont meadows. Since that day Lotta had been altogether different, and had never ceased to taunt the heart-broken Linda with having been the cause of the fate which had overtaken Hugh upon that occasion. She was always throwing reproaches at her, and urging her even now to accept the suit of Roger de Horn, lest some worse thing should happen; and Linda grew more pale and tearful as week after week passed by, and no news of the absent Hugh reached either her or any in the city.

He seemed to have been spirited away as if by magic. His body had never been found, and it was generally supposed that he had been alarmed by the magnitude of the fight, and fearing for the consequences to those concerned, had quitted the city and betaken himself elsewhere, as was often enough done by those who feared the result of any act of violence. He had been one of the most valiant of the tilters in the tourney, and might perhaps fear lest his name should be brought before the Chancellor or the King as having been a leader in the fight that had followed.

For there had been great displeasure aroused in high places at this lusty and bloody battle. The Chancellor had closed the schools for a while, to make inquisition on the matter; and the clerks, in affright at seeing their privileges withdrawn, had made a collection of money, and had sent presents to the King and Queen and Prince of Wales, in the hope of obtaining pardon.

The King had, however, given a stern reply, to the effect that money could not buy back the life of even one loyal subject wantonly slain; and had it not been that his Majesty was too much taken up with troubles in Wales and with his own Barons at home, more serious steps might have been taken.

As it was no mandate followed, and gradually the life of the place resumed its former course; but it may be understood that, at a time of so much excitement and anxiety, the disappearance of a single student created but little stir. Had his dead body been found, there must have been inquiry, and search made for the authors of the crime, as Hugh was a gentleman's son, and the companion and friend of young De Montfort; but since he had simply vanished, it was concluded that he had done so of his own free-will, and only a few of his nearest friends harboured dark fears as to his safety.

Linda had good reason for believing that he had met with foul play, and though for a while she cherished the hope that he would come back as suddenly as he had left, the hope was dwindling away little by little, so that Lotta's last words brought a start of mingled dismay and hope.

"If thou dost know nothing, why dost thou speak thus?" she cried, clasping her hands tightly together.

"I speak but the fantasy that sometimes fills my mind. I verily believe even now, if thou wouldst hear reason and mate thyself with Roger, that Hugh might be brought back again as from the dead."

"Thou dost believe he yet lives?"

"Marry, how can I tell? I know no more than thyself. But men put not their heads within a noose for small cause. Were I in thy place, I would see if I could not save my lover, even though I might never wed him."

"Thinkest thou that he would reckon life a boon had I been false to him?" spoke Linda, in very low tones.

Lotta's hard laugh rang out mockingly.

"Thou vain and foolish child! thinkest thou that there is a man upon earth who would not choose life rather than love? Thinkest thou that thou art the only maiden in the city worth the wooing? Go to for a veritable fool an thou dost! Let him but taste the sweets of liberty again, and I trow that he would console himself for thy desertion, and that right quickly;" and Lotta flashed a meaning glance at her own reflection in a small mirror of burnished brass that hung against the wall.

Linda shivered again. She read her sister's meaning all too well. Yet what would she not be willing to do to win liberty for her lover, were he indeed alive?

"If thou wouldst but tell me what thou dost know!" she said again.

Lotta threw herself along the couch beside the window, and looked down into the street below. It was plain that she was excited and disquieted, but Linda had no clue to her thoughts.

"I know naught," she repeated; "but I have my thoughts. That something is afoot I cannot doubt. Hast seen how strange Tito is of late—how little he is at home after dark—how he and Roger consort more and more together? Something is hatching between them; what its nature is I know not. But I have my thoughts—I have my suspicions. And is not Tito ever on at thee that thou shouldst forget Hugh and wed with Roger? And doth he not tell me to urge the same upon thee, and throw out strange hints that the sooner this be done the sooner some other good will follow? I verily believe that hadst thou the spirit or the heart of a mouse, thou couldst save him whom thou dost profess thou lovest. But if thou wilt not make sacrifice for him—well, such love is not worth the having! I would cast it from me with scorn!"

Linda buried her face in her hands and sobbed. She was bewildered and distressed above measure by Lotta's words. If indeed Hugh were living, what would she not do to obtain his release from the power of the evil men who had captured him? but to pay the price asked of her for this! Oh, it was almost more than she could bear to think of! And yet might it not be her duty—that duty she owed to him whom she loved more than life?

She was in a grievous state of doubt and dismay, and upon the first opportunity she sought counsel of her friend Joanna Seaton, who had been her confidante throughout.

Joanna looked very grave at what she heard, but warned Linda very seriously against taking such a false step as that of listening to the suit of Roger de Horn.

"Thou dost hate and fear him; it could never be right to wed him. We may not do evil even for good to come. The holy friars have at least taught us that, albeit the monks may not have done so. Thou mayest not swear falsely, Linda."

"Not even to save him from—oh, I know not what?"

"Not even for that. Moreover, thou dost not know that he is living, or in the power of his foe. I fear me that Lotta is not true to thee nor to her better self. She has let the demon of jealousy possess her, and she is now seeking to work upon thee and to get thee to wed with

Roger. I fear me she has some evil purpose in her head.
I would not have thee put too great faith in her words,
Linda."

"But if she should be right!" urged Linda feverishly.
"Oh, could we not save him?"

Joanna was silent, revolving many matters in her mind.
Linda suddenly spoke again.

"Joanna, to-morrow doth begin the Fair of St. Frideswyde."

"Yes, truly; but what of that?"

"Listen, Joanna. Dost thou not remember that there
come to the fair year by year those who practise magic—
who read the future from the stars, from the cards, from
crystal bowls? I have never sought to such before, having
never cared to pry into the future. But now, ah now, if
they could but tell me that one thing—if they could but
say whether he were alive or dead!"

Joanna looked struck by the idea, and a little excited.
Living in an age of superstition, the girls were not free
from the belief in magic which lies dormant in almost
every nature. Truly if they could discover by occult
means what they so greatly desired to know, it might put
a weapon in their hands which they could use with effect.
Many were there in the city who would fly to the rescue
of Hugh, were it but known that he lived, and where was
his hiding-place. If they could but once discover this
much, the rest might follow, and the prisoner be released.

No event could better facilitate their design than the
approaching Fair of St. Frideswyde. Formerly it had

been held in July, upon the feast of the translation of St. Benedict, and the five days following; but within the memory of the present generation it had been changed to the vigil and feast of the saint himself, and occupied a whole week, from the eighteenth to the twenty-fourth of October inclusive. Not only was a great fair held in the streets of the city all through these days, but the whole authority of the place was handed over to the Prior of St. Frideswyde's. To him the Mayor surrendered the keys of the city; the courts of the town were closed in favour of the Piepowder Court, which was held by the steward of the Priory, and before which all disturbers of the peace were brought during the week of the fair.

Persons of every sort thronged into the city during the week. The hostels were full to overflowing; a general holiday was observed. Housewives stocked their larders and wardrobes for the winter; young folks made merry together at mummings and shows of every kind. Clerks and scholars thronged into the fair so soon as they were free of the schools. The streets were lighted by torches, and frolic and merry-making lasted far into the darkness of the autumn night. Mummers, jugglers, fortune-tellers crowded into the place to gather a harvest there; and if any youths or maidens desired to consult the stars, have their fortunes told or their horoscope cast, that was the season when this could be managed without trouble or risk.

The fascination of the supernatural has a great hold upon the young imagination. Linda and Joanna had not discussed this matter long before both were burning with eagerness to put the matter to the test. It had been already rumoured that a noted astrologer from foreign parts would visit the town during the Fair of St. Frideswyde; and if this were so, he was the very man of all others to be consulted. He could know nothing whatever respecting the character or history of the persons who consulted him, and therefore, if he could tell or show them somewhat concerning the fate of Hugh, his prognostications might be looked upon as true, especially if he could give some sign whereby those who consulted him should be able to prove the efficacy of his magic.

Others besides Linda and Joanna awaited eagerly the opening of the fair. Alys de Kynaston was never weary of questioning her father about it, and begging permission to wander through it when the time should come. Edmund was keenly curious too, but he could not hope to see much, though he meant to ride into the city, and go through such places as his horse could carry him. Leofric was not able to tell them anything about it, as he had not seen one himself as yet; but he picked up all the information that he could on the subject, and both he and Amalric resolved to see everything possible, even at the expense of their studies during that week.

Different as was their rank in life, Amalric and Leofric had become great friends of late. Their anxiety for Hugh was one link which had drawn them together, and their love of study was another. Amalric attended a number of the same lectures as Leofric. He often joined the readings in the Castle, and profited by Leofric's scholarship, which was certainly rapidly increasing with all this exercise. At other times he would mount Leofric upon one of his own horses, and they would ride forth together and scour the country for miles round, enjoying the rapid exercise and the free companionship. Amalric was fond of weaving fancy pictures of their future life, when Leofric and he should ride forth together to win their spurs of knighthood, and meet with those adventures which befell all true gallant youths who went forth in the cause of chivalry.

In spite of his scholarly tastes, he had soldier blood in his veins, and did not mean to settle down altogether to a life of study. There was glory to be won in the far East in the Crusades, as well as against the Turks upon the seas, even if not nearer at home. Amalric had his dreams of warlike glory, and Leofric shared them also. He would be the esquire—Amalric should be his knightly master. Together they would do and dare great things; and thus planning and castle-building, their souls were knit together, and a deep and lasting friendship sprang up between them.

At the fair they were always to be seen together, sometimes in attendance upon the maiden Alys, who delighted to obtain permission to go afoot into the crowd with them. Her father, finding that there seemed little danger of any untoward disturbance just now (the memory of the King's recent displeasure being still fresh in men's minds), was pleased to gratify her whim, and Amalric was always eager to be entrusted with the care of one who was becoming

daily dearer to him. So with a servant or two in close
attendance, but with Amalric and Leofric one on each side,
the eager maiden visited the fair and made numerous little
purchases, greatly to her own edification and the admiration of the spectators.

Thus it chanced that she came one day face to face with
Linda, whom she had not seen since the day of the joustings,
and she was greatly struck and grieved by the change in
her looks. The citizen's daughter would have passed by
with a simple reverence; but Alys put forth her hand and
drew Linda towards her.

"I am glad to see thee once more; but thou art sadly
changed since last we met. My father ever says that Hugh
will come back again. Lose not altogether heart and hope."

"Ah, sweet lady, I thank thee for such kindly words;
but thy noble father knows not all that we know. And
I have not lost all hope, either, albeit I almost tremble.
Hist! I can say no more here; but anon I shall learn
somewhat, and then will I tell thee all—if indeed there be
aught to tell. I have heard a whisper of hope. Perchance
it will become something more anon. I must wait—I
must wait—with what patience I can. On the last day
of the fair I shall know all."

With these rather mysterious words Linda pressed Alys's
hand and glided away, whilst the maiden stood looking
after her with wondering eyes, and turning to Amalric
asked,—

"What doth such speech portend?"

Amalric shook his head; but Leofric, who had heard

much of the gossip of the fair from Jack, who was always in the thick of things, made answer,—

"Perchance she has been asking the oracle of him. Men say it is right wonderful what he doth tell; but they speak not too openly of the matter, lest the monks and canons of the city arise and drive him forth. The black arts are not encouraged, albeit there is always juggling and fortune-telling enow at these fairs. But this magician from foreign lands is something different. All men who have gone to him are whispering of the wonders he doth show, and the strange fashion in which he reads the thoughts of their hearts. For myself I have not had any desire to seek to him. Brother Angelus has warned us against such things. He says that half of it is trickery, unworthy to be practised by honest men; and that what is really magic is of the devil, and should be shunned by those who call themselves children of God. But for all that, many men who live upright and godly lives will, from sheer desire to see and hear the man, go to consult him or ask a question. These ofttimes come away with puzzled or troubled faces. For my part, I desire not to have dealings with either a trickster or an emissary of the Evil One."

Alys shivered slightly. She had been on the point of asking to be taken to the magician; but these words had the desired effect of checking the impulse. Nevertheless, she felt considerable curiosity to know what Linda had heard or seen, and greater still would have been her curiosity had she known what was about to take place.

Linda had consulted the oracle, who sat within a small

tent just within the south gate, his face shrouded beneath
a deep cowl, from under which his eyes gleamed like live
coals. By day he sat and answered questions put to him
in a deep, dreamy voice, which seemed to come from somewhere far away; but there were those who had asked to
see certain things, or to look into the crystal globe or into
the magic bowl, and they were bidden to meet him at an
appointed time without the city gate after nightfall; and
those who came back from these interviews spoke with
bated breath of what they had seen and heard, and that
only in whispers, lest the thing should reach the ears of
the Prior.

Linda was one of those who, in a strange ecstasy of
trembling and hope, were awaiting their turn to lift the
curtain and see beyond the veil.

The oracle had divined her question ere it could leave
her faltering lips. He told her that she came to ask
news of one she loved—of one who might even be beyond
the reach of human power—sleeping the sleep of death.
Linda had given a little shriek at hearing these words;
but the magician had gone on to say, in the same deep,
monotonous voice, that if living his face could be called
up in the magic mirror, and that thus alone could she learn
whether indeed death had taken her lover for his prey.

Did she desire to inquire further? Linda, in an agony of
terror and expectancy, declared that she did; and Joanna,
though more frightened than she had anticipated, and half
afraid of the approaching ordeal, would not leave her
friend to face it alone.

It was not difficult, in the confusion attendant upon the fair, to slip out of the house after supper, unknown to those within; and it was easy enough to find the emissary of the magician, who, habited in a long gown and cowl like those of some monk or friar, stood without the gate to conduct those who had appointments to that other secret place, where the magic arts were practised beneath the cloak of night.

But first he tightly bandaged the eyes of the girls. That they had heard was always done; so that no man knew in what spot stood the strange curtained place where these mysteries were carried on.   Linda held Joanna's arm tight, and both girls shook and trembled as they were led along what seemed an interminable road, till at last they were made to halt, and they heard a curious knock upon some panel that sounded like that of a door.

The next moment they were pushed within an archway, and they heard the door clang to behind them.   For a moment their hearts almost failed them; but the burning curiosity to know what would come next aided them to rally courage, and in a few seconds they felt themselves pushed into seats, and the bandage removed from their eyes.

At first all was so dark about them that they saw little more than they had done when blindfold; but in a few minutes there was a slight rustling sound, and then a little tongue of flame seemed to shoot up, and they saw by its light that the magician sat before them, a small table only between himself and his visitors, and that he was feeding the flame in a small brazier before him, which emitted not only a little light, but also a scent almost like that of incense, and a light smoke that dimmed the air.

Above the head of the magician was a mirror, placed at a curious angle, so that it reflected nothing in the room. Indeed there seemed nothing that it could well reflect. The walls appeared to be only black curtains, whose sombre hue absorbed almost all the little light there was, whilst the chill vault-like atmosphere lay like an oppression upon the lungs of the visitors. They felt almost as though stifling, and could not have spoken had their lives depended upon it.

But speech did not appear to be demanded of them. The magician after a long silence, during which time he was feeding the brazier with various drugs which he had arranged upon the table beside him, addressed himself suddenly as if to some unseen presence.

"Go!" he said, in a tone of inflexible authority, "look into the heart of yonder maid, and see whose face is engraved there. If that face be yet in the land of the living, show it upon the mirror. That is thy task this night. Go—begone!"

Dead silence followed this strange command. But in a moment a sound of music arose as if from the ground at their feet—a strange, weird, low cadence that rose and fell and filled the room; then the cloud of incense grew thicker, and for a moment the face of the mirror was dimmed and blurred.

Then the air cleared. The mirror shone out again, and

reflected in its shining surface was a face—the face of a man—wan, white, death-like, with closed eyes and ashen lips.   But it was the face of Hugh for all that.

"He lives," said the voice of the magician; "but he will not live long, unless the woman who loves him best on earth will sacrifice herself for him."

Linda uttered a strangled scream, and fell senseless to the floor.

CHAPTER XI.

THE MAGICIAN'S TOWER.

"I TROW there was no magic in it at all—or no magician," cried Joanna, with suppressed excitement of manner; "I believe it is nothing but some devilry and trickery of Tito's and Roger's. The more I think of it, the more certain do I become. They are an evil pair, and are capable of anything."

Joanna was standing in the midst of an eager and interested group. The whisper had gone out in certain quarters that a strange thing had happened, and that news might be had of the missing Hugh. Amalric de Montfort had heard as much, and had begged of Leofric to take him to see the maiden who could tell what had befallen. Gilbert and Jack were also gathered together to hear the tale. The Fair of St. Frideswyde had just concluded; the city was resuming its normal condition; lectures for the day were just ended, and Gilbert had conducted his friends to the citizen household, that they might hear from Joanna's own lips the story of the mysterious visit which had resulted in the unexpected apparition of the face of Hugh le Barbier in the magician's mirror.

It was an age of superstition, and the belief in magic was deeply implanted in the minds of men of all classes. Nevertheless, in this particular case, a sceptic doubt had arisen, and when Joanna boldly spoke out her opinions, a murmur as of assent passed round the ring.

"Devilry without doubt," said Amalric, with an emphatic gesture. "The only question to my mind is, Whose is the devilry? and what chance have we of catching the perpetrators thereof, and wresting the truth from them?"

"If it be a real magician from foreign parts, he may already have left the city," said Jack; "folks are flocking away, now that the fair is over, as fast as they were flocking in a week agone."

"If I be right in my conjecture," said Joanna significantly, "the mysterious magician and his associate will not quit Oxford. Neither will they altogether cease their dark practices; they find them pay too well."

Hal Seaton, the brother of Joanna, who was also in this secret, looked out to be certain no one was listening, and then locked the door, signing to the company to be seated.

"Now, sister," he said, "tell to these our friends all that thou didst tell to me upon the night after we had carried to her home the swooning Linda. For if thou be right in what thou dost surmise, Hugh le Barbier is yet alive, and in sore need of help from without, which we must give him without delay. Wherefore speak, and speak freely, for we are all friends here."

Joanna told them of what had befallen her and Linda

when they sought to learn more of the fate of Hugh—
how they had been taken blindfold into the presence of
the magician, and how the wan and wasted face of Hugh
had appeared before them in the magic mirror.

"Linda at that moment did faint away," said Joanna,
"but in the darkness the magician seemed not to know it.
He made some strange passes with his hands, and then the
lips of the mirrored face moved, and a voice which sounded
far away spoke in urgent accents, bidding Linda forget
him, and do all that was desired of her, as thus and only
thus could she save him from a fate that was worse than
death. Linda did not hear one word of this; but I heard
all, and methought I knew whose was the voice that
spake these things."

"Whose was it?" was the eager question.

"Tito Balzani's," was the reply. "We all know the
power Tito possesses to throw his voice here, there, and
wherever he chooses, and to imitate the voices of others.
We also know well that he has some knowledge of magic
and the black arts. His mother was accounted a witch,
as I have often heard, and she bequeathed to him certain
books and properties the use of which he has been
studying of late more than some folks think wise. There
be always those who would seek to pry into forbidden
things, and Tito is one of such. He could play magician
well, methinks, an he had the mind; and I verily believe
it was he and none other who so astonished and awed our
townfolk during the week of the fair."

"That might explain much," cried Jack, "for all men

were aghast at the things the magician told them about themselves, which smacked mightily of mystery if it were a stranger who thus spoke, but would easily be explained if he were their own townsman. But leaving that matter, how could he have deceived your eyes by the trick of the magic mirror? How could he have gotten the face of Hugh reflected there?"

"What I believe," answered Joanna, gravely and earnestly, as she glanced round the faces bent upon her, "is that Tito Balzani and Roger de Horn have made a prisoner these two months of Hugh le Barbier, and are practising some of their devilries upon him—Roger from jealous rage and hatred, because Linda scorns his suit and has given her heart to Hugh; Tito because he desires that his friend should wed his sister, and because a living subject can ofttimes be of such great use to one who is practising the black arts of magic and mystery. Thou knowest, brother, that the traveller who once chanced this way and told us of many strange things he had seen in far-off lands, said that human blood was needful to many of those experiments which sorcerers delight in. If that face were truly Hugh's which we did see in the mirror, truly methinks he has been bled within an inch of his life."

Amalric started up in great excitement.

"If that be so, we must fly to his rescue ere they do him to death with their foul spells."

"It is to talk of that that we are here together to-day," answered Gilbert, whose face was stern and resolute. "But first we must find out where they have hidden him; for albeit many of our townfolk did go forth beyond the gates to inquire further of the magician, all were fast blindfolded both in coming and going, so that none can say where the place stands which hides his guilty secrets."

Amalric turned eagerly upon Joanna once again.

"Canst thou tell us aught of this? And when didst thou first believe that it was trickery and not magic that was being practised upon thee? Hadst thou suspected aught ere thou wentest forth?"

"The doubt had just crossed my mind," answered Joanna. "I knew well that Roger was bent upon obtaining Linda's hand in marriage, and I believed that he had slain Hugh the better to obtain his object. Then when Linda spoke of her doubt as to Hugh's death, I could not but wonder how far Roger and Tito were concerned in his disappearance. But it was not till I was within the magician's cave—for such it appeared to be—and heard that voice urging upon the unconscious Linda to do the will of those two evil men, that conviction came home to me. Then like a flash I seemed to see it all—how they had not dared to kill Hugh, lest inquiry and discovery should follow, but had made a prisoner of him, and were now seeking through the medium of pretended magic to break Linda's resolve, and hurry her into lifelong misery as the bride of Roger. For if she could be convinced that her lover's life and liberty depended upon the sacrifice, she might be willing to make it, when no other consideration in the world would drive her to the step. This, then, was the meaning of all this pretence of magic and occult power. Linda was to be terrified into a rash promise, the magician working upon her and foretelling life to her lover if she did but comply. And I verily believe they would have succeeded but for that timely fainting fit, which rendered her helpless and speechless, and angered them into words which betrayed the plot to me."

" What did they say ? "

" I can scarce repeat the words. All was darkness and confusion and haste when they saw Linda lying like one dead before them. But I heard some muttered oaths, only too like what I hear from Tito Balzani in moments of anger; whilst the strength exhibited by the other man in lifting and carrying Linda away was little like that of the bowed and aged man which he had appeared to be, and I was wellnigh certain that it was Roger. I was more than half afraid he would spirit her away next; but I kept fast hold of her dress, even after my eyes were bandaged, and the other man walked beside me guiding my steps. Just at the South Gate they set down Linda, and vanished in the darkness. I pulled off the bandage, and found myself alone with her, leaning up against the wall. The sentry at the gate heard my call, and came and helped to carry her home. He said that several half-swooning maidens had been left there during these last days after dark. For his part he should be glad when the fair was ended and the magicians had gone their way. He did not hold with honest citizens being scared out of their senses. And having carried Linda home, he departed."

"Would he know where the magician had his place of resort?" asked Amalric eagerly. "Didst thou ask him?"

"Yes; but he could tell nothing. He said the less he meddled in such matters the better. Methinks the magicians had scared him somewhat. He was right glad to think they were going. I have asked of many if they could tell; but none can say. Those who went forth were led blindfold, and all they can say is that the way seemed long and tortuous, and that the place was like a cave, albeit none can remember going down steps. Yet it is true that there was a damp, cave-like scent in the air, and one seemed to pass beneath an arch as one entered."

"It could not be any of those buildings which pertain to the Black Friars; the danger would be too great," said Hal, "for the friars are no friends to magic. There are many mills along Trill Mill Stream, but one can scarce see how the mock magician could weave his spells there. By day they are used, and men work early and late. Besides, how could they keep a prisoner there—if so be that Joanna is right, and Hugh has been kept in durance vile during these many weeks? It is hard of credence; and yet how else could his face appear in the mirror?"

Here Leofric, who had listened to every word spoken, and had been thinking deeply, looked up to say,—

"There is the tower—Friar Bacon's tower—close to the Grandpont, beyond the South Gate, beyond the mills and the buildings of the Black Friars. That tower hath an evil report. Men fear it even by day; by night all give it wide berth. I have heard men say of late that strange sounds have been heard issuing forth, and that it is a place unholy and to be avoided. Can it be possible that these evil men have broken in, and used it for the practice of their wicked arts? It might suit them well, since they can study the stars from thence, cast horoscopes, and practise many forbidden arts safely within its walls. And if they had a mind to keep a prisoner there—"

Amalric had started to his feet in great excitement.

"The Magician's Tower—that is what I have heard it called! Verily, good Leofric, methinks thou hast gotten the key of the mystery this time! What place could better suit these evil creatures wherein to practise deeds of darkness? As we know, men shun the spot even by day; but at night none will pass by who can avoid it. Doubtless Friar Bacon left behind him some things which might be useful to the pretended magician; and he may have implements of his own for practising his black arts. Where better could he carry on his practices? Where more secure could some hapless prisoner be kept? And the sounds which men have heard proceeding thence! Why did we not think of it before? Surely it must be the voice of Hugh, seeking to call for aid from those without! Let us fly to his rescue without delay! We will take a sevenfold vengeance upon his persecutors if we find matters as we believe!"

"We must have a care," said Hal, looking round with an air of caution; "we have two clever and unscrupulous rogues to deal with. If we are to catch them as well as their victim, we had better lie low till night has fallen, and then sally forth and see if we cannot take them red-handed in some of their villany. If we breathe a word of this abroad, we shall find that they have escaped—and perchance have made away with their victim, or hidden him elsewhere—and we shall be foiled in our purpose."

"And we do but suspect the hiding-place," said Leofric. "If we are wrong, and have given them warning, we shall lose them utterly. We shall have much ado, methinks, to catch them as it is. If we make any stir and let them hear so much as a whisper, they will be off, and we shall see them no more."

"True," said Amalric, whose first impulse had been to speak to the Constable of the Castle and ask for a guard to go and search the tower; "we might defeat our own ends by publicity. And then if our surmise were to be wrong, they would have time to remove their prisoner and betake themselves elsewhere before we discovered our error. We will band together, all of us, and to-night we will meet here once more, and set forth on our errand. Meantime let us not breathe outside these walls one word of what has been resolved upon. Let us spend our day as we are wont to spend it; but let each man revolve in his mind some course of action, and come provided with that which he judges to be most needful to the success of the enterprise. Arms, of course, each must carry, and anything else that may seem well. To-night at curfew— or perchance an hour later—we will meet, and then make for the tower with all speed and secrecy."

They rose with one accord as if to go.

"Then," said Hal, "let our meeting-place be just without the South Gate, under shelter of the wall hard by St. Michael's. There in the shadow none will note our gathering; and the sentry knows us all, and will let us pass without comment."

"So be it," said Amalric, who from his rank naturally took the lead in this matter. The young men saluted Joanna, Amalric thanked her for her information and praised her for her courage, and then they went forth one by one, to note that Tito Balzani, lounging in the door of the inn a little higher up the street, watched their exit with lowering brows and a sullen mien.

Leofric and Jack passed him by as they walked towards their own quarters. He looked at them with suspicion.

"Whither away so fast?" he asked, with an air of would-be good fellowship; "come and have a drink, and tell the news. What has taken thee to Master Seaton's house to-day? The city is as dull as a stagnant pool after the fair."

"How goes it with Mistress Linda?" asked Leofric, ignoring the question; "we heard from Joanna but now that she was sick of some fever of the brain."

"It is naught but a maid's folly and fantasy," answered Tito, with an ugly scowl; "marriage with an honest fellow who would keep her from her whimsies and puling would be the best cure for her. So I tell my father, who has promised to think of it."

Leofric passed on, seeing that Jack's face had flushed all over, and that he only restrained himself with difficulty from betraying his real feelings towards the Italian youth.

"He is a young scamp himself!" cried the farmer's son, as they hastened towards their lodging. "If we can but catch him to-night, I would gladly wring his neck for him! But I fear he will be as slippery as an eel. Nevertheless, let me but get a good grip of him, and it will go hard that I shake not the breath out of his body!"

"Gently, good Jack," said Leofric; "we must not take life without good cause. But if things be as we suppose, I trust we shall bring both him and his accomplice to the punishment their evil deeds deserve."

To the impatient Jack the time seemed long before night came and they could start forth on their quest. But the darkness fell early at that season, and at the appointed hour the pair sallied forth, avoiding the High Street, where Tito might possibly be on the watch (if he were not already at the Magician's Tower), and skirting along the wall till the South Gate was reached and passed. The walls of St. Michael's rose up immediately before them, and here had already gathered the eager party, all armed, and all resolute and full of courage.

"Tito and Roger passed through the gate together an hour ago," said Hal Seaton; "I have been watching and dogging them ever since our meeting broke up. Fain would I have followed them farther; but they were full of suspicion, and I feared to be seen, and so spoil everything. They scuttled along like hunted foxes, sly and cunning and crafty. So far as I could judge, they went straight down as if towards Grandpont. I truly believe that the tower is their place of resort."

Amalric took the lead. Bidding his followers walk very softly—which it was easy to do in the thick mud of the low-lying road—he made his way rapidly yet cautiously in the direction of the tower, and before long they could see the lonely building standing out against the sky just at the head of the bridge.

All was dark and silent as they approached; but Jack had made a little detour, and had found his way down to the very edge of the river. Now he came flying back to say that from that side a glimmer of light could be detected in an upper window, visible only from the river, and looking blue and ghostlike as a corpse candle. Nor had they actually reached the wall before a sudden cry, wild and strange, rang through the silence of the night. The whole party started, and Amalric ground his teeth; but they could well understand how the ordinary passer-by, hearing such a sound, would hurry past in terrible fright, believing it the wail of a lost spirit, or a demoniac yell.

"Here is the door!" spoke Gilbert, in smothered tones, "but it is fast locked and bolted. They will take good care of that."

A long-drawn sobbing wail seemed to come from within, and Amalric's face grew hard and stern.

"Break it in, then—a truce to secrecy!—there is no time to lose!" he cried; and the next moment the silence of the night was rent by the sound of blows against the solid door, which soon sent it crashing inwards.

"A light!" cried Amalric; and Hal flashed a concealed lantern within the opening forced. In a moment the five youths had vaulted in, drawing their daggers as they did so. They found themselves in a dark, vaulted chamber, hung round with black cloth; and for some moments they could see no way of getting into the upper part of the tower. The magic mirror hung upon the wall, and various curious-looking implements lay upon the table, doubtless used by Tito when practising upon the credulity of those who sought him.

"This way!" cried Jack suddenly. He had discovered in the wall a narrow spiral stairway. Recklessly dashing upwards, stumbling in the darkness, but closely followed by his comrades, and holding his dagger fast in his hand, he suddenly found himself brought up short by a locked door, and behind that door he could hear whispering voices.

"Stand back a moment!" he yelled to those behind; and they fell back, not knowing what was to happen next. Jack had armed himself beforehand with a mighty club, which in old days he had often wielded with good effect, and which since his arrival in Oxford had been his favourite weapon in those matches of skill and strength in which the hearts of the students delighted.

Raising this formidable weapon, and bringing it crashing against the lock of this door, he forced it open before him. A stream of light burst forth for a single second, almost dazzling their eyes. The next instant they were enveloped in black darkness, whilst a sound of scuffling steps and of angry words in the room beyond them told that they had surprised the evil-doers in their work.

Hal sprang forward with his lantern, and Jack exclaimed,—

"Catch them! catch them! they are getting out by the windows!"

Springing forward, he caught at the legs of one, but received such a violent kick upon the cheek that he let go his hold for a second. The other fugitive was grappled by Gilbert, but he was more than half-way out before he was seized, and he wriggled so dexterously and fiercely that he too drew away, and the next moment both figures had vanished.

"After them down the stairs!" cried Hal; and he, Gilbert, and Jack dashed down through the darkness, leaving the light for any one who desired it.

Amalric caught it up, flashed it round the room, and then uttered a short, sharp exclamation. Leofric had seen a ghastly figure stretched upon a pallet in a corner. The next moment both he and Amalric were bending over the prostrate form of Hugh le Barbier.

Hugh indeed it was, though worn almost to a skeleton, and looking like death. One arm was extended, and blood was oozing from a vein that had evidently been recently opened. A number of other scars plainly showed how frequently this operation had been repeated. His eyes, though half open, seemed to take in no impression from without. He was cold and almost pulseless. Amalric, bending over him and feeling his heart, said between his clenched teeth,—

"We are only just in time!"

They stanched the wound. They forced strong spirit down his throat. They chafed his cold limbs, and finding warm garments, left behind by the fugitives in their hasty flight, they wrapped him in them, and set light to the fire upon the hearth, and laid him down in front of it to get the full heat of the blaze.

In moving him, they found that he had been chained by one ankle to the wall, and they had to file through the fetter before they could free him, their hearts meantime swelling with indignation and fury.

"If we can but lay hands on those miscreants!" muttered Amalric between his teeth.

All this while Hugh lay lifeless and unconscious, although his pulses still beat faintly. When he had for the third time swallowed the cordial forced upon him by Leofric, he slowly opened his eyes, at first with shrinking and horror in them, which changed gradually to great wonder and joy.

"Amalric!" he said faintly, as though speaking in a dream—"Leofric! Heaven send this be not another dream!"

And having so said he put out his hand, as if to assure himself by touch of the presence of friends; and after having so done he once more lost consciousness, the very shock of joy being too much for his weakened frame.

CHAPTER XII.

WINTER DAYS WITHIN THE CASTLE.

ALL Oxford was thrown into excitement by the news. Hugh le Barbier, whose disappearance after the jousting in Beaumont meadows two months before had created a certain stir in some quarters, had now been found in fetters in the Magician's Tower, as people sometimes called it, and had been carried off to the Castle for security by the Constable.

It was in all mouths that the foreign magician, whose doings and wonders had attracted no small notice during the Fair of St. Frideswyde, was none other than the Italian youth Tito Balzani, who had grown up in their midst, and had therefore an intimate knowledge of those who consulted him. It was further said that both he and Roger de Horn had been in the plot for abducting and imprisoning the missing man, and that they were now being searched for all through the neighbouring forests, to which they had most likely fled for safety so soon as they found themselves discovered.

Jack Dugdale was forward to tell the tale to the gaping throng who surrounded him whenever he appeared in the streets.

He had spent pretty nigh three days himself searching for the fugitives, and had often been hot upon their trail; but they had eluded him and the other pursuers with a cunning which had in it almost a touch of the supernatural, some thought, and now the chase had been reluctantly abandoned, and it was admitted that the quarry had escaped for the present.

But the excitement did not immediately die down. The story was in every one's mouth. Pedro Balzani's house was thronged with guests, all eager to learn what was to be known; and though the house was watched closely by the authorities, the man himself was not interfered with. He had made it plain that he was ignorant of the doings of his son, and as he himself bore a good character, the misdeeds of Tito were not visited upon his head.

But great anger prevailed against that young man throughout the town. Numbers of the citizens, and still more their wives and daughters, had consulted the magician, and had paid him what to them were large sums for scraps of information which had seemed to them marvellous as coming from the lips of a stranger from beyond the seas, but which lost all their value when it was known that Tito was the speaker. Others had been lured by him to the tower, and had paid heavily for a glance into the magic mirror, the crystal bowl, or that other bowl the thought of whose dark contents now made them shudder. Some still declared that he had dealings with the Evil One, and that the things they had seen could only be produced by the co-operation of spirits; but others vowed that it was nothing but trickery from first to last, and longed to see Tito brought back into the city, that he might be made to disgorge his ill-gotten gains, which doubtless he had kept securely fastened upon his person, so as to be ready for any emergency.

As for the other members of the Balzani household, the mother was deeply indignant at the trick which had been played upon her daughter by the girl's half-brother and his friend. She saw clearly that they sought to impose upon her credulity, and to induce her by that means to pledge her hand to Roger de Horn as the price of the life and liberty of her lover, Hugh. The mother learned much from the delirious ravings of the girl, who had been stricken with brain-fever, and lay in a most precarious condition. Indeed so dangerous was her state, and so imperative was it that she should be kept perfectly quiet, that after three days she had been conveyed by water up the river to the little village of Eynsham, where her mother's sister lived; and there, far away from the tumult of the city, which always set up excitement and paroxysms of fear, it was hoped she would recover from the shock to her system, and regain her normal health.

"And learn to forget the past," spoke the mother to her sister, before leaving the patient in her kindly care. "She is full young for thoughts of love. Methinks in these troublous days the less a maid dreams of such things the better. Hugh le Barbier is a goodly youth, and I desire none better for child of mine; but he is above her in rank. When he sees more of life and of the world, he will make more fitting choice. It would be better that they should not meet—that both should learn to forget. Naught but trouble and peril have followed from their early affection. Better it should be put aside and forgotten. Wherefore I will the more gladly leave Linda here, where, amid new scenes and surroundings, she may well forget the past, and cease to think of him for whom she is no fitting spouse in the eyes of the world."

Bridget Marlow, who had no child of her own, was willing enough to have the care of her sister's daughter. She promised to guard her jealously and tend her lovingly, and to keep her as long as her mother could spare her.

"I always said, when I did hear of thy twin daughters, that one ought surely to be mine," she said with a smile. "Fear not for her, sister—I will guard her like the apple of mine eye; and she shall find a second father and mother in us. In this quiet place few, save the good monks of the Abbey hard by, pass our way. My husband, as thou dost know, acts as porter of the gate by day; and living as we do neath the shadow of the cloister wall, we are not molested by the comings and goings of worldlings from the city. The maid will have peace and quiet here, and may well forget the troubles through which she has passed."

So Linda was, after a few days, left in that quiet place by her mother, in the fond hope that she and Hugh would now forget one another, and that the troubled dream of love would be effaced by illness from her daughter's brain.

Lotta nodded with approval when she learned what had been done.

"She had better take the veil herself, and live the life of a nun," she said, tossing her handsome, haughty head. "She is not fit for the battle of life. She is a poor, puling creature at best! She is not fit to be the bride of any save a man of dreams and books. The clash of arms turns her cheek white; the thought of peril to one she loves drives her out of her senses. She had better forget Hugh, and he her. They are no fitting mates one for the other."

As for Hugh himself, he had been carried to the Castle by order of the Constable, when his case had been made known there. A guard had been sent to search the tower, to take possession of everything found there, and to convey the young man to the Castle, where he received every attention and care.

The father of Hugh and the Constable of the Castle had been friends in their youth, and Sir Humphrey was not only interested in Hugh for that reason, but was deeply indignant at the treatment he had received, and the trick which had been played upon the authorities of the city by these two lawless youths.

For some days Hugh was unable to give an account of what had occurred, lying in a state of exhaustion which was almost like that of trance. Indeed so strange was his condition that Brother Angelus (at the earnest solicitation of Leofric) was asked to come and look at him; and he shook his head somewhat gravely over his state, and spoke words not altogether understood by those about him.

In those days the friars were the best leeches and surgeons to be had. Their work amongst the sick poor

gave to them a skill and insight not always found amongst
those who professed greater lore. Brother Angelus had
no small store of knowledge regarding sickness, and it was
well for Hugh that he was called to his side ; for he strictly
forbade any further bleeding (always the favourite remedy
for fevers), declaring that this fever was itself the result
of excessive bleedings practised with an unholy purpose,
and he detected other symptoms about the young man
which caused his face to take a stern and anxious aspect.

" He has been made the unwilling accomplice in deeds of
darkness," he said, as he observed the comatose symptoms
which often seized the patient. " They have sought to
subdue his spirit and will, and to throw him into those
unhallowed trances wherein men see and hear things
which our Maker has thought it good to hide from us.
There are ways by which one man may obtain this un-
righteous power over his fellow, and this is what yon evil
men have sought to do with their captive. By weakening
his body they have sought to gain ascendency over his
spirit. But it is plain that he has resisted manfully, and
to the very last. God be thanked for that ! We will pray
that the malice of the enemy may in this case be frus-
trated ! "

And daily, before he left the bed of the patient, the
friar would kneel down beside him, whilst those in the
room would follow his example ; and he would pray
earnestly against those wiles which had been used upon
him, and ask release for the spirit which had been in some
sort fettered and bound.

Mysterious as all this was to those who saw and heard, it was plain to them that Hugh responded better to the ministrations of Brother Angelus than to any skill of leeches.   In presence of the friar he was never tormented by harassing dreams, nor did he start up as though in answer to some call unheard by others.   He grew calm and tranquil, and would fall into a natural sleep; and at the end of ten days the fever fits left him altogether, and he wakened to a full knowledge of his surroundings, and an interest in life.

When this advance was made, he was permitted to pass the day with Edmund, in the pleasant upper chamber hard by his own, where, lying upon another couch in the cheerful glow of the fire, he could enjoy the society of his friends, and by-and-by tell them of those things which had happened to him since his mysterious disappearance on the day of the joustings.

"I was suddenly and furiously set upon by three of those strange black figures which we had noted moving in the crowd.   There was such a tumult all around that I scarce knew what was passing, nor who was friend or who was foe; but it was plain that these men were bent upon my destruction or overthrow, and I set myself to the task of fighting them, though calling for assistance the while. But I seemed to be in the heart of foes, for none heeded my cry, and though I laid low one of the fellows, I presently felt a heavy blow upon my head which made me reel in the saddle, and the next instant I was lying upon the ground with a hand upon my throat, and just as my senses deserted me I thought I saw the fiery eyes of Roger de Horn glaring into mine through the holes in his mask."

"Ah! I thought as much," said Amalric, through his shut teeth. "Would that we could lay hands upon the villain now!"

"And what befell you then?" asked the fair Alys, who had grown mightily interested in Hugh during these past days, and was as eager as any to hear his tale when he should be allowed to tell it, which he had not been at first.

By this time Hugh seemed quite like an old friend; he had been at the Castle for a considerable time, and both Edmund and his sister felt towards him almost as though he were a brother. Any comrade and friend of Amalric's would have been welcomed, but Hugh was liked for his own sake, and for the romantic history of which he was now the hero.

"That I cannot say with certainty, fair mistress. For I lost my senses then; and when I recovered them, it was to find myself bound by an iron fetter to my ankle, in a strange circular chamber with a dome-like roof, the like of which I had never seen before."

"The Magician's Tower!" whispered Alys, with a little shiver of horror.

"So I afterwards made out, from the words of the men who haunted it, and from mine own knowledge of the city. I could sometimes hear the wash of the river, or the voices of men in boats by day. But though I cried aloud whenever I thought I might be heard, never an answer came;

and my captors, if they heard me, would punish me with
blows and kicks, if not with more refined forms of cruelty."

"These men were Tito Balzani and Roger de Horn?"
questioned Amalric sternly.

"Yes; and soon I became aware that they were engaged
upon other matters than those which directly concerned
me, and that I was to be made useful to them in the
practice of their evil arts. I will not speak too much
of these things. The thought is hateful and repulsive.
Suffice it to say that they were eagerly pursuing the study
of certain black arts, and that they had books and instruments, either belonging to Tito, or found by them in this
strange tower, whereby they sought to prosecute their
studies. They had dupes too, who visited them, and strove
to peer into the future, and they would use incantations
and burn strange pungent drugs, and methinks they ofttimes so bewildered their visitors that they imagined they
saw in the smoke wreaths strange things which were
never there at all. However that may be, there were
some who came again and again, and brought gold with
them each time. And as the conjurors grew bolder they
would ask larger fees. I trow they have grown rich upon
the proceeds of those weeks of fraud and devilry."

"And how didst thou come to hear and see so much?"

"They grew careless of my presence in the upper
chamber, where everything was prepared. As I grew
weak from hunger and from loss of blood—for blood
seemed a necessity to them for every experiment, and
it was part of their purpose to reduce me to a mere

shadow—they spoke freely of all they did and wished to do. I am certain they never intended me to escape their clutches; and I believe that upon the night of the rescue, had you been but a few minutes longer in forcing the door, they would have taken my life without pity, so fearful were they of what I might reveal. But they could not spare time in their haste to collect their gold, and as it was, they were almost caught as they climbed through the window-slits."

"And was it real magic?" asked Alys in a low voice; "or was it all trickery and jugglery?"

"That is hard to tell," answered Hugh; "but methinks they did all in their power to invoke the aid of the Evil One. I trow well that they sought to throw me into trances, that I might aid them in this. They studied their books, and tried their wicked spells upon me; and there were moments when I felt them succeeding, albeit I fought might and main. If I could keep my mind fixed on holy things, and continue to pray, I was safe from them. But there were moments when I was so weak that I felt my hold slipping away, and I trow that then I did fall in some sort beneath some evil spell; and the horror of it is but passing away now, since Brother Angelus has spoken and prayed with me. Trickery there was in much they did. I know my face was shown again and again in the magic mirror, and that I was dressed up to look sometimes as a maid, sometimes as an aged man, sometimes as a mailed warrior—my face painted and my hair arranged to suit the part. This was when I was wellnigh dead through loss of blood, and could not resist them. They had gained such power over me that ofttimes I could not make a sound, greatly as I longed to do so. When I guessed, from what they had said in my hearing, that Linda was to be brought to see my face in the mirror, I strove might and main to cry aloud, and tell who and what these men were; but my voice would not obey—no sound could I utter."

"If we can but catch them," cried Amalric, "they shall pay for their devilries!"

But Roger and Tito were too wary to be caught. They had fled beyond the precincts of Oxford, and pursuit was abandoned at last as hopeless. Hugh recovered his wonted vigour with more rapidity than could at first have been anticipated; but he showed no disposition to return to his old quarters at Dagville's Inn. Once he asked after Linda, and on hearing what had befallen her he heaved a long sigh.

"Methinks that I have brought her nothing but woe and sorrow," he said; "she will be happier there than in the tumult of this strange city. Some day I will see her again; but for the present let her remain in peace and safety. I am glad she should be in so tranquil a place."

But the house of the Balzanis had lost its charm for him. He had no wish to face the father of Tito or the witcheries of Lotta, of which he was not unconscious.

"Stay here within the Castle," said Amalric, "and enter at St. George's, as I have done. There be a few poor, turbulent Welsh students there, but for the most part we

are a quiet and studious company. We will make you
welcome amongst us. Come and be my comrade there."

Hugh was easily persuaded to this course. St. George's
in the Castle was a very ancient building, dating back from
the reign of William the Conqueror. It had been founded
by Robert d'Oilly for secular Canons, and his successor had
transferred it to the Canons Regular of Osney. Subse-
quently it had become a house for University students,
although it remained to a certain extent under the jurisdiction of the Abbot of Osney.

This was shown by the fact that there was a Custos or
Warden appointed from among the Canons of Osney to be
over the College of St. George's in the Castle. He was
not a permanent resident there, but paid a domiciliary
visit about Christmas time, which was regarded as a part
of the season's festivities.

"Thou wilt join us in a good time," said Amalric to
Hugh, when the latter had installed himself with as much
comfort as might be in those days in his new quarters,
having arranged to share a small and fairly commodious
chamber with young De Montfort: "for upon the Feast of
the Nativity, or a few days later, the Warden will come
from Osney, to remain to the Feast of the Epiphany; and
we shall go forth with torches and songs to welcome him,
and bring him hither in state. They say we live right
merrily whilst he is with us. Fair Mistress Alys is all
agog to see the torchlight procession. I trust the night
will be fair and fine, that she be not disappointed."

Alys, indeed, was all alive for any bit of entertainment

in her pleasant but rather monotonous life. The Christmas revellings were not of a character greatly to attract one of a gentle spirit. She knew that she would scarce be permitted during those days of feasting to sally forth into the city at all. Riot and disorder too often characterized the events of that season. The lectures of the Regent Masters were suspended for a short period, although other lecturers continued their discourses. Some amongst the richer scholars, or those from the neighbourhood, went to their homes; but the greater number remained in the city, and made night hideous with their revellings and disorder. A Lord of Misrule was chosen for the occasion, and misrule was the order of the day. The citizens themselves were little better behaved at this holiday season, and for a week disorder and roistering prevailed in defiance of any action on the part of the authorities. If they could prevent an open riot or a pitched battle in the streets, it was as much as they could hope to do; and Alys knew that she would be kept closely within the Castle walls. Indeed, after her experience of a students' holiday once before, she had little desire to witness another.

Hugh was not sorry himself to be free of the turmoil of the city, his health being not altogether what it had been before his strange captivity. The greater seclusion and quiet within the Castle walls better suited him, and companionship with Amalric and the Constable's children was pleasant. He rather liked, too, the small solemnities with which he was admitted to be a scholar of that place. He was taken before the high altar of the chapel, and bidden to swear to be faithful and obedient to the Warden and to the Abbot of Osney, and not to raise debates between them, not to clamber over the Castle walls at night, or to be guilty of nocturnal vagaries ; and if promoted to wealth in after life, to leave something to the College. Then he paid some small fees for the registration of his name, for a supper to his fellow-scholars, and towards the common stock of money ; after which he became a scholar of the College, and shared in the life of his companions.

Three days after Christmas, upon a clear starlight night, the scholars sat down to their supper attired in their best habits, each of them being provided with a torch dipped in pitch and resin.

That meal having been disposed of, they all marched in procession to Osney in decorous silence, and with their torches yet unlighted. They were admitted into the courtyard by a silent monk, and once there they drew up in a circle round the enclosure, and waited, mute and patient.

But they had not to wait long. A door in the building was flung open, and out stepped the Abbot, and by his side was the Warden of St. George's, the Canons Regular being grouped in the background. At sight of these reverend men the scholars all bent the knee in token of respect, and the Abbot advancing a few steps forward gave to them his blessing.

Then the Warden stepped forward, and saluted the scholars in Latin, they replying in the same tongue, after which two of the seniors advanced, lighted their torches, and placed themselves before him.

The rest of the scholars drew up in rank behind, their torches yet unlighted, and the procession filed out of the courtyard, and along the wet, muddy road which led towards the Castle. Midway between the Abbey and the Castle a halt was called. Rapidly and in orderly fashion the scholars kindled their torches and struck up the appointed hymn. The procession formed up again, and passing between rows of gaping citizens, who had come out into King's Meadow to see the show go by, trooped across Quaking Bridge and through the gateway, till they found themselves within the precincts of the College itself.

Here a new hymn was sung, and the Warden was conducted with great ceremony to his own lodging, where he bid farewell to his body-guard and dismissed them with kindly words of thanks.

Alys from her upper window watched the picturesque grouping of the gowned scholars, and the flashing of torches in the open space below; and as Amalric and Hugh looked up and held theirs aloft, they were rewarded by the waving of a slim white hand, which told them they had been seen and recognized.

CHAPTER XIII.

KENILWORTH CASTLE.

THE summer sun shone bravely down upon a small band of travellers journeying leisurely along through the leafy lanes of Warwickshire.

Of this little band, two members rode ahead of the rest, sometimes silent, but often engaged in earnest conversation. One of the pair was richly dressed, and the horse he rode was a fine animal, fit for a battle charger; the other was well mounted, but his dress was sober, and suggested that of an ecclesiastic, albeit the sunny locks of the rider flowed to his shoulders, and bore no sign of the tonsure. Both riders were young, neither being over twenty years of age; but those were days when youths were ranked as men at eighteen, and there were even warriors in the battle ranks who counted less years than that, whilst few comparatively of those who lived a stirring life in the midst of stress and strife lived to see their hair turn grey.

The younger of the pair, he of the more knightly aspect, was none other than Amalric de Montfort. His companion was Leofric Wyvill, who had been for years his chosen comrade and friend.

13

The young men had just passed through a memorable period of their academic life, and had been invested with the cappa of the bachelor. They had successfully passed through their Responsions and their Determinations. They had ably disputed before a large gathering, and had acquitted themselves to the admiration and satisfaction of all. At Amalric's cost they had given a banquet to the Masters and scholars, and had now attained to the status of Bachelors of Arts; and Leofric, at least, had every intention of continuing his career at the University, and was to give a series of cursory lectures there upon his return.

But for the present he was taking, in company with Amalric, a well-earned holiday. Ever since his first arrival in Oxford, as an impecunious clerk, he had remained there, year in, year out, working hard to support himself and carry on his studies, and this was the first time he had quitted the city either on business or pleasure.

One year of academic life much resembled another; and little change had come into Leofric's condition, save what was brought about by his increasing intimacy with young De Montfort. He and Jack Dugdale still occupied their little turret chamber, which had gradually become more and more comfortable and habitable. Leofric had earned a steady income by his illuminating work upon the vellum he was enabled to purchase, and by assistance to Edmund de Kynaston in his studies. Jack kept the larder supplied, and hung their chamber about with the dressed skins of the creatures he had slain, thus protecting them from the winter's cold, which down in that marshy place was severe and prolonged. The life had been a busy and a happy one, and Leofric found it hard to believe how fast the months and years had sped by. Looking back upon his life as a clerk, it seemed to him to have been very short indeed.

There was still a considerable interval before he could take his degree as Master, and from that go on as inceptor in theology if he had a mind to do so; but he had already won the favourable notice of many persons in the University, and a brilliant career had been prophesied for him if he did but persevere, as he had every intention of doing.

The Determinations had taken place in Lent, as was always the case, and for a while afterwards he and Amalric had remained in Oxford; but they had long planned a holiday together when the summer should come, and a few weeks back they had started off together to see something besides the inside of lecture-halls and the familiar sights of Oxford.

Amalric was determined that Leofric should see London, and their first journey had been to that great city, which was seething in the excitements of that unquiet period, when the struggle betwixt the King and his Barons was becoming ever more and more acute, and when far-seeing men began to predict that the matter would never be settled until swords had been drawn and blood shed on both sides.

After a week spent in that place, the friends had journeyed northward. Leofric had paid a visit to his old friends and fathers the monks of St. Michael, who were delighted to see him and to learn how great success he had achieved. Now they were on their way to the Castle of Kenilworth, Amalric's home, and the youth was growing excited at the thought of seeing again his mother and his sister, who were certain to be there, although he was far less certain of meeting with his father and brothers.

Just latterly the young students had been too much engrossed in their studies to have a very clear idea what was going on in the world around. Now, however, they began to feel a keen interest in these outside matters, and Amalric, as was natural, strove to obtain and piece together every scrap of information he could gain from high or low, eagerly discussing each matter with Leofric, and growing in enthusiasm for the cause to which his father was pledged as day by day passed on.

The arguments upon both sides were strong. The King's party urged that the King should be free; that he is no longer a King if he does not rule as he pleases. He has the same right to rule the kingdom that the Barons have to rule their own estates, and those who would interfere to make a slave of him are robbers and worse, for they are laying unholy hands upon the Lord's anointed.

The Barons' arguments were also culled from Holy Writ, and proved how deeply the teachings of the Franciscans were working in the hearts of the people. The kingdom has to be protected as well as the King. If the King listens to false counsellors, his Barons must guard him from such. Obedience to law is not slavery, and God's laws are for monarch as well as for peasants. True freedom consists in abstaining from evil. The King's people are God's people, and must be ruled in His fear, not in a spirit of greed and oppression. As Christ laid open all things to His disciples, so should a King consult on all weighty matters with his nobles. If he dishonour them and oppress his people, he cannot wonder if he is hated and disobeyed.

These arguments sunk deeply into the minds of the people, and they looked to De Montfort as their hope and deliverer. The past years had been full of trouble and vicissitudes. The King had escaped from the tutelage and restraint imposed upon him, had made himself practical master of London and even of the kingdom for a while, and had set at open defiance the Provisions of Oxford. His son, Prince Edward, had opposed him in this; had said that he, for his own part, could not reconcile it to his conscience to break the oath which he had sworn on that occasion; and had in effect joined himself to the party of the Barons. This had alarmed his father, who perhaps felt that his son was a better leader and stronger spirit than himself, and Edward had been sent off to Gascony to his duties there. As it happened, however, the De Montforts, his cousins, were there also at that time, and the Prince spent most of his time with them, thus adding to the disquietude of his father.

Henry himself had been over to France carrying on the negotiations with Louis concerning his renunciation of his futile claims upon that realm; and upon his return he had asserted himself by summoning a Parliament in the old form, quite irrespective of the Provisions of Oxford, and by seeking to obtain from the Pope a bull absolving him from the oath taken in that city under the compulsion of the Barons.

The Pope, always ready to take the part of so pious a son, and one who had been so useful to him as a tool, was ready enough to grant this absolution, which was couched in characteristic terms by the wily prelate :—

" We therefore, being willing to provide for your dignity in this matter, with our apostolical authority, in the plenitude of our power, from this time forward entirely absolve you from your oath. If, however, there should be anything in those statutes concerning the advantage of prelates, churches, and ecclesiastical persons, we do not intend to make such void, or in any way relax the said oath in that respect."

It was, perhaps, small wonder that the English people, with a lover of freedom and constitutional liberty at their head, should revolt from the rule of a monarch who could place himself beneath the sway of a Roman Pontiff, and accept at his hands such favours as these.

Of all these things and many others Amalric and Leofric spoke as they rode through the sunny country during these long summer days. Everywhere they met the same sort of talk, the same sense of insecurity, the distrust of the King and the enthusiasm for De Montfort which was agitating the hearts of the people everywhere.

The nearer they approached to Kenilworth, the greater did this enthusiasm grow ; and when they were so near that the face of Amalric became known, he was received with open arms by all, and was eagerly questioned as to the doings of his noble father, and whether he also were coming to dwell amongst them again.

But of his father's doings at this particular juncture Amalric knew little. He had returned to England—so much he had heard in London—and was doubtless busy somewhere, but whether at Kenilworth or in other districts the young man could not say. It was one of those things he was eager himself to learn.

The golden light of evening was lying over the level plains and wooded slopes as the riders drew near to the Castle, and Amalric suddenly drew rein and pointed to the great tower rising bold and massive from the waters of the lake-like moat and the surrounding park and forest land.

"See," he cried—"see, Leofric, there is my home! Is it not a lordly pile of which one may well be proud? And look at yon white sail upon the lake! that is our own sloop, wherein we have been wont to take our pastime. Ah, happy, happy days of childhood spent within those walls! I wonder if the future will hold anything half so sweet!"

Leofric looked in admiration and amazement at the finest building it had been as yet his lot to see, save perhaps the great Tower of London itself.

Although Kenilworth Castle in those days was not the magnificent pile which it became when the Lancaster and Leicester buildings were added to it, it was yet a very majestic structure, well fitted to be the home of the King's

sister, and of the foremost noble of the land. It was a
fortress as well as a castle, the walls being in many places
from ten to fifteen feet thick, whilst the principal tower
—Cæsar's Tower, as it was called—was considered wellnigh impregnable. It had a double row of ramparts, and
the moat which lapped the walls upon the south, east,
and west sides was more of a lake than a moat, and could
be carried round the north side if necessary. Boats were
kept upon this lake, where the family disported themselves, and the suite of rooms used by the Earl and Countess
were washed by the waters of the lake, and a boat was
kept at the water-door for their use and behoof.

The banqueting-hall was capable of seating two hundred
persons; and Kenilworth had, besides its innumerable
suites of living-rooms, its prison, its mill for grinding corn,
its brewery for the manufacture of beer, its weekly market
for the interchange of commodities with the neighbouring
peasants, and even its courts of justice. For Kenilworth
was privileged to hold assize of bread, beer, and so forth, to
regulate the prices for these, and weights and measures for
other provisions; it had its court-baron for the recovery
of debts and the punishment of minor trespasses, and its
court-leet for that of more serious crimes. It even had its
gallows, which stood frowning upon the castle walls, ready
to make an end of any unlucky wight doomed to death by
the voice of the court. Such was the life of those days
in a place as strong and as important as the Castle of
Kenilworth.

But this evening all was sunshine and peace and beauty.

Amalric pointed eagerly out to his companion objects of interest in the Castle and grounds as they rode onwards, and eagerly scanned the approaches to the place, if haply he might see some familiar face, or catch a glimpse of mother or sister taking an airing outside the walls.

The gardens themselves lay within the extensive buildings and walls, which formed two immense enclosures, capable of containing, in addition to gardens and orchards, a tilt-yard and courtyard of ample dimensions. Kenilworth was in effect a small township, complete in itself; and there was stabling for above a hundred horses, which stables were often full to overflowing when the Earl and his retinue arrived.

But apparently he was not here to-day, for there were few signs of active life about the place, and even the sentry upon the wall seemed slumbering at his post, so that their approach had not yet been observed.

Suddenly Amalric shaded his eyes with his hand, and gazing towards the waters of the moat, exclaimed,—

"In good sooth I am certain that yon figure in that white-sailed boat is that of my sister Eleanora! Come, good comrade, let us leave the road and ride up to the water's edge! Let us take her by surprise!—my pretty, dainty little sister Nell. She will not have forgotten me, I trow, though I have not seen her for three years and more."

Spurring his horse eagerly forward, and closely followed by Leofric, Amalric galloped towards the edge of the lake, upon whose placid bosom a little white-sailed sloop was idly rocking, the wind having scarce power to drift it from side to side.

As they drew near they could see that the only occupant of the boat was a young maiden of perhaps twelve summers, though she looked more, being tall and slim, and possessed of a high-bred grace and self-possession which her training had given her. She had just observed the unceremonious approach of these riders, and was about to direct her craft towards the opposite bank as a mark of her displeasure, when something in Amalric's dress and bearing arrested her attention, and she gazed earnestly at him, whilst the boat drifted nearer and nearer inshore.

"Sister mine, dost know me?" cried the youth, springing from his horse and running to the very edge of the water.

She looked at him with wide eyes full of wonder, which kindled into joy as she recalled his face.

"Amalric, dear Amalric!" she cried, stretching out her arms to him; and the next moment he had drawn the boat ashore, and had her fast in a brother-like embrace.

"Amalric! how comest thou thither? Is our father with thee? Art come with news of him?"

"Nay; but to get news of him, and to see thee and my mother, and to take a holiday after all these years of study. Art glad to see me again, little Nell?"

"O brother, yes! I missed thee sorely when thou didst go away; and now thou wilt be so learned I shall almost fear to talk with thee. But I too have learned to read the Latin tongue; and my mother has given order

for some fine vellum to be bought for me; and I am to
have a breviary of mine own when we can find some clever
scribe who will transcribe it for me. But tell me now,
Amalric, who is thy friend who stands thus modestly by?
for methinks he has a gentle air. He is not a servant,
but a friend, I trow."

"Thou art right, sister; a friend in good sooth. It
is the same as I have written of, if thou hast received
the letters I have writ to my mother as occasion has served.
I would present him to thee—my faithful friend and
comrade, by name Leofric Wyvill. Thou wilt give him
welcome, I doubt not, for my sake."

"Ay, and for his own," said the little Lady Eleanora, or,
as she was universally styled (probably to distinguish her
from her mother), the Demoiselle. The Countess of Leicester was always spoken of in her household as the Lady
Eleanora; for although the sister of a King, no higher title
had as yet been accorded to the Princesses of the blood
royal, at least in the common round of everyday life. The
only daughter of the Earl and Countess, therefore, had her
own distinguishing title of Demoiselle, by which she was
universally known throughout the Castle of Kenilworth.

As she spoke she held out her hand with an air of
gracious dignity, and Leofric bent the knee and raised it
reverently to his lips. The maiden smiled, innocently
pleased with the homage, and addressed him in friendly
tones.

"We have heard of you, fair sir, and you are welcome
to Kenilworth.—Amalric, let us give our mother a surprise.

Come into the boat with me—yes, and you also, sir—and let us across to the water-door, and enter her apartments without announcement! I trow she will give us joyful welcome. We are looking from day to day for the arrival of our father and his retinue. Thou dost seem like a herald of his approach."

Leofric's skilful management of the boat drew forth the approbation of the Demoiselle, who permitted him, with a charming smile, to hand her ashore at the wide stone landing-place, upon which opened an oaken doorway studded with brass plates and heavy bolts. The door, however, opened readily to the touch of the child's hands, and when she had pushed aside a curtain, the trio found themselves in a vast and beautiful apartment, so much more luxurious than anything that Leofric had ever seen that he stood mute and spell-bound at the sight. But the Demoiselle, laughing gaily at his silent bewilderment, called to them to follow, and pushing aside a rich curtain of sombre hue, she beckoned to them to pass within into a smaller second chamber.

This room was very bright, for a western oriel window let in a flood of glory. Seated near to this window, some fine embroidery in her hands, was a stately and dignified figure, at sight of whom Leofric instinctively retreated a step; for he knew without any telling that he was in the presence of the Lady Eleanora, wife of the great De Montfort and sister to the King.

Amalric and the Demoiselle sprang forward, uttering their mother's name, and the next moment Amalric had dropped upon his knees at her feet, to be clasped in her fond arms.

Whatever faults and failings Eleanora possessed—and that she was proud, extravagant (at least in early life), and wilful no one who reads her life can deny—in her relations as wife and mother her loyalty, tenderness, and unselfishness shine out in no dim colours. Her husband loved and revered her; her children almost worshipped her. She had always a warm and loving welcome for them, and was never so happy as when she could gather them about her, albeit in those troubled times these opportunities were growing rarer and more rare.

Leofric, standing just within the curtain, could not but gaze with admiring eyes at the queenly woman before him. Although the Countess was very plainly habited in a russet robe with no other trimming than white lamb's wool, and had no ornament upon her person save a golden clasp to her girdle, there was yet in her aspect such dignity and high-born grace that he could not take his eyes from her beautiful face, and the story of her romantic secret marriage with De Montfort (which Amalric had often told to him) came flashing into his mind, and he could not wonder that the Earl had dared so much to win that noble woman for his wife.

The Lady Eleanora's face was thin and worn with anxiety, and her eyes had that peculiar light which bespeaks a life of anxious watching. Her life had not been a smooth one, for she had shared in all things her husband's cares and troubles. Yet with all that she had not lost the gracious sweetness of manner which had been hers from girlhood, and when at last she beheld Leofric standing mute and shrinking just beside the door, she made her son present him, receiving him with a gentle courtesy and kindness which put him at once at his ease, and made him her devoted servant from that time forward.

She would not dismiss him to the quarters of the retainers, albeit his rank was humble. She treated him as the friend and equal of her son, and the fact of his having been of much assistance to Amalric during his course of study gave him a standing at once. For the Lady Eleanora had a great respect for learning, and all her children were well educated for the times they lived in. Her sons had all received instruction from such celebrated men as Robert Grostête and Adam Marisco, and scholars, even if humble by birth, were always well treated within the walls of Kenilworth.

So when refreshment was served for Amalric in a neighbouring chamber, Leofric was made to sit at table with him, and was given a room close by that of his comrade. He made one of the little party that gathered in the small oriel room after the more formal supper had been eaten in the hall below, and he listened with the keenest interest whilst the Countess related to her son the events of the past years and months, and the condition of public affairs as they now stood.

" I pray God," she said, " that my brother the King will be advised for his good, and that this land may be saved from the miseries of war. But I greatly fear me that he will

refuse to be bound by the Provisions of Oxford, even as
our father refused to be bound by the terms of the Great
Charter. If that be so, there is but one remedy for the
evil—the appeal to arms; and from that your father will
not shrink, if he knows his cause to be a righteous one."

"And where is he now?" asked Amalric eagerly.

"He is in England; but more than that I do not know.
He returned from Gascony a short while since, and he has
been conferring earnestly ever since with our friends in
various parts of the country. I am looking for him daily
now at Kenilworth. Every day that passes brings him one
day nearer."

CHAPTER XIV.

THE GREAT EARL.

"MY father is coming! my father is coming! the watchman has sighted his approach! Come and see him arrive with his train! it will be a right goodly sight, methinks."

So spoke the Demoiselle, rushing in hot haste into a great hall, which might perhaps be termed the library of the Castle, where certain books and manuscripts were stored in carved oaken presses against the wall, and where Leofric spent a portion of each day in transcribing for the little Eleanora the breviary which she was so eager to possess.

The Countess, at a hint from her son, had offered this task to the young scholar, and Leofric had gratefully undertaken it. The Demoiselle took keen interest in the work, and had already established very friendly relations with her brother's friend. A child at heart, despite her graceful and self-possessed manners and queenly little ways, she delighted in listening to stories of Oxford student life, and in watching the skilful pen and brush of the young bachelor as he copied the text or the illuminations from the scrolls in the library. Little Eleanora was greatly delighted at being able to choose her favourite designs for reproduction in her own breviary, and she danced in and out the library like a veritable sprite, directing and admiring, chattering freely to the scribe as she grew intimate with him, and letting him into a great deal of the family history of the De Montforts during the years of Amalric's absence.

Amalric himself was often present, and then brother and sister would converse freely and eagerly together. Leofric was treated as a friend and equal by both, and greatly enjoyed this experience of life in a nobleman's castle. It was like stepping forth into a new world or learning a new language.

The arrival of the Earl of Leicester had been for some time expected. His wife knew that he was in England upon a flying visit for political reasons, and daily was he looked for at Kenilworth; but so far no definite tidings of his movements had reached her, and the household lived in a state of expectancy and impatience.

It was no wonder that, when the Demoiselle rushed into the library with this piece of intelligence on her lips, Amalric and Leofric should start at once to their feet, and hasten with all speed to the great courtyard, where already the men-at-arms and the retainers were mustering.

It was a beautiful and picturesque sight. The Countess, with her little daughter and her handsome son beside her, stood at the top of the great flight of steps which led into the banqueting-hall, opposite the great gateway. All round the spacious courtyard were grouped the armed retainers and servants of the household. The sentinels and men-at-arms mounted the battlements, or drew up in martial array about the gateway, and the herald rode forth to meet and greet his master and bring him in in triumph.

The sense of expectancy deepened as the minutes passed by; then a great shout was raised as the trampling of horses' feet was heard within the outer courtyard. The next minute the great Earl, bare-headed, as he responded to the enthusiastic greetings showered upon him, rode through the gateway and across the court; and a cry went up that seemed wellnigh to shake the walls, as Kenilworth welcomed back its long-absent lord.

The eagle face of the Earl had grown thinner and browner since Leofric had seen it last. There were lines there which had been traced rather by anxiety and sorrow than by the hand of time. But the light in the eyes was unquenched, and the carriage of the haughty head betrayed the undaunted and resolute spirit of this leader of men.

His glance softened at the sight of his wife and daughter, and with a quick and skilful turn of the reins he drew up his charger at the foot of the steps, and leaped lightly to the ground. The next minute he had embraced his wife before the eyes of the assembled crowd, who were making the welkin ring with their plaudits; and little Eleanora was clinging to his hand, half shy, yet intensely eager for the notice of her sire, of whom she had seen but little, and that only on brief visits, paid as occasion served, and he could be spared to enjoy the pleasures of home life.

Leofric's eyes wandered over the goodly company filing into the courtyard after its lord. Immediately behind their father rode Henry and Simon, his eldest sons, now knights, and youths of handsome person, albeit lacking their father's nobility of aspect and charm of manner. Behind these again rode Guy, the third son, and side by side with him was a young man of noble aspect, very richly dressed, and plainly of no small importance in the eyes of the great De Montfort himself; for even before his own sons had had time to embrace their mother, he beckoned up this youth to the top of the steps, and presented him with much ceremony to his wife.

Leofric noted that quite a number of the men who followed wore the badge and the livery of this person. For a moment it crossed his mind that it might be one of the King's sons; but upon putting the question to one who stood by, he was answered in the negative.

"Nay, it is not the Prince. The Prince is a kinglier youth than that. That is Gilbert, the young Duke of Gloucester, and a right royal welcome will be accorded him at Kenilworth; for if he had followed his father's footsteps, and taken the side of the King, great hurt and loss to our party must have ensued. We cannot afford to lose the support of Gloucester."

This enlightened Leofric considerably as to the situation, and he added his voice to those raised in lusty cheering for the young Earl Gilbert. He had heard much about the father of this young man, recently deceased, and how, after joining in the cause which the Barons had at heart, he had quarrelled again and again with the Earl of Leicester, and had finally gone over to the King's side. Up to the present moment it had been feared that this young son, a youth of nineteen, now Earl in his father's stead, might follow that father's example and join the King's party; but his appearance at Kenilworth to-day, in company with De Montfort and his sons, showed plainly that he had thrown over the old Earl's policy, and had cast in his lot with the Barons: so the hearts of all were made glad, and cheer upon cheer rent the air as Leicester presented his youthful compeer to his loyal retainers here.

Preparations were instantly set on foot for a banquet of more than ordinary splendour. The Countess had been prepared for some such emergency as this, and the vast kitchens of the Castle could be depended upon for an ample supply of those substantial dainties under which the tables of our forefathers were wont to groan. The waters of the moat supplied fresh-water fish and wild fowl in abundance. Kids and goats and calves, oxen and sheep and swine, had only to be fetched in from the stores in the Castle. Venison from the forests around, as well as small game of all sorts, was supplied by the huntsmen; and in the household roll of the Countess are to be found abundant entries concerning spices, saffron, rice, figs, ginger, cinnamon, and raisins, showing that the variety afforded in those days was considerable.

But Leofric still stood watching the entry of the gay company which came with the Earl in martial array. It seemed as though there was no end to the following of

knights and esquires who attended these two great nobles.
They filed in one after another in endless array, till the
youth wondered how even the walls of Kenilworth could
accommodate them all.

Suddenly he gave a great start of surprise, and pressed
a few steps forward. A small group had just come into
the courtyard, seemingly in the rear of the followers of
the Earls, and Leofric recognized the face and form of
Sir Humphrey de Kynaston, Constable of Oxford Castle;
whilst riding at his side, upon a pretty little barb, was fair
Mistress Alys, his daughter, now grown to be a most
beauteous maiden, the light of her father's eyes; and these
two were accompanied by four stout serving-men, who
wore the livery of their master.

What could Sir Humphrey be doing here? asked Leofric of himself in no small wonder; and pushing a way
through the moving crowd of horsemen, who were filing
off towards the stables and quarters allotted to them, he
made his way to this little group just within the great
gateway, and doffed his cap respectfully before them.

A little cry of delight from Alys told him he was recognized.

"Father, it is Leofric—our good Leofric!" she cried.
"I remember now that Amalric was to bring him to
Kenilworth. Now this is a good hap indeed; for we feel
like fish taken from the water in this strange company.—
Prithee, good youth, be our friend and counsellor, for methinks our noble host has forgotten that he has made us
his guests for the nonce."

A few words from Sir Humphrey explained what had happened. He had been taking his daughter on a little riding expedition through the country, some business of his own having obliged him to quit Oxford for the space of a few weeks. They were journeying back, when they had fallen in with the Earl of Leicester, who had cordially invited them to be his guests for a few days. Then he had only had a small company with him; but that very day he had been joined by the Earl of Gloucester and his following, and so many knights and gentlemen had added themselves to his train upon his approach to Kenilworth, that he and his daughter had betaken themselves to the rear, and were disposed to think themselves forgotten; so that the sight of a familiar face amid all that strange throng was hailed with pleasure and relief.

But the Earl had a better memory than Sir Humphrey had supposed, and at this moment Amalric came hastening up to give a hearty welcome to the Kynastons, and to escort them to his mother's apartments, where Alys was to be lodged during her stay. She was eagerly received by the Demoiselle, who was always delighted to have a girl friend to stay with her; and before an hour had passed away the two maidens were fast friends, and little Eleanora had promised Alys to take her into the gallery overlooking the banqueting-hall, to see the fine company sit at table, and hear the address which her father was certain to give them.

"And Leofric shall come with us," said Eleanora, with one of her imperious little gestures; "Amalric cannot. He must sit at table as one of my father's sons. But

Leofric can stay with us, and I trow he will like it better than sitting for hours stuffing himself with all those strange dishes that the cooks send up at feast-times. I will send and tell him that we desire his attendance. Thou dost know him—he is thy brother's friend; I have heard tell of thee from him. He is my brother's friend likewise, and I trow he is a very goodly youth, and a good one too. I care not if his birth be humble; we might have been born peasants ourselves!" and the niece of the King tossed her dainty head, airing the democratic fancies of youth with a petulant grace characteristic of her varying moods.

"My father loves the people, and fights for their rights," she added more seriously, after a moment's pause. "He loves the King, and would well like to be his faithful vassal; but if he does wrong, my father withstands him. Sometimes he says it may cost him his life one day; but he never shrinks back from what is his duty."

Leofric obeyed the behest of the Demoiselle with alacrity.

There was, in addition to the minstrel's gallery over-looking the great hall, a smaller private gallery, leading from the quarters occupied by the Earl and Countess and their personal guests. Sometimes when the Earl entertained a company of nobles, the Countess sat here and looked on without taking part in the feasting; but to-day she would sit at table with her lord, and he would fain have had his daughter too, had not Eleanora pleaded the weariness she always felt at these lengthy functions, and obtained grace for herself and Alys to have their own supper privately served, and to look on as spectators only at the banquet.

It was in truth a goodly sight. The great hall was filled from end to end with nobles, knights, and squires of varying degree, who occupied tables arranged according to their rank, and made a proud and gay display with their costly dresses and flashing jewels. The Earls of Leicester and Gloucester, with the Countess between them, occupied the places of honour at the highest table raised on a dais, and Leofric looked with admiration upon the noble face and grand figure of the great De Montfort. Without doubt his was the kingliest figure of all those present to-day; and his voice when he spoke was clear and sonorous, and might be heard from end to end of the hall.

The tables shone with massive silver plate; serving-men hurried to and fro, bearing huge silver dishes containing viands of every description. Huge barons of beef were borne in between two stalwart attendants; boars' heads with gleaming white tusks, and peacocks with spreading tails, formed dishes more ornamental than edible, though some favoured them, and laughing plucked out the peacocks' plumes and stuck them in their belts. Huge pasties, both savoury and sweet, found ready custom; and as for the hogsheads of beer and wine that must have been consumed, the household roll speaks eloquently of the capacity of our ancestors in the matter of strong drink. The watchers in the gallery laughed merrily at the sight, and wondered how long the stores of Kenilworth would stand the strain.

Towards the end of the banquet the Earl of Leicester rose to his feet, flagon in hand, and in clear loud tones, which dominated the clamour of voices around him, gave the toast,—

"His Majesty the King!"

In a moment the whole company was on its feet, and the loyal toast was drunk with acclamation.

When the hubbub had subsided, the Earl motioned to his guests to be seated, and himself remaining standing, made a long and eloquent speech.

He spoke of his own affection for the King—his desire for the peace and welfare of the realm—his hatred of bloodshed and confusion. Men had said of him, he exclaimed, with a flash in his eagle eyes, that he desired himself to be monarch of the realm, and the King to be a mere tool in his hands. That charge he utterly and fiercely denied. He was the loyal servant of the King, so long as his Majesty would abide by his plighted word, and would regard the liberties of his subjects and the terms of the Great Charter. The Provisions of Oxford were in themselves nothing new; they were but the means by which the Great Charter could be upheld. The King was not the only person in the realm who had rights to be cherished and guarded. The liberties of all classes must be considered; and if a monarch, through weakness or lack of judgment, surrounded himself with false and scheming men, who persuaded him to acts of tyranny and rapacity, it then behoved his loyal subjects, who wished to do him true service, to remove from his side these false sycophants, and to furnish him instead with true and able counsellors, who could advise him for his own good and for the good of the realm.

This was in effect what the Barons' party (as it had come to be called) were doing. They would not stand by passive and idle whilst England's wealth and England's honour were being handed over to foreign powers, whilst the country was being bled to death to fill the papal coffers, and every lucrative place, as it fell vacant, was heaped upon some foreign adventurer, whose handsome face had attracted the King's admiration, or whose relationship to the Queen gave him a supposed claim upon his royal kinsman.

The Prince knew all this as well as any man in the kingdom. He had remonstrated with his feeble father times without number. He had sworn to the Provisions of Oxford, and had refused to cancel his oath even when the King repudiated his own, and had bribed the Roman Pontiff to grant him absolution therefrom. The Prince was the true friend to his country, and when he should sit upon the throne all would be well. Meantime the most true and loyal servants of the King were those who sought the true welfare of the realm, and would withhold him from spoliation at the hands of foreign hirelings.

Then holding his head very high, De Montfort spoke of the taunt sometimes levelled at himself of being a foreigner. He admitted freely his foreign birth, and pointed out how he had been the first to deliver up his castles of Kenilworth and Odiham after the Provisions of Oxford

had been agreed upon. He had even retired altogether to
Gascony after a stormy quarrel with the Earl of Gloucester; and were it for the good of the realm, whose welfare
he had so deeply at heart, he would return thither willingly, and never again set foot on these shores. But
over and over again he had discovered that he was
necessary to the welfare of the party. At this moment
he had been summoned across the seas to help in their
deliberations. No one had the true welfare of the English
nation more at heart than he; and alien though he might
be by birth, he loved the land of his adoption with a
changeless and passionate love, and would live for her or
die for her whichever might be for her good. He had put
his hand to the plough; he had pledged his honour and his
reputation to save her from papal thraldom and the spoliation of self-seeking men; she should have her Great
Charter, for which men had bled and died before, or he
himself would leave his dead body upon a blood-stained
battlefield!

Roars of applause followed this masterly speech, spoken
with all that charm of manner and lofty dignity of which
De Montfort was master. Not one word did the great
Earl speak of the personal wrongs inflicted upon him by
the capricious monarch. Every one present knew how
greatly he had suffered from the injustice of Henry—how
he had spent money like water in his service in Gascony,
only to be reviled and abused upon his return by a master
who gave greedy and credulous heed to every word spoken
against one whom he ofttimes feared and hated.

True, there were moments when the old affection would break forth, when the love for his sister was in the ascendant, and a temporary peace was patched up. But far more often was the Earl the butt for the King's injustice and extortion, and the troubles over the payment of the Countess's dowry added to the chronic friction between them.

But of this the Earl made no mention. He spoke always of the King in terms of loyal affection, only deploring and denouncing a state of things which made him the prey of foreign extortion, and the tool of those who would have him grind his people to the very dust to supply their endless demands. From this condition of affairs the kingdom must be rescued at all cost; and even if force alone would do it, that last and fearful remedy would be better than the curse of slavery and foreign tyranny.

His hearers were with him to a man. Cheer after cheer went up, making the great rafters of the hall ring again. Even the youthful Demoiselle clapped her hands and joined her voice with that of others, and Alys's fair face flushed and paled with varying emotions as she listened; and she turned impulsively upon Leofric and asked,—

"Oh, surely it will never come to that! The King will not suffer himself to be so led astray!"

"The King is a puppet in the hands of his Queen and her relations!" cried the Demoiselle, with the assurance of extreme youth. "I have been to Court; I have seen it all.

And there are all the De Lusignans, his half-brothers—
they are more to him than his true kindred. He has them
ever about him—them and the Queen's relations, who are
legion. They stuff his head with all sorts of falsehood.
They foster his pride and folly, and they prey upon him
like vultures. Only when my father and his friends can
get speech of him and take him away from these harpies
does he ever behave himself as a monarch should. As
soon as he makes his way back to them, they make of him
their tool and their slave. And then he seeks to sink
England into slavery like his own !"

It was amusing to hear the child speaking thus, with
sparkling eyes and a mien oddly like that of her noble
father. She had all the spirit of her sire and her royal
mother, and her companions regarded her with admiration.

"If his Majesty the King had but half the spirit of my
lady mother," cried the child once more, "all this trouble
would speedily be at an end. Methinks Providence made
a blunder in fashioning him the man and her the woman.
Had it been the other way, things in this realm would be
vastly different now."

The stir within the hall had drowned the sound of
another kind of tumult without; but had the revellers
been less excited by the great Earl's speech and their own
enthusiastic reception of it, they might have been aware
of some unwonted stir going on in the courtyard. The
stone pavement had been ringing to the clang of horses'
hoofs; voices had been raised in eager challenge and
greeting.

At this moment a servant quickly entered the banqueting-hall, and made his way up to the Earl, to whom he spoke in a rapid undertone. Leicester rose instantly and spoke to his wife, who also rose to her feet, a look of surprise upon her face, though none of displeasure.

"What can have chanced?" questioned the Demoiselle eagerly; "it is no trifle that would cause my father to rise and stride from the hall at such a moment as this. And see! all at the high table have risen, and are looking towards the door; and now the whole company is afoot. Some strange thing is about to happen; what can it be?"

They were not kept long in suspense. The great doors at the bottom of the hall were flung wide open. A trumpet note rang through the building, till the rafters themselves echoed to it; and it was answered by the shout from hundreds of voices as the company saw whose was the stately figure that the Earl had gone forward to meet.

The Demoiselle suddenly clapped her hands, and waved her scarf in token of joyous greeting.

"It is my noble cousin, my well-loved cousin!" she cried, in tones of childish rapture; "it is Prince Edward himself!"

CHAPTER XV.

PRINCE EDWARD.

THE Demoiselle was right. The tall and kingly-looking youth now striding up the great hall of Kenilworth, greeting first his uncle the Earl and then the Countess his aunt, was none other than the King's eldest son—that Prince Edward who was to play so great a part in the history of the English nation.

At that time he was a youth of some two-and-twenty summers, and had long been held to have arrived at man's estate. He was becoming a power in the kingdom, and was developing an aptitude for government which sometimes delighted and sometimes alarmed his father. He was no favourite with his father's foreign flatterers, and was an ally of those who upheld the gradually moulding constitution and the liberties of the people. He had subscribed willingly to the Provisions of Oxford, and had remonstrated hotly with his father when the latter resolved to ignore his oath, and later on to obtain absolution from it.

Prince Edward at that time had practically embraced the cause of the Barons, although taking no public action

against his father. Henry, in dismay, had sent him to
Gascony; but the move had not been a happy one, for it
had thrown him into the society of the young De Montforts, his cousins, who were also there, and had increased
his intimacy with that dread man their father. His appearance at Kenilworth at this juncture was startling to
all, for he was believed by the Earl and his family to be
still in Gascony, and they had not the smallest premonition
of this visit.

But the Prince had been at Kenilworth before, and was
fond of the fine old place and of the life led by its inhabitants. It was nothing very wonderful for him to come
hither, though the manner of his arrival to-day was somewhat startling.

Standing upon the daïs, and looking round upon the
assembled company with his keen, fearless gaze, the
Prince motioned to the guests to be seated.

"I come hither, as it seems, in a good time, my friends,"
he said, his face, naturally stern of aspect, softening to a
slight smile; "for I see here to-day many gathered together
to whom I have a word to speak. I have come from
France in part for that very purpose; and I am glad that
not only do I find here my noble Uncle of Leicester, but
others who are bound together with him in a cause that
is dear to the heart of this nation. He has himself
but lately addressed you. Methinks I can guess full well
what he has said. In sooth, I heard the final words
of his speech through yon open window as I rode into
the court."

The Prince paused for a moment, his eyes sweeping round the hall, and resting upon several faces there with a curious, searching expression. The knights and nobles were still as death, hanging upon the words of the Prince. After a brief pause he spoke again, very clearly and trenchantly, and in tones that all might hear.

"My lords and gentlemen," he said, "I am not come at this moment to England to enter into the dispute which is ever waging between the King, my father, and those of his subjects who form the so-called Barons' party. I have come, by my father's desire, to quell the troubles in Wales, and thither am I bound. I have, however, made this deflection in my line of march that I might have speech with mine uncle before I go thither, and I am well pleased that what I have to say should be said in the hearing of this goodly company of his adherents."

The Prince paused for a moment and then took up his discourse.

"All men here assembled know right well that I have the welfare of this nation deeply at heart. All know that I have been a friend to the friends of liberty, and that I have even opposed the King, my father, when I have thought him wrong. I have observed my oath as sacred, even to mine own hurt. I have sought in all things to do the right. If I have failed, my youth and ignorance have been in fault, not my will. Have any here present aught to bring to my charge?"

The answer to this strange challenge was a ringing cheer. Prince Edward was always beloved by those who knew him personally, whilst his dauntless courage and his high sense of honour had brought him into esteem with all men. Every person present regarded him with admiration and respect, and all were proud to know that he was with them at heart, however small a share he had taken in the dispute.

"I thank you, my friends," said the Prince, as the cheers died away. "And now, having done me thus much honour, I will ask you to have patience whilst I speak a few more words. It is said by some, it is feared by more, that ere the kingdom sees peace and stability once again, the sword will be unsheathed, and Englishman will meet Englishman upon a field of battle. I pray God that this may not be. War with a foreign foe is a glorious thing, provided the cause be just; with those of our own race and name it is a horror and a disgrace! But such things have been before, and they may be again. I stand before you this day, whilst the realm is still at peace and before that peace has been broken, to say a thing in your ears from which I shall not go back when the day for action comes. You know that I love liberty and hate oppression. You know that I honour and respect the men of the realm who have made so bold a stand for liberty. I have been one with them—I have their cause at heart still. But listen again. I am the King's son. He is my father; I owe him filial love and obedience. If his subjects take up arms against him, thus breaking their oath of allegiance, I, his son, repudiate my own oath sworn at Oxford, and I fly to his side to help him with all the power that I have. At such a moment as that, if it come (which God forbid), it could not be that I should stand by an idle spectator. I must and I will join myself to one side or the other; and here I tell all ye assembled that no power on earth shall induce me to take up arms against my father and my King. The moment danger of personal violence menaces him, I, his son, fly to his side, and in his cause I fight to the last drop of my blood!"

The Prince stood perfectly still for several seconds after he had spoken these words, his head slightly thrown back, his eyes full of fire.

Dead silence reigned in the hall. Not a man there but felt the power of the challenge thus thrown down, and a sense of reverence for the royal youth who had uttered it. But to many the words seemed those of evil omen, for these men were bound heart and soul to the cause of the Barons, and they had begun to count upon Prince Edward as their ally, and even to whisper sometimes between themselves as to the possibility of setting him upon the throne in his father's place.

The minute after the Prince had spoken these words his face changed. A kindlier, softer look came into it, and turning towards his uncle and aunt with a courteous mien, he said in an altogether different tone,—

"And now a truce to these vexed questions of state. Let us forget all but that we are closely akin, and bound together by cords of love.—Why, Amalric, thou hast grown marvellously since I saw thee last, and art like enough a notable scholar by now.—Guy, I have a pair of rare coursing dogs for thee, with which we will hunt together in Kenilworth forests ere I move towards the Welsh marshes. I must needs wait awhile for my forces to reach me.—Thou wilt give me house room at Kenilworth meantime, wilt thou not, fair aunt ? "

The Prince was a great favourite at Kenilworth—that was patent to all. The Earl of Leicester was eager to do all honour to his young kinsman, despite the bold challenge thrown down by him on his arrival.

The best rooms in the castle were put at his disposal ; he was made much of alike by uncle, aunt, and cousins. The little Demoiselle showed him marked favour, and was ever to be seen riding beside him, or showing him through the gay gardens, dancing a measure with him in the hall after supper, or playing some game in one of the many long galleries.

The Prince was the most congenial of companions, and seemed to enjoy the free life of Kenilworth not a little. After the departure of the bulk of the guests whom the Earl had brought with him, the life within those massive walls partook of a free and family character very pleasant to all concerned. Sir Humphrey was pressed to remain, but he was almost the only guest not immediately connected with Kenilworth ; and Alys was delighted to stay in this stately place, and cement her friendship with the little Demoiselle, who had taken so great a liking for her.

The Demoiselle was, however, considerably taken up with her cousin Prince Edward, and Alys was often left to the companionship of the Countess. That lady was availing herself just now of Leofric's presence in the Castle to have some of the writings of authors past and present read aloud to her, as she sat at her embroidery or tapestry frame; and Alys seemed to delight in being present at these readings, and taking her part in the discussion which often arose.

The Lady Eleanora was a woman of much culture and insight, although she was not fond of the trouble of reading for herself. She was also familiar with the Latin tongue, and was seldom obliged to interrupt the young scholar, or ask him to translate the passages read. Not unfrequently Amalric was one of those who sat in the pleasant oriel room and listened and discussed, although the sharp eyes of the Demoiselle, who flitted all over the Castle like a veritable sprite, detected another reason for his love of study.

"Thy sweet eyes, methinks, are the book that Amalric loves best to read," she said to Alys one day, as the twain sought the room they shared together. "My cousin Edward marvels that he comes not a-hunting in the forest with the rest; but I know what it is that keeps him thus within the walls of home."

Alys coloured crimson, and put her hand to the lips of the laughing maid.

"Nay, nay, thou must not speak so. I am but the daughter of a humble knight. Thy brother is a King's nephew and the son of a notable noble. Such thoughts would never come to him. It is not well to speak so recklessly."

But the Demoiselle only laughed, and skipped round her friend.

" I can see what I can see ! " she answered merrily ; and as she looked into the face of Alys, through her long, dark lashes, she wondered what had brought there that look of sudden pain and bewilderment. Surely she must have known ere this that she was the light of Amalric's eyes !

However, she spoke no more upon the subject, only saying in her heart,—

" I wonder if she does think more of the gentle, chivalrous Leofric than of the knightly Amalric ! It might be so. One may never read the heart of a maid, as I have often heard say. But I fear me that her sire would be sore displeased at such a thing. Methinks he has noted Amalric's amorous regards, and is well pleased thereat."

It was not altogether strange that the Demoiselle should have shrewd notions of her own on these points, for marriages in those days were often arranged between mere children, and her own hand might at any time be solicited in wedlock. Association with her seniors had ripened her powers of observation somewhat rapidly, and she had come to have a certain belief in her own shrewdness. Moreover, her cousin Edward had asked her about Amalric and his indifference to sport, and that had set her sharp eyes to work to some purpose.

The Prince himself, however, was very well disposed towards learning, and often engaged Leofric and Amalric in conversation, asking with interest of the student life of

Oxford, and professing himself well pleased with the scholarship of his cousin.

He was much interested also in the stories of the strange life there, and was greatly entertained by what he heard. He declared that if he had not been born a prince, he would be an Oxford scholar; and the tale of Hugh's kidnapping and escape was listened to with the keenest attention.

The Prince, however, had not come on a mere visit of pleasure, and although he was detained longer than he had expected by the delay of his forces to muster at the appointed place, he spent much time closeted with the Earl, talking over the situation in Wales, and making plans for the subjugation of the unruly sons of the mountains and marshes, who were for ever causing trouble in the west.

Nevertheless he was too fond of the pleasures of the chase not to take advantage of the forests of Kenilworth, and when news was brought, just before his departure, that a marvellously large wild boar had been sighted in the forest, he must needs go forth for one last expedition, to strive to slay that monster of the woods.

The young De Montforts were ardent sportsmen, as the household roll testifies, entries being made for the feeding of six-and-thirty dogs belonging to Lord Guy, and again for forty-six belonging to Lord Guy and Lord Henry. Entries also occur for the keep of their horses when stabled at Kenilworth.

So as soon as the Prince expressed his wish for one more

grand hunt in the forest, preparations were at once commenced, and the Demoiselle rushed eagerly to her mother
to obtain permission to accompany the hunt.

"Prithee let me go, sweet mother! I do so long to see
the great fierce boar which has escaped the huntsmen these
many years. Old Ralph says he has known him ranging
the woods longer than any other of his kind; but he is so
artful and so strong that he has ever eluded chase before.
Now they think they have so managed that he cannot
escape them. I would be there to see; and my cousin
Edward has said that I shall not be in their way, and that
he will take care of me."

The Countess smiled as she smoothed the child's hair;
but she came of a fearless race herself, and desired that her
daughter should be fearless also.

"Thy cousin Edward will forget all when he sees the
fierce creature face to face; but if thy brother Amalric
will ride at thy side and take care of thee, I will let
thee go."

Amalric eagerly assented, looking the while towards
Alys, and then he said to his sister,—

"But thou must ask thy friend and playmate to ride
forth with thee to see the sight. Methinks Mistress Alys
scarce knows what a hunt in our forest is like."

"Oh, she will come, I doubt not," answered the Demoiselle
gaily; "and Leofric shall come too, and ride with us, so
that we may be well escorted even if our servants be all
lured away in the ardour of the chase, as is ofttimes the
way."

All this was speedily settled. The orders went forth for the huntsmen to make a cordon round a certain part of the forest, enclosing the lair wherein the great beast had been known to secrete himself for many days past. It was to be their business to see that he did not break bounds, and escape to the more distant portions of the forest; whilst the Prince, at the head of his hunting-party, was to follow and track him down, and seek at last to slay him.

It was like to be an exciting day's sport; for the fierce old boar was a wily customer and a tough one, and he would probably give no small trouble to dogs and men alike.

This, however, only added to the ardour of the chase, and it was with feelings of elation and excitement that the party rode forth from the gates of Kenilworth on that bright summer's morning, long before the dew was off the grass—dogs baying, horses prancing, riders exchanging gay sallies as they took the road to the forest under the direction of the head hunstman.

For the moment the Demoiselle rode ahead with the Prince her cousin, Lords Henry and Guy being of the group. A little behind them was Amalric, keeping close at Alys's bridle rein; whilst Leofric rode at his side, enjoying the exhilaration of the fresh morning air and the excitements of the gay scene.

He knew the country in the immediate vicinity of Kenilworth pretty well by this time; but he had not often penetrated deeply into the forest tracks, and to-day he was greatly impressed by the grandeur of the stately woodland trees and the beauty of the long glades of grass and bracken, where deer browsed or scampered off at their approach, and small game scuttled away in hot haste at sound of the horses' feet.

But though several tempting quarries crossed its path, the hunt turned neither to right nor left, but pursued its way along a narrow track which seemed to lead to the very heart of the forest.

They were now approaching the region where the boar was known to be lurking, and the dogs began to whimper and show signs of uneasiness. Old Ralph, an aged huntsman who had lost an arm, but whose sagacity and fidelity were always to be depended upon, here rode up, and told the Prince that the boar was in a thicket not far away. Then he coaxed the Demoiselle and her companion to separate for a time from the rest of the party, and put themselves under his protection; and he promised them that if they would but obey and follow him, he would place them where they should see the end of the hunt, without peril to themselves or embarrassment to the huntsmen.

The child was rather loth to accede to this, but Prince Edward advised her to do so; and finally, whilst the rest of the party rode onward warily towards the thicket, the two girls, together with Amalric, Leofric, and Ralph, pursued a different and circuitous path, being only made aware by the baying of the dogs and the shouts of their men that the quarry had been found, and that the chase had begun.

"We shall miss it all! we shall miss it all!" cried the Demoiselle petulantly; but old Ralph assured her to the contrary.

"Bide a bit, my little lady, bide a bit, and you shall see the best of the sport yet. Think you, fair ladies and brave gentlemen, that yon old brute will be slain in half an hour? Nay, but the chase will be long and sore, and many a good dog will get his death-wound ere the savage creature falls to rise no more. Pray Heaven no hurt come to the brave young Prince; for men have been done to death ere this by savage boars of the forest. Yet methinks he has stout heart and cunning hand, and a score of good riders to come to his aid."

The Demoiselle might pout and fret in impatience, but there was nothing for it but to follow old Ralph, who could guide his horse cleverly enough with his left hand, though helpless now to draw bow or wage war with any fierce denizen of the wood. But he had strung to his saddle a steel-pointed spear of wonderful sharpness and temper, and several times he excited the admiration of his companions by the skill with which he threw it, and brought to the ground some small beast against which he had launched it.

Talking with old Ralph and hearing his woodland stories made time pass fast, and the Demoiselle was quite coaxed from her fit of ill-temper ere sudden sounds broke upon their ears telling them that they were approaching to the hunt or the hunt to them once more.

"It is as I thought!" cried old Ralph, in some excitement.

"They have brought him to bay in the elves' hollow! I knew he would take them there at the last. Now come quickly this way, my little lady, and you shall see what you shall see."

They cantered their horses up the brow of a wooded knoll, and all in a moment the scene of the hunt broke upon their eyes. The hunt indeed! for there was the fierce old boar down in the shallow pool, with the rock behind him, and five dogs, dead or dying, lying on the banks or in the blood-stained water. He was there, and a handful of hunstmen in a ring round him; but of these one was wounded, several more were weary. It looked indeed as though the monster of the woods were getting the better of his adversaries.

But with a sudden shout as of triumph the Prince came charging down the hillside. He sprang from his horse and seized his spear, and before any one could hold him back he had sprung into the water, and was facing the furious creature, who looked ready and able to tear him in pieces with his gleaming tusks.

"Nay, but that is madness!" cried old Ralph; "the Prince will lose his life!" Others, it seemed, were of the same opinion; for there was a forward dash amongst the group around, some seeking to withhold the Prince, others to plunge their weapons in the body of the boar. A scene of wild confusion ensued, in which more than one sharp cry of human suffering rang out; and Amalric, unable to contain himself longer, rushed down to join the fray, crying out in his dread,—

"The Prince! the Prince! have a care for the Prince! Pray Heaven he be not wounded!"

The face of old Ralph was white, and working with emotion,—

"Would that I had the strength of my good right arm!" he cried; "then would I give the monster his quietus."

"How?" asked Leofric, shaking with excitement. "Tell me, and give me thy good spear; I trow I could wield it well!"

It seemed time indeed that something should be done, for the furious creature was goring and fighting like a mad thing, and one blow from those terrible tusks might mean death to man or dog. The Demoiselle had covered her face, and was shrieking with fear; whilst Alys, white and wild-eyed, felt as though turned into stone.

Eagerly did old Ralph talk to Leofric, giving him the pointed spear and filling his ears with directions and cautions. Thus fortified did Leofric creep quietly down the little bluff on which they were standing, fetching a circuit, and approaching to the scene of the fray from behind the rock, against which the boar had planted himself. With snake-like movement did he work himself upon the rock, the sound of his approach being lost in the hideous din of the fight; then suddenly springing to his feet, he drove the sharp-headed spear into the shoulder of the savage monster, who turned suddenly upon his new assailant with an impulse of awful and ungovernable fury, and in making a furious lunge at him with his bloody tusks, fell helplessly into the crimson water and expired without a groan.

"By the arm of St. James," cried Henry de Montfort, using a favourite expression of his father's, "that was well and bravely done!"

Next moment Leofric felt his hand taken by that of the Prince, who said in a low voice,—

"Leofric Wyvill! methinks that thou hast saved the life of the King's son this day. Thou shalt not find him ungrateful if the occasion when he can serve thee shall arise."

CHAPTER XVI.

BACK AT OXFORD.

THE narrow streets of Oxford, the crowds of clerks and scholars, the grey old walls and the frowning Castle—all looked wonderfully unchanged as Leofric, after hard upon a year's absence, returned to his *Alma Mater.*

He had seen something of the world during this time of absence. He had had a glimpse of warfare under the auspices of the young De Montforts and Prince Edward in Wales. His ideas upon the political situation had considerably enlarged. He had also earned a very fair sum of money, sufficient to enable him to cover all expenses of tuition for a considerable time to come. The breviary he had transcribed for the Demoiselle had brought him a liberal reward; he had also received remuneration for his readings with the Countess and her daughter.

Leofric had spent the greater part of the winter at Kenilworth Castle, after having been into Wales with the Prince. The King's son had taken a strong liking to Leofric after the incident of the boar-hunt, and the young student had been glad to accompany him into

Wales, to gain new experience in that strange, semi-barbarous land. Amalric had been one of the party, as well as his brother Guy; and having been wounded in a fray, he was put in charge of Leofric and sent back to Kenilworth, where the two had remained together during the winter months.

It had been a very happy season for those within the walls of the great fortress. The Earl and his sons were away in France again; but the Countess and her daughter remained in England as usual, and Alys de Kynaston had been persuaded to remain and be the companion of the Demoiselle, who had formed so strong an attachment for her.

In addition to this, at the instance of the imperious little lady, Edmund had made by slow stages the journey to Kenilworth, and had been one of the party. The change had been beneficial to him, and upon the return journey he had been able to ride the whole way without trouble or pain. They had journeyed by easy stages, and reached Oxford safely and without adventure.

It was a very different arrival from that which Leofric could well recall when as a poor lad, with his way in life to make, he had entered the city, scarce knowing where he could find shelter or how he could maintain himself.

Now he had many friends, some of them the highest in the land; he had won a certain modest renown by his scholarship, and had small fear of failing to attract pupils to his lectures when he should commence them. The

Master under whom he had studied rhetoric and logic had invited him to teach in his school; and as he would still have his own lectures and studies to prosecute with diligence, if he were to go on to the degree of Master, upon which his mind was set, he would have his time and thoughts pretty well filled, and require more than ever some quiet place of study.

His thoughts turned lovingly towards that little spot where he and Jack Dugdale had made a home so long. Would Jack be there still? What had he done with himself all these months? Naturally he had heard nothing from his friend during his absence; but he hastened his steps eagerly as he approached the Smith Gate, and was rewarded by hearing a regular whoop of joy as Jack suddenly dashed out to meet him and fell on his neck in a rapture of greeting.

"I have been on the watch for thee all day, good comrade. It was told to me that Edmund of the Castle and Mistress Alys had returned, and methought it like that thou hadst come with them, since they said there were others in the company. How good it is to see thy face again! But thou hast come to be so great a man now thou wilt never deign to dwell again in our humble little chamber with poor Jack."

"Nay, but I have been longing to see again thy face, good Jack, and the little turret chamber where so many happy hours have been passed. I have no wish to lodge in any other place. Let us go thither, and talk of all that has chanced since we parted. Art thou a bachelor thyself by this time? Thou shouldest have determined this late-past Lent!"

Jack made a wry face. Study was pleasant to him up to a certain point, but he lacked the courage to present himself for the ordeal of Responsions and Determinations. He was ready enough to learn, but shrank from the thought of becoming in any sort a teacher; and, moreover, in the absence of Leofric he had been taking something of a holiday himself, and the woods and streams had of late seen more of him than the schools and lecture-rooms.

"I could not travel away like thee, Leofric," he said, apologetically, "but methought a holiday would be no such bad thing. What says the wise old adage? All work and no play makes Jack a dullard."

Leofric had no mind to chide his friend and comrade, albeit he thought it would have been wiser had Jack postponed his holiday till he had passed the ordeal of Determinations.

"Now that thou art back, I will study might and main, and next year will dispute with thee, good friend, so that men shall flock to hear us;" and Jack laughed aloud in the happiness of his heart, knowing that many long months had to pass by ere he would be called upon to stand up and maintain a thesis or proposition in the teeth of his opponent's arguments, and in the hearing of all who chose to come and listen. He had listened with admiration and delight to Leofric when he had won his academic spurs (if the term can be permitted), and so delighted was he at his friend's prowess in argument, that he had many times dashed out into the streets to invite the passers-by to come in and hear the candidate for bachelorhood holding his own so gallantly and brilliantly.

Jack's loving admiration was very sweet to Leofric, who felt he had in him a true brother. This fraternal welcome was further displayed in the simple preparations made for his return—the fresh rushes upon the floor, the brightening up of the familiar chamber, the simple luxuries set out upon the little table, and the flowers filling the empty hearth.

Leofric looked round with brightening eyes, delighted to find himself once more in this home-like place. Tiny indeed did it appear after the spacious apartments of Kenilworth; and yet it had the charm of being his own— here he was no guest, no hireling, but a joint-owner of the primitive abode. Here he could keep his few precious books, study in quietness, and be secure from interruption.

"Ah, it is good to be at home once more; I want no better home than this!" he cried. "And now, whilst we set to upon this excellent dinner, tell me all that has betided in Oxford since I left. How goes it with all our friends —and foes? Has aught been heard of Tito Balzani or Roger de Horn? And has Hugh been molested in any wise by them? But, indeed, that was a matter almost forgotten before I left the place."

"Yes; I trow the fugitives might now return, and nothing would be done to them. Men quickly forget such matters, new stirs and quarrels ever cropping up that require adjusting. But I have seen naught of the

men, and Hugh has likewise been away for a time with
his father. But he is back now, and is studying hard,
for he would become a Master in Arts ere he quits Oxford,
and he thinks his father desires his presence at home ere
long."

"And Gilbert?"

"Oh, Gilbert is a bachelor, and he is betrothed to
Joanna, the Seaton maid. His father came to see the
damsel, and was pleased at his son's choice. Master
Seaton will give her a dowry, and they will be wed
anon, and go and live in the seaport of Southampton,
where Merchant Barbeck's business lies. He thinks his
son has now wellnigh scholarship enow, and that he had
better soon begin to learn the secrets of the merchant's
trade. So we shall lose one of our comrades."

Before the pair had finished telling and hearing the
news of the place, there was the sound of a hasty footfall
on the stair, the door was burst open, and Hugh le Barbier
strode in, grasping Leofric by the hands, and embracing
him with all the delight of a brother.

"I heard at the Castle that thou hadst returned!" he
cried, "and methought I should find thee here, back in the
old place. And so thou hast been the friend of nobles
and princes, and the guest of the greatest man in this
kingdom! Well, thou dost merit all the good that comes
thy way; for thou art a good and godly youth, and right
glad shall we all be to welcome thee back."

Hugh looked a very fine specimen of youthful manhood. He had been moving about with his father from

time to time during the past years, and·his studies had
been somewhat interrupted. Still he had made excellent
progress even in these, and was regarded as a very promising youth, who could wield sword and pen alike with
dexterity and force.

" Let us upon the river," he cried, when the first greetings and exchange of news had died down ; " I have much
that I would say, and what better place for talk than the
silent reaches of the upper river ?—Bring thy rod and net,
good Jack, and thou shalt fill thy creel with fish for
supper. I have seen wondrous fine trout in the stream
above. Come, and I will show thee the best of pools."

Jack was known as a skilful and ardent fisherman, and
was always perfectly happy when engaged in his favourite
pastime. The light boat which he and Leofric had
fashioned long ago was often in demand by their comrades and friends. Hugh had of late borrowed it oft
for many hours, and he had lately contrived a small sail
by means of which he could fly through the water at a
greatly increased speed.

To-day, after they had left Jack, abundantly happy
amid the sedges which lined a most promising-looking
pool, Hugh hoisted sail, and soon the little boat was
slipping rapidly along against the sluggish current of the
river, the low-lying banks on either side gliding past them,
and the wild fowl rising at their approach, and skimming
away with short, harsh cries.

" Leofric," said Hugh, after they had navigated several
reed-grown reaches, and were now in more open water,

"hast thou ever visited the Priory and little hamlet of Eynsham?"

"No," answered Leofric; "the way is something long for oars—a matter of seven good miles at least. Sometimes we have gone forth with the resolve to push there, but some tempting reach or shallow has always caught Jack's eye, and we have halted. Why dost thou ask?"

"Because that is our destination to-day. Leofric, dost thou remember Linda Balzani?"

"Ay, verily I do," answered Leofric quickly; "but methought thou hadst learned to forget her."

"I tried to do so," answered Hugh, a flush mantling his bronzed cheek. "After that terrible time of which I scarce cared to think for many a long month, I told myself that it were better, both for her and for me, that we should see each other no more. She had suffered nothing but trouble and pain from my love; and now that she had found a safe asylum in some peaceful spot, I vowed that I would leave her alone, and let her forget. They said that the memory of that time seemed to be blotted from her mind; and if that were so, it were better she should forget."

"Perchance so," answered Leofric thoughtfully: "she is scarce thine equal, for thou wilt surely rise to be a gallant knight ere many years have passed, and she is but a city burgher's daughter, albeit a very fair maiden."

The flush in Hugh's face deepened a little; he spoke in a strange voice.

"Is an angel from the heavens the equal of any sinful

son of this earth? If I am to wait till I can claim equality with Linda, I shall go to my grave unwed."

Leofric looked at him with surprise.

"Then thou hast seen her again?"

"Yes, truly I have. I have avoided the house of the Balzanis for many a year, thinking it better not to revive associations which must be painful. But I have heard men speak of Lotta—the beautiful, daring Lotta. Many there be who would serve for her, even as Jacob for Rachel; but it seems that she will none of them. Hearing always of Lotta and never of Linda made me question within myself whether that maid had died. I asked, and found that she had never returned to Oxford, but remained with her aunt at Eynsham, having grown to be as a daughter to her. I scarce know what it was that first awakened within me the desire to look upon her face once more, but once awakened the wish would not sleep, and at last I accomplished my purpose."

"Thou hast seen her again?"

"Yes, verily; not once, but many times. Leofric, I am taking thee with me to-day, that thou mayest see her too; for if ever the foot of angel trod the paths of men, that angel being is the lovely Linda of my boyhood's and manhood's love."

Leofric was greatly surprised, having believed, with all the rest of his comrades, that the youthful infatuation of Hugh le Barbier for Linda Balzani had quite passed away.

Her name had not crossed his lips, so far as any knew, since the excitement following upon his rescue from the

Magician's Tower had died down. The whole episode seemed to have come utterly to an end, and those who knew Hugh's circumstances thought it well, as he was of the stuff which might cause him to rise in the world.

The boat was riding at a fair rate of speed through the water, and the Priory walls of Eynsham gradually loomed in sight. It was a quaint, lonely, old-world spot, this little community lying hidden in the winding valley, far away from any other abode of man. There was a charm in the low-lying meadows, in the grand old trees, in the herds of deer that came down from the forest to drink at the river. Fish and wild fowl abounded in these solitudes, and the appearance of a white-sailed boat wrought astonishment and commotion amongst them. It was a place where life might well be dreamed away in pious meditation and contemplation. It was an ideal spot for a monastery; but Leofric had come to feel of late that more was desired of man than mere contemplation and meditation—more even than mere study and the acquiring or propagating knowledge. The life of the cloister had never greatly attracted him; now he felt that it would be nothing better than death in life.

A little winding backwater opened before them at this point, and Hugh, furling the sail, took up the oars and rowed quietly into the dim, narrow place. As he did this he uttered a low, sweet whistling call, not unlike that of some bird; and very soon Leofric became aware of a fluttering of white drapery, and a low, soft voice spoke out of the fringe of alder bushes,—

"Beloved, is that thou?"

The next minute Hugh had driven his boat up against a fallen willow that lay athwart the stream, barring further progress, and leaving it to Leofric, had sprung ashore, and had taken in his arms the slim form in the white robe that had come to the margin of the stream to meet him.

Leofric busied himself with the boat for a few moments, and only turned his head when his name was spoken.

Then indeed he saw before him the remembered face of Linda Balzani, but so etherealized and beautified that he could not wonder at the way in which Hugh had spoken of her. The deep, dark eyes shone like stars, the dusky hair waved round the small and well-shaped head like the aureole round the head of painted saint; and so pure was the expression upon the lovely chiselled features, so sweet the lines of the exquisite mouth, so graceful and sylph-like the slim figure, that Leofric gazed with wonder and admiration. It was Linda who spoke first.

"Thou art Leofric; I remember thee right well. I have heard from Hugh of thy prowess and success. Thou art welcome, as any friend of his must be; but thou art doubly welcome as being beloved by him."

She would have led them to her aunt's house and refreshed them; for Hugh was courting in no clandestine fashion, but had won the esteem and affection of Bridget Marlow and her husband. Linda was now their child by adoption, and they were responsible for her future. If Hugh were not ashamed to wed with a simple burgher maiden, they would not say him nay. They were simple-minded folks, and Hugh made light of his own prospects.

So far he was nothing but the son of an esquire, and a scholar and bachelor of Oxford. Linda was his one and only love, and that she was his in heart and in soul all who saw them together could not fail to recognize fully.

But to-day Hugh would not come in. They had not much time, and he spent the precious moments with Linda beside the rippling water, Leofric remaining in the boat and idly observing the objects about him. His eye was caught by the grey habit of a monk, who was seated amid the alders with a rod in his hand. Leofric observed that he seemed little engrossed by his fishing, and certainly caught nothing. Perhaps he was engaged in meditation or the telling of his beads. At any rate he sat wonderfully still and quiet; indeed he never moved at all until Hugh and Linda wandered away a little farther from his secluded nook, whereupon, to the surprise of Leofric, the cowled figure rose up and crept stealthily after them.

True, it might be the way back to the Priory, and surely a cloistered monk could have no interest in the lovers' raptures of a youth and maid; but Leofric noted and rather wondered at the action, though he forgot it again when Hugh returned, and they set to work to row down stream with long, sweeping strokes.

It was indeed several days later before he thought of the matter again, and then the incident was recalled by a remark made by Hugh as they were pacing the familiar streets together after morning lecture.

" Leofric, I have a curious and perhaps foolish fancy

that I am watched and followed. It must be the merest
fantasy, and yet I cannot rid myself of it."

" Has it been long so with thee ? " asked Leofric
quickly.

" Not very long—so far as my suspicion goes. But
how or when it commenced I cannot tell ; nor would I say
with certainty that the thing is not now the fruit of a disordered fancy. But I cannot rid myself of it."

" What form does the following take ? "

" I have a fancy that a certain grey-cowled monk is
often near at hand watching where I go and what I do.
There be so many of these monks and friars in the streets
of Oxford, that I sometimes laugh at myself for the
thought ; and yet methinks there is one—tall, and slim,
and active—who is more often in the same street with me
than chance can quite answer for. Thou dost start,
Leofric ; what means that ? "

" Only this, that as thou didst wander with Linda by
the backwater at Eynsham that day when I was with thee,
a grey-cowled monk was sitting beside the stream ; and
when ye twain moved a little off, he also moved and
seemed to follow, though I lost sight of him in the bushes
almost at once."

Hugh looked rather perplexed.

" And there is another whom I seem always to be meeting—a powerful fellow in the habit of a clerk, but with a
bearded face, and a scar across his cheek which perhaps
gives to him an evil aspect. Often when I turn suddenly
round in the street I see him behind me, but whether there

be anything beyond and behind I cannot tell. At first I heeded it little, but there are moments when I grow uneasy. Last time that I and Linda exchanged vows of love, some evil power threatened us, and seemed like to separate us altogether. Is it that, thinkest thou, that makes me fear, and puts fancies in my head for which there is no warrant?"

"I know not," answered Leofric; "but I would have thee be watchful and prudent. It is ill work stirring up strife and jealousy. If Roger de Horn were in the city, I should fear for thee. He was always thy bitter foe, and they say that he was very greatly bent on having Linda for his wife."

"Roger de Horn," spoke Hugh thoughtfully; "could it by chance be he? Methought once there was something familiar in the gleam of the eyes of that bearded fellow, but the scar has changed him if indeed it be so. I did not recognize him. He seldom meets me face to face. Perchance that is the reason;" and then Hugh's face became clouded with anxiety, and he said between his teeth,—

"If indeed that wild hawk has flown back thither, it behoves me to warn and watch over my tender dove. If hurt should come again to her through me, I should never forgive myself."

Leofric's suspicions were aroused, and he kept his eyes and ears open. He took counsel with his kind friend the Franciscan friar Brother Angelus, who had a warm welcome for him on his return; and he made inquiries amongst the other brothers, and amongst those whom he visited and tended. But none had heard a word of Roger de Horn since his disappearance after the discovery of Hugh's imprisonment in the Magician's Tower. Men were of opinion that he would hardly venture back into the city, in case he should be called upon to answer for his misdeeds there. Brother Angelus was of opinion that Hugh had better exercise prudence and discretion, and keep his eyes open. It was certainly a strange coincidence that this thing should be just when he and Linda had renewed their vows of love; and yet if any other suitor had desired the maiden's hand, why had he not come forward during the years when Hugh had been seeking to forget his love?

That was a question which Leofric could not answer, and just now he had many other matters to think of which drove Hugh's affairs into the background of his thoughts. He took up the academic life with renewed zest and energy, and in his studies and pleasant intercourse with kindred spirits passed many happy weeks. Hugh went about free and unhurt, and gradually the fear for his friend which had assailed him once died down into oblivion.

CHAPTER XVII.

THE BELL OF ST. MARTIN'S.

IT was the day of the bi-weekly fair, and the High
Street was considerably crowded as Hugh walked
along it on his way back towards his quarters in the Castle.
He had passed by the vendors of hay and straw gathered
near the East Gate with their horses and carts, and was
picking his way through the motley crowd who were
chaffering on the one side of the street with the sellers of
poultry, meat, and fish, and on the other with the sellers of
gloves, hosiery, and those other articles of which mercers
were the vendors. The street was encumbered with stalls
set up by country folks for the sale of greengrocery,
scullery-wares, and fruit or cakes. At Carfax itself the
sellers of white bread set up their stalls and called their
wares; opposite All Saints' Church stood the tables of
sellers of gloves, earthenware, and ale. Altogether it was
a busy and animated scene, and although Hugh was well
accustomed to it, he could not but look about him with
amusement, and pause now and again to listen to a piece
of unwontedly animated bargaining.

Clerks and scholars, and even some of the higher dig-

nitaries of the place, were abroad in the streets; and as
the evening was approaching, those who still wanted to
buy were pressing forward eagerly.

Hugh was detained for a time by meeting with one of
the Masters who had something to say to him, and the
pair stood for some little time beneath the shadow of All
Saints' whilst they conversed.

Meantime the aspect of the streets changed considerably :
tables and stalls were broken up and taken away by the
country folk, who streamed off through the various gates ;
town tradesmen took in their wares, and began to close
their shops ; and the purchasers hurried home with their
goods, talking and laughing, and comparing notes upon
their bargains.

The shadows were falling in the narrow thoroughfares
as at length Hugh pursued his way eastward. There were
plenty of passengers still afoot, but the crowd had thinned
somewhat. As he passed by the bull-ring in Carfax, he
thought he heard the sound of a small tumult from the
direction of the North Gate, where the cordwainers and
mercers congregated on market days ; but he paid little
heed to it, and continued his way to the Great Bayly,
where the drapers were putting up their shutters for the
night.

Suddenly the great bell of St. Martin's overhead boomed
out through the startled air, and immediately all was
hurry and confusion.

The tolling or ringing of the bell of St. Martin's was
always the signal for the citizens to rally against the

University, and showed that some collision between clerks and townsmen had occurred. Hugh quickened his steps, having no desire to be mixed up in one of those senseless outbreaks of anger and jealousy which were constantly disturbing the peace of Oxford.

Just lately these riots had been more frequent than ever, the disturbed state of public feeling seeming in this place to take the form of incessant rioting in the streets. Several persons, both citizens and clerks, had recently been killed, and a number more injured more or less severely during the past weeks; and Hugh had heard the Constable of the Castle speak in no measured terms of the need to take stronger measures against the delinquents.

Within the last few months a new Chancellor had been appointed to the University, the celebrated Thomas de Cantilupe, who had just arrived at the University (where he had previously taken the degree of Doctor of Canon Law), and he had joined issue with the Constable for the preservation of order. Indeed he had already adventured himself into the streets to interpose between some riotous spirits of North and South who had come to blows, and had himself received some injury in seeking to pacify the insensate youths.

It was said that he was about to make some fresh regulations, in the hope of putting a stop to this perpetual nuisance; but so far his decision had not been made public, as he had been obliged to keep to his rooms till his bruises should be healed.

Hugh, however, had heard and seen enough to feel

indignant at any fresh outbreak, and he quickened his steps in order to avoid any contact with a gathering crowd. Already citizens were hurrying towards Carfax, eager to learn what was betiding; several brushed past Hugh as he walked; and then, before his very eyes, a strange and terrible thing happened.

Suddenly he was aware that in a dark doorway close at hand a cowled figure was standing. Then the figure moved, and Hugh saw the glancing blade of a long, murderous stiletto flash out. It was plunged up to the hilt in the body of a citizen hurrying by towards Carfax, and the hapless man fell dead at Hugh's feet without so much as a groan.

The young man stood stupified with astonishment and horror; then in a moment he realized the peril of his own position.

"Seize him! seize him!" yelled a dozen furious voices; "he has slain one of our townsmen! Seize the murderer! Do to him as he hath done! Take him red-handed in the act, and we will see that justice is done upon him!"

"My good friends," said Hugh, looking at the angry faces surrounding him, and striving to keep his head in face of this very real peril, "I am innocent of the death of this unhappy man. I do not even know who he is. The murderer was a man disguised in the habit of a monk, loitering in yon doorway. Search, and you will find him yet, and I can testify to the blow he struck!"

Angry and excited, the crowd would scarce hear him. No such figure as he described was to be found. No one had seen a monk in the street, nor could Hugh declare in

what direction he had fled after committing the crime, so
bewildered had he been by the suddenness of the deed, and
by its tragic sequel. His words were received with hisses
of scornful discredit; the angry townsmen, some of whom
were neighbours to the murdered man, clamoured more and
more fiercely for the blood of the destroyer. Overhead
the bell of St. Martin's swung in the air, increasing the
excitement with every clang. The street was full of
wrathful burghers; yells, curses, threats, rent the air.
Hugh believed that in another moment the crowd would
fall upon him and tear him in pieces, and had almost given
himself over as lost, when a loud voice dominated the
others in the throng, and yelled out lustily,—

"Take him to the Bocardo prison; lock him up there
for the night, and then let the Mayor and the Chancellor
deal with him. They will avenge us of the death of our
neighbour. Let us not fall upon him ourselves, or we
shall, perchance, have our liberties again curtailed."

Many grumbled, and showed a disposition to resist this
counsel, crying out that it were better to deal with the
miscreant then and there, for that clerks and bachelors
were always let off far too easily by the authorities. But
the older men of the city knew well that the slaying of a
clerk was regarded with severity by those in authority,
and had sometimes been punished by the King himself in
the withdrawal of certain liberties and privileges from the
city charter. If a clerk fell in open fight, that was one
thing; but for the citizens deliberately to doom him to
death, and to dispatch him with their own hands without

form of trial, was another; and it was this sort of summary justice which brought the citizens into trouble.

"To the Bocardo then, to the Bocardo!" cried the wiser of the onlookers; and despite the mutterings of the malcontents, Hugh was hustled along, not without receiving many sly blows and kicks by the way, in the direction of the North Gate, where the Bocardo prison was situated.

It was getting very dark by this time. Breathless, spent, and bewildered, the clothes half torn from his back, his purse and clasp and finger-ring filched from him by thieving hands, Hugh was thankful when the gloomy gateway was reached, and he felt himself thrust up a dim stairway and flung with scant ceremony into a dark and ill-smelling room.

A faint ray of light stole in through a grating overhead, and revealed a small stone chamber with a truss of straw in one corner as its only plenishing. He was given over to the custody of a surly-looking fellow, who merely answered his questions with a grunt. Hugh greatly regretted the loss of his purse, as he felt sure that a gold piece would have worked wonders upon his custodian. He wanted to send a message to Leofric, to Edmund, to the Constable himself; but at the very mention of this wish the man broke into curses, and said he had other things to do than run errands for prisoners. He could wait till he was brought out for trial, and then see what was said to his fine tales!

With that the jailer deposited a pitcher of water and a modicum of bread within the door, and going out banged and locked it behind him, leaving Hugh to meditate in silence and darkness upon the thing that had befallen him.

Little sleep was there for him that night, and the tardy daylight brought small increase of comfort. He listened eagerly for any sounds from without that should tell of approaching deliverance; but hour after hour passed, and nobody came near him save the sullen jailer, who put down the rough fare of his prisoner, and did not deign so much as to answer a single question.

Such treatment was hard to bear, and Hugh, unaccustomed to it, chafed not a little against the helplessness of his position. He wondered whether his friends were in ignorance of what had befallen him. Surely if they knew they would do something for his release. It seemed monstrous that he should lie under the imputation of this foul crime. Surely no man of any standing in the city would believe him capable of it. And yet how could he prove his innocence, when his foes would make it appear that he had been caught red-handed in the act?

His was certainly no enviable position, nor did his thoughts tend to increase his peace of mind. He recalled his previous uneasiness with regard to a tall grey-cowled monk, and could not but believe that the figure lurking in the doorway had been that of the same person as he had seen so often in the streets before or behind him. He remembered what Leofric had said as to a monk at Eynsham spying upon him there. A thrill of fear ran through his heart lest Linda should once more be endangered—and through him. And then, again, had not he seen that

scarred and bearded face amid the rabble crowd that
thronged and maltreated him? Had not that man, so
often seen of late, been one of his foremost foes? He
felt in a maze of perplexity and dread. Was he to be
the victim of some new plot, which had for its object to
separate him and his beloved?

He paced his narrow cell hour after hour in mute
misery and disquietude. When would he be brought to
trial? When would his friends find him? He could hear
the familiar sounds in the streets below. He could hear
the sentries at the gate relieving one another. Why did
nobody come near him? How long was he to be left
thus?

Gradually the hope of seeing any face (save that of the
jailer) upon this day faded from Hugh's mind. The light
began to flicker and grow dim. The prison chamber
became dark as night. At last even the outline of the
grating above his head became indistinguishable. Hugh,
with a groan of disappointment and weariness, threw himself upon his sordid bed, and after a time found oblivion
from his woes in sleep.

How long he slept he knew not, but he was suddenly
awakened by the sound of a stealthy movement outside
the door. He started up and held his breath. Yes, he
was certain of it. Somebody was outside, feeling over
the walls and door as if in search of the fastening; and
presently he heard a key softly fitted into the lock.

His heart beat fast as he heard the door open and a
soft rustle bespeak the entrance of some human intruder.

Then followed a deep silence, broken by the sound of a voice—a voice which like new wine sent the blood coursing through the young man's veins.

"Hugh—my beloved—art thou there?"

"Linda!" he cried, in wild amaze, and the next moment had groped his way across the intervening space, and had encircled her with his arm—"Linda, my heart's joy! how comest thou here?"

"Hush, dearest! speak low, lest we be heard. I have come to set thee free—to fly with thee beyond the reach of pursuit. Dearest, wilt thou trust thyself with me?"

He pressed her hand to his lips. He thrilled from head to foot. But how had she come to him in this dread place? He was enwrapped by the sense of mystery.

"Linda, sweetheart, how hast thou made thy way hither? Art thou a being angelic, to whom closed doors offer no obstacle? How hast thou penetrated hither?"

"That will I tell thee anon, dear love. Dost thou not know that love will ever find out the way?" She spoke in low, whispering tones, and he followed her example, guessing well the need for caution and secrecy. "Thou hast friends without these prison walls, and thy friends are working for thee. Nevertheless thy case is somewhat perilous; and if thou canst not make good thy flight, there are grave fears for thy life, since there be many to swear thee guilty of the crime, and both Constable and Chancellor are greatly resolved to make an example of any disturber of the peace, be he citizen or clerk."

"What then shall I do?" asked Hugh.

" Listen, beloved," she answered. " How I have got access
to this place I will tell another time, for we may not linger
here. But I have brought to thee the habit of a monk. I
am likewise attired in cowl and gown. Once free of this
prison, we can walk the city streets without fear; for the
good friars of St. Francis go about their works of piety
and charity by night as well as by day. Only we must
not linger in the city, but must flee forth ere thine escape
is discovered; for there will be hue and cry after thee,
since thou hast at least two vindictive enemies, who are
sworn to thy destruction—and to mine undoing !"

She shivered as she spoke, and Hugh muttered something between his teeth. He had been about to say that
he would take her back at once to her aunt at Eynsham;
but these last words seemed to show that she would not
now be safe there.

" Are they molesting thee, sweetheart ? " he asked.

" It is that evil Roger de Horn again," she said, with
a slight tremor in her voice; " he has come back under
another name. It is he who is the disturber of the city's
peace. He has found me out, and I am no longer safe
with mine aunt. If thou art in danger, beloved, so am I.
Can we not both seek safety in flight ? "

" Yes, if thou wilt marry me, so soon as we can find
some holy man to join our hands in wedlock ! " cried
Hugh eagerly. " Then will I carry thee to my father's
house, and I will seek to win my spurs in the service of
King or Prince, whilst thou at home dost play a daughter's
part to my sweet mother, who will, I trow, receive thee

with open arms, when she shall know what thou hast done and dared for my sake."

All this had been spoken in rapid whispers, and now Hugh hastily donned the monkish garment, which was in fact the habit of a Franciscan friar, and entirely covered his whole person. The cowl was drawn over his head, and he was completely disguised, although in the pitchy darkness they could see nothing, and had to trust to the sense of touch.

Then the soft hands guided him down the narrow stairs —he had discarded his foot gear the better to personate a friar—his companion softly locked the door behind him, and the pair glided down and unfastened the outer door which opened upon the street.

Close at hand, in a tiny chamber, sat the guard of the gate, sunk in sodden sleep, an empty wine-flask lying at his side. The slender cowled figure stole toward him, and replaced the keys at his girdle, whence they had plainly been detached; and then, gliding forth again, she took Hugh by the hand, and they made their way along the shadow of the wall till the Castle loomed up before them.

"Sweetheart," said Hugh suddenly, "why should we go farther? Within these walls we shall find shelter and safety, and here we may be wed ere we fare forth into the world together. I know my friends will not desert me at this perilous moment, and Alys will be as a friend and sister to thee till I can make thee mine own. The sentry at the gate will know me and let me pass; or these habits will suffice to win us our way. Come, beloved; I would not have thee wander longer through the darkness of the night. Trust thy dear self to me, and all will be well."

"Ah no, no!" cried his companion urgently; "thou wilt only run thyself into greater peril. I have planned all. Come only with me. I will lead thee where thou shalt be safe. Only do not delay!"

At the sound of those words Hugh's heart suddenly stood still, and a qualm of fear and mistrust shook him from head to foot.

Was that indeed Linda's voice? Was it like his gentle, timid Linda to refuse such safe shelter for the perils of the road and the uncertainties which must lie before them? When the voice had spoken only in whispers, he had never for a moment doubted; but now—now—his brain felt on fire. He was bewildered—dismayed—apprehensive. If not Linda, who could it be? Who save her twin sister could personate her thus? And was it possible that any good purpose could be designed by those who were practising this fraud upon him? Would not Linda have been the first to snatch at the thought of seeking safety with the gentle Alys, of whom they often spoke together? She might have braved much to get her lover out of prison; but once free from those walls, and maiden modesty, as well as her natural timidity, would have urged her to accept this suggestion with gladness. Hugh knew the nature of his sweetheart too well to be deceived.

But the companion of his flight seized him by the hand and cried eagerly,—

"Come with me! come with me! all is ready—all is planned. There is no need for protection for me. I am safe with thee; and the priest already awaits to unite us in wedlock. Come; I will guide thee to the place."

"Nay, now I know well that thou art not Linda!" suddenly cried Hugh, throwing back his cowl and gazing intently at his companion by the light of a dying moon. "Who and what art thou, who hast come and succoured me under her name? Thou canst be none other than Lotta, for thou hast her voice and her form. What is the meaning of the masquerade?"

With a fierce gesture Lotta flung back her cowl, and stood before him with flashing eyes.

"So thou hast discovered me? I said that thou wouldest; that I could never play the part of puling love-lorn maiden such as Linda was ever wont to be! But I hold thee to thy plighted word. This very night shalt thou marry me. I have saved thy life, and thou art now my prey."

"Nay, Lotta," answered Hugh, with manly dignity of bearing, "I am grateful for thy help. I will not forget my debt, and I will be a true brother to thee to my life's end. But not even if I stood at the point of death would I forswear myself, and vow to love and cherish one I cannot thus love. I am the betrothed of thy sister. To thee I can be nothing but a brother; but I will remember always what thou hast done for me, albeit I will sooner return to my prison walls than be false to mine own true love."

"Fool!" hissed Lotta between her shut teeth, "dost think thou wilt ever wed her? I tell thee she has already been lured from Eynsham by means of thy signet-ring, stolen from off thy finger by Roger de Horn. The same priest who will wed thee and me will wed Linda and Roger ere the day be done. I have loved thee always, Hugh. Even now when thou goest far to make me hate thee, I love thee with a fierce and passionate love which brooks no bounds. From my window I have watched thee go to and fro in the city these many years. Though thou hast forgotten me, I have never forgotten thee; and now when thy life was threatened by evil men, I have offered to save thee at this price. Marry me, and they will cease to fear and hate thee, and will receive thee as kinsman and friend. Refuse, and thy life will pay the forfeit! And make haste in thy choice, for already we are waited for; and if thou dost longer delay, thou wilt be set upon in these dark streets, and not even my voice will avail to save thee."

There were urgency and passion in Lotta's voice, and a part of her words had filled the heart of Hugh with a great fear. Was it indeed true that Linda had been lured away? It might well be, since she would know the signet-ring of her lover, and might take it to be a token from him. His heart seemed to stand still within him; his brain felt benumbed by horror. He attempted no reply to Lotta's rapid speech; and noting his silence, she suddenly grasped his arm and shook it in her impatience and urgency.

"Come!" she cried, "come! Better a bridegroom than a dead corpse; and I am as fair as Linda, and as meet a bride for thee. Come, I say, come!" She paused for a moment, and then in more urgent accents cried, "If thou dost not consent, thou art undone. Here come Tito and Roger to look for us."

And indeed at that moment Hugh plainly saw two figures creeping along towards them—the grey-cowled monk and the bearded man with the scarred face.

That was enough for him. His only reason for standing thus long in talk was his chivalrous dread of leaving a maiden alone in the streets of the city. Now that her brother and his comrade were close at hand, he did not hesitate a moment.

They were just beneath the Castle walls. The Gate was half-way between him and his foes. They might chance to reach it as soon as he, did they guess his intentions. But he knew the place well, and knew of a small postern close to the end of Bedford Lane (New Inn Hall Street now). Making therefore a quick dash in the opposite direction, he fled like a hunted hare, and a few loud knocks obtained him entrance from the soldier on guard.

"I am pursued! Shut it after me!" he cried; and the man instantly obeyed, for he thought he was succouring a holy friar from the attacks of some wanton roisterers, too drunk to reverence the habit of their quarry.

And thus it was that Hugh le Barbier escaped from prison and found his way within the Castle walls.

CHAPTER XVIII.

THE NEW CHANCELLOR.

"LEOFRIC, Leofric! hast thou heard the news?"
"I have heard the bell of St. Martin's," answered
Leofric, scarce raising his head from his task; "I trow the
new Chancellor will have cause for displeasure and stern
judgment. This is the third time there has been a disturbance since he arrived within the city."

"But listen, Leofric, there is worse than that. They
say that our good friend Hugh has been dragged off to
prison for the murder of a citizen, and the whole place is
clamouring for his blood—all the citizens, that is!"

Leofric was aroused now, and started up in excitement.

"What—what!—Hugh charged with such a crime?
Impossible! It must be some mistake."

"Or some foul play," said Jack significantly. "I could
not get at him for the press, but I got near enough to
hear them say he declared the murder had been done by a
man in a monkish habit, lurking in a doorway, who had
vanished the moment the crime was committed, leaving
the murdered man lying at Hugh's feet with the stiletto
in his heart. But not one word of this story will the

crowd believe, and Hugh has been haled off to the
Bocardo prison!"

Hardly had Jack finished these words before Gilbert,
together with Hal Seaton, hurried in full of the same
news.

"It is some vile plot against Hugh!" cried Gilbert.
"Have we not suspected for long that his enemies have
returned, and are plotting evil against him? For my
part, I have long believed that Tito Balzani has returned,
and is masquerading beneath the cowl of a monk; and
that yon evil-faced, bearded braggart whom men are beginning to know and note in the streets, is none other
than our old friend Roger de Horn—much changed by his
three years' absence, and by staining his face and growing
his beard. If those two are in league together again, be
sure they are after no good."

"And it behoves us to do something, and that something
quickly," said Hal, "if Hugh is to be saved from disgrace,
if not from imprisonment or worse. For upon the day
after to-morrow the new Chancellor is to hold a court, and
all turbulent citizens and clerks are to be brought before
him. I trow if Hugh is charged before him with murder
in the open streets—and there be some ready to swear to
seeing him strike the blow—it may go hard with him.
For all men say that the Chancellor is an upright and
just man, and will not favour the clerks more than those
of the city; that he has spoken stern things as to the riots
so frequent here, and has resolved to put them down with
a strong hand."

Leofric stood lost in thought, revolving many things in his mind. The original cause of jealousy between Hugh and Roger had been Linda Balzani. So long as she played no part in Hugh's life it had been undisturbed; but directly he recommenced his wooing, he began to feel himself watched and spied upon, and now this evil thing, carefully and craftily plotted, had happened to him. Did it not all point to some jealousy with regard to the beautiful Linda? They had contrived that her lover should be helpless to fly to her aid; did not that show that some evil was purposed against the maid herself?

Quickly and anxiously did he communicate these thoughts to his companions, and as he spoke Jack smote his hand against his brow and cried excitedly,—

"Now I think of it, I heard somewhat but just now which goes to substantiate thy suspicions, Leofric. I was wedged into the crowd, and seeking to press up towards Hugh, when that black-browed fellow whom we all believe to be Roger de Horn came elbowing his way out, and went up to the side of some tall fellow, whose face I did not see in the press, albeit we were close together; and to him he spoke in a hissing sort of whisper, every word of which I heard. 'I have the signet-ring,' he said; 'now we can get her into our power easily. She will go anywhere at sight of that!'"

Leofric and the others uttered in low tones exclamations of wrath, whilst Jack continued quickly,—

"I did not heed the words at the time—I did not think they concerned our friend Hugh; but verily I believe that it was his ring they plundered, and that they mean to use it for some evil scheme of their own."

"Which we must frustrate!" cried Leofric excitedly; "we must to the boat as soon as the day dies, and we must be at Eynsham with the first light of dawn. They will not appear there before daylight to-morrow. They will not desire to raise suspicion by appearing at untoward hours. We shall be before them, and I trust we may circumvent them yet; but we shall have a pair of wily foes to deal with."

*   *   *   *   *

Oxford was in a ferment of excitement. It was known all over the place that Hugh le Barbier had escaped from the Bocardo prison, but had surrendered himself to the Constable of the Castle, claiming his protection against false imprisonment, and desiring to be brought before the new Chancellor to tell his tale and be confronted with those who dared to accuse him of the murder of an unoffending citizen.

It was also said that the Constable was determined to make the most searching inquiry into the matter, in which the Chancellor would aid him. Both were greatly disturbed by the state of chronic feud that was growing up betwixt citizens and clerks, and were resolved to put down with a high hand this perpetual rioting. The court was to sit in the largest building which could be found in all Oxford, and the citizens and clerks were to attend in a mass, and hear what the Chancellor and the Constable had to say to them. All the ringleaders in the recent riots would receive some sort of trial and punishment, and the case of Hugh le Barbier would be thoroughly investigated.

There was a feeling of considerable excitement throughout the town, and the ways to the place of judgment were thronged to suffocation upon the appointed day.

Of course it was impossible for all the city to throng into one building; but a very large concourse was admitted there, whilst the streets and open places in the vicinity of the Castle were thronged with eager faces, and the space within the Castle walls was one sea of heads.

Within the great hall were seats for Chancellor and Constable, and in a place set apart stood a number of citizens and clerks who had been specially called upon to attend. These were stationed somewhat apart from the rest of the crowd, and upon the faces of some could be read a certain anxiety and apprehension.

For the most turbulent spirits within the city had been gathered together and summoned to answer for their conduct. It had been whispered that the new Chancellor intended to make a protest against the habit of carrying arms which prevailed almost universally at that time amidst persons of all classes. It was this habit which led to such constant bloody quarrels. Men in the heat of argument would suddenly break into abuse and invective, and then it was but a short step to blows, which if from fists would matter little, but when struck with sharp, shining blades became quite another matter. Peaceable citizens declared that they were forced to carry arms for self-defence amid the hordes of savage youths who infested their streets, calling themselves clerks and scholars. But if the more turbulent of these could be denied the use of arms, then they would willingly consider laying down theirs.

These and such like things were passing from mouth to mouth whilst the expectant crowd waited for the judges to appear, and gazed curiously upon Hugh le Barbier, who occupied a seat by himself near to the daïs of the Chancellor and the Constable. His face looked somewhat anxious, and he kept searching the crowd with his eyes, as though looking for faces which he had expected to see, but had missed. It was only upon the past night that he had escaped from the Bocardo prison, and speculation was rife as to how the matter had been managed.

A stir and a rustle and a surging movement through the crowd showed that the judges were coming at last, and every face was turned towards them, and every eye fastened upon them as they took their appointed places amid a deep silence.

The aspect of Sir Humphrey was familiar enough to all; but many had scarcely set eyes as yet upon the new Chancellor, and these fixed their regards steadfastly upon him, the guilty and rebellious clerks in particular being full of anxiety to learn what they could of the temper of this new dignitary, in whose hands so much power lay.

He was attended by the Proctors and a number of the Doctors and Masters in their robes, and he wore his own state robes of office. Sir Humphrey was accompanied by some knights and gentlemen of his household, and the face of Amalric de Montfort could be distinguished amongst these, though the young man detached himself from the group round the chairs of state and placed himself near to Hugh le Barbier, who greeted him with a smile.

The Constable spoke first. He addressed himself mainly to the citizens, who were regarded as being under his control. He rebuked them for their readiness to fight— for their impatience and irritability with the clerks and scholars, who, when all was said and done, were a source of profit to them and of prosperity to their town. Instead of setting them a good example, they fell into all the wild ways of raw lads who might not have had opportunity to learn better. He chid them severely for this, and warned them that they were seriously in danger of the royal displeasure, and of infringements of their charter, if they continued in this turbulent manner to disturb the peace of the realm. They had felt this sort of displeasure many times before. Why could they not learn wisdom and discretion, and strive to put down these disgraceful scenes, instead of taking an eager share in them, and being no better than the youths to whom they ought to set an example ?

After the Constable had spoken in this key, the new Chancellor arose. He had a dignified mien, a tall and commanding figure, and a face which at once inspired confidence and affection. He could look stern and kindly at the same time, and his sonorous voice, which penetrated right through the hall and into the open space without, was full of fire and earnestness ; yet there was

withal something so winning in his address that all eyes
were riveted upon the speaker, and men held their breath
to catch his every word.

He first spoke of the pleasure he had in this return to
a city he had always loved, and of his promotion to a position in which he hoped he would prove of service to it.
He spoke of changes for the better which he had noted,
but quickly passed on to his deep regret at finding matters
in nowise better betwixt the citizens and scholars, and
betwixt the clerks themselves. He had been shocked and
grieved to note the violence with which quarrels raged
and blows were struck upon the smallest provocation, or
upon no provocation at all. That was a thing which must
and should be stopped. Valuable lives must not be
sacrificed, nor lifelong injury inflicted, just to satisfy the
wanton passions of the moment. Two men had been
killed, and quite a dozen more injured, in street brawls
during the brief space in which he had resided amongst
them. Against such a state of things as this strong
measures must be taken, and any delinquent convicted of
deliberate crime must be punished with impartial justice,
be he citizen or be he clerk. Their good Constable was of
one mind with himself on that point.

Of the two men who had lost their lives, one had been
killed in open fight in the streets, rather by accident of
the riot than by deliberate intention. With that matter
he would presently deal, as no person in particular was
charged with the crime. But the other was altogether
different. A peaceable citizen had been stabbed to the

heart by an act of deliberate murderous intent. Hugh le Barbier had been found beside the murdered man, and had been charged with the deed, and even imprisoned somewhat informally in the Bocardo. But he was not only a gentleman and bachelor of good repute in the University; he also solemnly declared that he had seen the blow struck by another hand, and he had proved his fearlessness of inquiry in having refused to fly from the city (on being released in a romantic fashion by some maiden, whose name he asked not to divulge), and in having placed himself under protection of the Constable, demanding that he might be heard in his own defence, and that the whole matter might be diligently investigated. This inquiry was forthwith to be made, and any person who had any knowledge of the matter was to stand forth and bear witness.

A slight commotion now stirred through the crowd, and certain persons pressed forward to give their evidence. Several bore witness to having found Hugh standing beside the murdered citizen, but none would swear to having seen him strike the blow, though several declared that there was a man who had seen the act, though he had not been seen in Oxford since. His name was Robert Holker, and little was known about him. He attended lectures, but had put himself under no tutor. He was known to be a good fighter, and had been mixed up in every riot in the place since his arrival there. Somebody testified to the fact that he had boasted himself able to hold his own against twenty adversaries.

The face of the Chancellor darkened slightly as this fact was elicited by questions from the Constable. Then a slight sensation was caused in the hall by the sudden stepping forward of Lord Amalric de Montfort, who asked leave to bear a certain testimony about this very man. He declared that he was very decidedly of opinion that this man's name was not Robert Holker, but Roger de Horn, a famous braggart and bully in Oxford during past years, who had been forced to fly the place on account of a murderous outrage upon the person of Hugh le Barbier; and he believed that his evidence against him now was all part and parcel of some fresh plot against the life and liberty of a good man and a faithful comrade.

Amalric as he spoke laid his hand affectionately upon the shoulder of Hugh, and immediately public opinion began to turn in favour of the supposed criminal.

A buzz of talk instantly arose. The former episode, long since forgotten, of the Magician's Tower and Hugh's imprisonment there by Roger de Horn and Tito Balzani was at once on all lips. The Chancellor desired to learn some details of that occurrence, and Hugh stood up and told the tale, carrying the sympathy of all hearts with him. When he went on to speak of the occurrence of two days back, and of the stealthy cowled figure in the doorway who had struck the murderous blow, his words, instead of being heard with scorn and disbelief, carried the convictions of all, and a voice in the crowd called out,—

"If thine accuser is indeed Roger de Horn, then mark my word, the accomplice-monk is Tito Balzani!"

A strange, strangled cry went up from the crowd. Sudden conviction of the truth of these words seemed to come home to many hearts. Voices were heard declaring that Tito had been seen in the streets of late—or one singularly like him. Others declared that they had certainly seen Roger de Horn, only they had not remembered whose the familiar face was under its beard and bronze. Excitement rose high; there was a call for these two men. Constable and Chancellor alike desired that if in the city they should be brought before them, and there was hurrying to and fro of many persons.

Then suddenly and unexpectedly a cry arose,—

"They come, they come! they are being brought bound and fettered before the Court. That is Tito Balzani in the habit of the monk, and there is Roger's sullen face glowering upon all! Who are these that be bringing them in? Leofric the bachelor, and honest Jack Dugdale, together with Hal Seaton, our good citizen's son, and his future brother-in-law, Gilbert Barbeck. Now this is a marvellous strange hap; and there be others of the company too. Who are they? and whence come they? Marry, but it is a happy chance that brings them here to-day!"

The crowd, uttering these and many like words, gave way right and left before the group of persons who had solicited the right of entrance to the Chancellor's presence, as they had a matter to lay before him that brooked no delay.

The leader of the band was a fine-looking old countryman, and just behind him walked a buxom dame, probably his wife, who led by the hand a maiden with veiled face, whose form could not be distinguished through the folds of the habit she wore. Behind these, again, walked the two bound prisoners, whose faces expressed the extreme of terror. One of the pair was guarded by Leofric and Jack, the other by Hal and Gilbert. As this strange procession made its way into the hall the crowd set up a great cheering, and Hugh le Barbier gave a violent start and fixed his eyes eagerly upon the veiled figure of the girl. For although he had spoken nothing of this matter, being unwilling to speak Linda's name in the audience of the Court, he had been suffering a terrible anxiety all this while on her account, wondering what had befallen her, and if, indeed, some evil plot menaced her. Amalric had vowed to ride across to Eynsham and make inquiries there directly the Court rose, but he knew that it was of the first importance for him to stand forth as Hugh's friend and champion here; for as a son of the great Earl his popularity in Oxford was immense, and the Chancellor himself had a great friendship and reverence for De Montfort.

Chancellor and Constable alike looked with surprise upon the group now standing before them. The weather-beaten countryman had bared his head, and having made a clumsy reverence, he began to speak in short, abrupt sentences, as though unaccustomed to the task, yet stirred by unwonted indignation and stress of feeling to make the effort.

" My noble lords and masters," he said, " I have come
hither to-day, hearing of the court to sit in judgment on
the misdeeds of certain persons in this town, to bring
before your worshipful notice the tale I have to tell. I
am a man of Eynsham. I carry water for the monks, and
keep the gate. My wife dwells with me hard by; and
we have a niece entrusted to our care. This maid is
virtuous and beauteous. She is the light of our eyes. In
her youth, when little more than a child, she was loved
by and she loved a student of this city called Hugh le
Barbier. I see him standing yonder. They were sepa-
rated by the machinations of evil men, and the maid went
nigh to lose her life. We cared for her, and she grew
sound again. A short while since her lover came back.
He wooed her openly before our eyes. We loved him,
and the maid loved him, and they plighted their troth
anew. Some happy months fled by. Nothing disturbed
her mind save a fancy, once whispered to my wife, that
one of the monks was ever watching her. We chid her
for this, knowing the monks to be godly men, and she
spoke of the fancy no more. Yester morn there came
in haste to us these four youths you see here, all of
whom have been known to us from coming sometimes to
Eynsham with Hugh le Barbier. They told us that a
plot was on foot against him, and they feared against
the maid likewise. They told us that they believed some
men would come ere the day was over, and seek by a
well-contrived plan to get possession of the maid, by showing the signet-ring of her lover. Not to make my tale

too long, I will only tell what, with much debate, we decided on. These youths I concealed in the house, taking their boat well out of sight. The maiden kept close to the side of her aunt; and things went on as usual in the house.

"Shortly after noon come yon two miscreants, the one wearing the cowl and habit of the monk, even as you see him. They bring with them a pitiful tale. The maiden's lover is ill. He desires to be soothed by sight of her. He sends his ring by a faithful messenger and a holy father confessor, who will bring her to him. My wife appears to hesitate, and-asks if she may not accompany her niece. Plainly they are prepared for this, and reply readily that she may do so. I know well what is meant by that complacency. They would wait until they had reached some place where the river runs smooth and swift, and then they would wind her clothes about her and throw her into the depths, and never a sign would be seen again of my good wife Bridget Marlow!"

A groan went round the crowd; the Chancellor's face grew stern, those of the criminals were blanched with terror. The man went rapidly on with his story.

"We had planned what to do. We gave them patient hearing. We showed no sign of distrust, and the maid and her aunt went to their room as though to prepare for the journey. I set food and wine before our guests, and they refreshed themselves, talking in low voices between themselves the while. Methought the man in the habit was strangely little like a monk; and, moreover, I saw in his girdle, from time to time, the glint as of some long, sharp weapon, such as certes no monk ever carries. Nor have I ever seen monk eat and drink as yon fellow did, albeit the ungodly are fond of jibing at them as gluttonous men and wine-bibbers.

"After they had refreshed themselves they desired to be going. They had come by boat, and would return the same way. I asked the monk if he would not like to visit his brethren of the abbey; but he replied rather uneasily that he had not the time to do so to-day. He was anxious above all things to return to the bedside of the sick man, and bring back with him the medicine which he knew would be the best cure—meaning the presence of the maid.

"Whereupon a great wrath seized upon me, and I suddenly rushed at him and pulled back his cowl, and then, seeing well his dark face and untonsured head—which ye can see well for yourselves—I cried out, 'Thou art no more monk than I. Thou art Tito Balzani, my sister's stepson, a dog of an Italian, who has been hooted out of Oxford before now!' Well, in a moment he had whipped out a long stiletto—I have it here to show you—and was at my throat like a tiger. But I had given the signal already, and yon four doughty lads were at my side in an instant. Even then, albeit we were five to two, we had no small trouble with them: for we did not desire their hurt, but only to take them prisoners; whereas they would have done to death the whole of us to gain their liberty, had we not been too quick for them. But at last we

overcame and bound them, and they have been bound
ever since.   I bring them here before your worshipful
presences, that ye may do with them even as ye list."

And here the narrative of honest Marlow came to a
sudden end.   He tendered to the Constable the long, sharp
stiletto he had wrested from Tito, and retired to the background.

CHAPTER XIX.

THE CHANCELLOR'S AWARD.

THE story was told. Amalric stepped forward and offered to the Chancellor a second long stiletto, the very fellow and counterpart of the one just tendered by Marlow.

" This was the weapon found buried in the heart of the dead man," he said; " I can testify that my friend and comrade Hugh le Barbier, whose room at St. George's I share, never possessed such an one. It is of Italian workmanship, and the two weapons are a pair from the same maker."

A low murmur had been for some time rising from the crowd; now the people broke forth into execrations and menaces. Somebody pulled the cowl from the head of the would-be monk, and when the untonsured head and foreign face was seen by all, the clamour of wrath and fury could not be kept down; indeed it needed all the authority of those surrounding the Constable and the Chancellor to restrain the angry clerks and citizens from setting upon the wretched criminals and tearing them limb from limb.

But the tumult was appeased after some little delay, and the Chancellor spoke in clear and ringing accents.

"Tito Balzani, you are here confronted with the evidence of your crime. Have you anything to say in your own defence?"

The wretched criminal, cowering with fear, confessed his guilt, only pleading in extenuation that Roger de Horn had been the leading spirit all through, and had devised the plot, whilst he had been only a tool in his hands.

The Chancellor heard these words with stern coldness, and, deigning no reply, contented himself with handing the culprit over to the Constable, as he had no jurisdiction over the persons of other than members of the University. Roger, however, claimed to be a clerk, and to be under the authority of the Chancellor; so whilst the hapless Tito was led away to the Constable's prison, to be dealt with hereafter by a different tribunal, Roger remained amongst the unruly clerks, who awaited the award of the Chancellor in some fear and trembling.

Every eye was fixed upon the face of the great man as he rose to speak. He had conferred for a while with the Constable, and now addressed himself in the first place not to the dark-browed Roger, whose face was a picture of lowering malignity and craven fear, but to the throng of minor defaulters who had been accused of indiscriminate rioting in the streets during a period of many weeks, and of acting as ringleaders in the disturbances which were growing almost intolerable.

The Chancellor spoke with moderation but with great firmness, pointing out the folly and danger of such conduct, the interruption to study, and the peril to the peace of the city. He then went on to say that he greatly reprehended the practice of carrying arms—a custom which, in a city surrounded by walls and inhabited by members of a peaceful fraternity, ought not to be needful, but which the lawless violence of the clerks had rendered necessary. He hoped that in days to come this custom would die out; but for the present he should not attempt legislation for the well-disposed and orderly members of the University. But he called upon all the turbulent clerks who had been convicted of disturbing the peace on many different occasions to deliver up their arms at once into his keeping, and to refrain from bearing them again until they had licence to do so. The names of these persons were to be taken; and if they were found with arms upon them after this injunction, they were to be brought before him by the Proctors, and would then be dealt with more severely.

The Constable then rose and said he should make a like rule for turbulent citizens; and the ringleaders of the recent riots were brought up one by one and bidden to lay their arms upon a table placed there for the purpose, after which their names were taken, and they were, as it were, bound over to keep the peace.

This act, which combined clemency with firmness, was very popular with the multitude, and the culprits themselves were thankful for having been treated with such leniency. A number of them left the hall on hearing this award, but others remained to hear what would befall their old comrade Roger de Horn, who had not been recognized by many in his changed condition, having in fact taken some pains to keep himself away from former associates until he had carried out his plans.

The braggart and bully was led in his turn before the Chancellor, his hands still bound, but the arms he had upon him still in their place. Roger was one of those men who always carried a sword, and was of the regular swashbuckler type so common in the Middle Ages. He looked a pitiable object now——fear and rage struggling for mastery in his face as he met the steadfast gaze of the Chancellor. His spirit had deserted him under his misfortunes, and his blotched face was white with craven fear.

"Roger de Horn, calling thyself Robert Holker, thou hast been caught red-handed in an act of unpardonable wickedness, and hast been (if thy comrade speaks truth) deeply concerned in a murderous plot. Thy case will be considered at leisure, and thy punishment made known when that of Tito Balzani is likewise decided. Meantime thou wilt be kept in restraint, and taste the wholesome discipline of prison. Take off that sword and deliver it, in my presence, to Hugh le Barbier, whom thou hast sought so greatly to injure. Thou shalt never wear arms in this city again. Thou wilt do well, if ever thou dost receive liberty, to quit Oxford and seek to live a different life in some other place. Here thy record has been nothing but one of black treachery and disgrace!"

A murmur of approbation followed these words. Gilbert Barbeck, who was standing guard over the prisoner, so far loosed his right hand as to enable him to obey the Chancellor's command. With sullen brow, and eyes that gleamed fiercely as those of a wild beast caught in the toils, Roger detached the sword from his belt and tendered it to Hugh ; but so malevolent was the look upon his face that a faint cry broke from the veiled maiden who stood nigh at hand, and drew the Chancellor's regards upon her.

"Remove the prisoner," he said sternly ; and Roger was led away, the hall almost clearing itself as soon as the people had seen the last of this procession.

Around the daïs at the upper end there still remained the knot of persons who had brought in Roger and Tito, together with those who had accompanied the Constable and the Chancellor. The latter turned towards Linda, and asked in a gentle tone,—

"What dost thou still fear, fair maiden ? "

She made a humble reverence and put back the hood of her cloak, permitting for the first time her fair, pure face to be seen. Her eyes looked like those of a startled fawn, and the flitting colour came and went in her cheek, but she spoke with a soft and gentle steadiness which bespoke a well-ruled spirit.

"I have come to fear those evil men with a great fear," she answered. "Twice have they sought to compass the death of him I love, and to obtain possession of mine own person. They are crafty and wily, as well as fierce. I fear them sorely. No place seems safe from them ; and yet one of them is mine own kinsman—my half-brother. But I fear me he has sold himself to do evil, and is the tool of a spirit more wicked than his own."

Here Bridget Marlow, who had been speaking apart with her husband, stepped forward and said,—

"Reverend sir, the maid speaks no more than the truth; and if Roger de Horn be let loose again, methinks peril will again threaten her safety and ruin the peace of our home. But for the promptness and courage of these young gentlemen, I trow I should have been murdered and the maid carried off ere the sun set yestere'en. Although I love her as the apple of mine eye, I fear me that our home is no safe place for her—or will not be when Roger de Horn is set at liberty. Wherefore we do ask counsel and help of thee what we shall do for her, for she was sent to us from her father's house because that was no safe place for her; and now our home seems little safer, and were hurt to come to her from thence, our grey hairs would go down with sorrow to the grave."

Edmund de Kynaston, who had been present at this function, had been seen a little while before to step to his father's side and speak earnestly with him for a few minutes; and now the Constable stood forth, and addressed himself partly to the Chancellor and partly to the kinsfolk of the maid.

"I have somewhat to say about that. This maid is of our city, and therefore has a claim to what protection I, as keeper of the city, can afford her. I grieve that twice over she has been subjected to the machinations of evil-

doers; and since the man who plans these evil deeds may
probably (since he has been artful enough to keep his
hands free from actual blood-guiltiness) be sooner or later
set at liberty, it behoves us to take measures to thwart
any further schemes on his part. So, my lord Chancellor,
I have a proposition to make. Within the walls of the
Castle the maid would be safe. I myself have a daughter
who has ofttimes begged of me to find for her a companion
of her own age and sex, to assist her in her tasks and be
her friend and confidante. This maid is virtuous and fair;
she is beloved by Hugh le Barbier, of whom all men speak
well. He is ready to make her his wife so soon as his
father shall be willing; and pending that time, I will give
her an asylum in my household, and my daughter will
make of her a companion and friend. Will that content
you, good people, who have played the part of parents to
the maid?"

The Marlows were overjoyed at the proposition. Greatly
as they regretted parting from Linda, they felt that their
home was no safe asylum for her, and that it was scarce
the fit home of one who was to wed with a scholar and
a gentleman in the position of Hugh le Barbier. Linda
herself, although with some tremors, gratefully accepted
the proffered boon; for she remembered pretty Alys of
old, and had always loved and admired her. To dwell
near to her, in a place where she could sometimes see her
lover, and have news from day to day of his safety, was an
enchanting prospect; and though she shed some tears at
parting from her kindly aunt and uncle, her face kindled

into smiles of hope and happiness as Edmund and Hugh presently conducted her into the presence of Alys, who started up from her embroidery frame with a little cry of surprise and pleasure.

Although she had charged Edmund to carry a message to her father when a rumour of what was passing below had reached her, she scarcely expected that the result would be so prompt and satisfactory. Ever since Hugh had recommenced his wooing of Linda, Alys had been to some extent in his confidence, and had been full of keen interest in the matter. Hugh's disappearance, and his sudden return with his story before dawn to-day, had filled all his friends with excitement, sympathy, and wrath; and his fears for Linda's safety had awakened in Alys the vehement desire to befriend her. Edmund had even gone forth to see if he could find any trustworthy friend to dispatch to Eynsham (marvelling what had become of Leofric, Jack, and Gilbert, who were wont to be forward with help where any comrade was concerned), when he had met the procession coming in, and had hastened to Alys with a hurried account of what he had gleaned from the brief explanations of his friends. After that he and Alys had made this plan of befriending Linda, and now she had been brought to her apartment to be her "friend," as the girl herself called it, though Linda declared that it was as tirewoman or serving-maid she had come.

"For I am but a city maiden, and thou the daughter of a noble knight," said Linda; whereat Alys smilingly rejoined,—

" Nay, but thou art the betrothed of one who will one
day win his spurs, and rise to be as great a man as my
honoured father. We love Hugh here even as a brother,
and I have so ofttimes longed for a sister."

So the gentle Linda took up her new duties within the
safe shelter of the Castle walls, and the life of Alys was
the brighter and happier in consequence. She was in need
of a friend and confidante of her own age and sex ; for her
mother kept her with strict hand, and now that she was
growing older, and Edmund was stronger than of yore, he
and his friends came less to that upper room which had
come to be called " the maiden's bower." Her brother was
able to go forth for some of his studies, and it had even
been thought that he might soon enter as a scholar at
St. George's in the Castle. Alys rejoiced in his return to
greater health and strength ; but it had left her somewhat
more alone, and she rejoiced greatly when Linda came to
be her companion, for she learned from her the soft Italian
tongue, and a greater proficiency upon the lute ; whilst
she taught her friend those things which she had studied
with her brother, till Linda felt that a whole new world
was opening out before her.

Those were peaceful and happy days for the two
maidens. Although the world without was full of strife,
the echoes of which sometimes reached them in their quiet
chamber, they lived with their books, their music, their
needlework, and their birds, seeing the familiar faces of
Edmund and his comrades day by day ; but jealously
watched and guarded by Dame Margaret de Kynaston,

who felt Linda now to be her charge, as well as her own
daughter, and was well pleased—after the first surprise at
Alys's " whim "—with the working of the arrangement.

It had by this time become pretty evident to the parents
that Amalric de Montfort was wooing their daughter, although he had not yet declared himself. Sir Humphrey
was well pleased, for he believed that the Earl of Leicester
was and would remain the greatest man in the kingdom—
not excepting the King himself. Dame Margaret, however, was less sanguine on this point, and had misgivings
sometimes as to the ultimate fate of the great leader of the
Barons' party. She was not anxious for her daughter's
hand to be irrevocably pledged, and did not encourage the
visits of Amalric more than the duties of hospitality
required. She was, however, willing that her Alys and
Linda should have instruction in book-learning, which
they so keenly desired ; and Leofric continued to come
from time to time to read to and instruct them, although
Edmund was not so regular at these readings as he was
when unable to attend lectures in the schools.

It was from Leofric that the girls learned the ultimate
fate of Tito and Roger. There had been talk of condemn-
ing both to death ; but since Roger had not struck the
murderous blow, and had claimed benefit of clergy (to
which, however, he was hardly entitled), he had escaped
with his life ; and it had seemed hardly just to take the
life of his comrade in evil, who had been his tool in this
crime. Also Balzani had made a great effort to save the
life of his son, and in the end the two men had been

sentenced to banishment—Tito from the realm altogether, Roger from Oxford and its environs. Both had disappeared promptly. Tito had been guarded out of the kingdom, and was outlawed, and it was thought that Roger had accompanied him; but although this was not certain, it was believed that Oxford had seen the last of him. If he came back, he would certainly be arrested, and some worse punishment dealt to him for his insubordination.

Hardly had these things taken place before all the city was thrown into a state of wild excitement by the arrival of the great Earl of Leicester, who came there on his way to the south coast, and was received with open arms by the University, from the Chancellor down to the rawest clerks fresh from the country.

By the people De Montfort was regarded as the champion of their liberties and the defender of the realm from foreign rule and foreign spoilers. The friars supported him, and their influence went far with men of all classes. Save for this many might have feared to give adhesion to the cause, for the papal part of the Church sided with the King. But the friars, and particularly the Franciscans, in this land were no tools and slaves of papal tyranny. They were thinking men of deep personal piety, lovers of mankind, and champions of the poor and oppressed. They were zealous advocates of the cause of constitutional liberty, of which De Montfort had made himself champion; and in Oxford, where their influence was widely felt, the Earl was certain of an enthusiastic welcome.

Many songs were composed in honour of the idol of the

city; and as he rode into it, escorted by a large following
of clerks who had gone forth to meet him, they burst into
the following ditty, sung in Norman-French, but which
may be translated thus :—

> " Right many were there men of fame,
> But all of them I cannot name,
>   So great would be the sum ;
> So I return to Earl Simon,
> To tell the interpretation,
>   From whence his name has come.

> " Montfort he is rightly called—
> He is the *mount*, and he is *bold* (fort),
>   And has great chivalry :
> The truth I tell, my troth I plight,
> He hates the wrong, he loves the right,
>   So shall have mastery.

> " Doubtless the *mount* he is indeed ;
> The Commons are with him agreed,
>   And praise is due to them :
> Leicester's great Earl right glad may be,
> And may rejoice full heartily,
>   To gain such glorious fame."

And then, excitement and enthusiasm working mightily
within them, the clerks commenced shouting and singing
all manner of couplets which had been made at different
times whilst the Provisions of Oxford had been under
discussion.

> " Totam turbat modica terram turba canum,
> Exeat aut pereat genus tam profanum."

Which may be rendered in English,—

> " A paltry set of curs is troubling all the land,
> Drive out or let them die, the base ungodly band.

The Earl received the adulation of the motley crowd with a courteous dignity; but he could not linger long in Oxford. It was part of his policy to make sure of the hearts of his friends, and show himself in various places where a welcome was certain. But just now he was on his way to Dover, which it was necessary to secure for the cause. He had been already in Wales and the West, taking practical possession of many cities—expelling the King's sheriff from Gloucester because he was an alien, and the Savoyard Bishop of Hereford on the same ground. It was small wonder that the clerks greeted him with songs of praise, or that the old couplet anent the " foreign dogs " should be lustily revived.

The Earl was in arms, and had a following of nobles with him, but as yet the peace of the country had not been materially broken. The Welsh war afforded excuse to the Barons for mustering under arms; although all far-seeing persons felt that it would scarcely be long before the sword was unsheathed in England also.

During the weeks and months which followed, news came in which kept the whole city in a tumult of excitement. From the fact that Amalric remained as a student in Oxford, it was natural that intelligence of the great Earl's movements should be brought regularly and constantly to the town. Sometimes it was Guy de Montfort who came himself, and stayed for a few nights at the Castle; sometimes dispatches were brought to Constable or Chancellor by a travel-stained messenger, and more than once the whole city and University had been on the tiptoe of excitement and uncertainty, expecting every day to hear that some collision had taken place, and that the long-expected conflagration had burst out.

Dover and the Cinque Ports had declared for De Montfort and the Barons. London had received him with open arms, and the King was practically a prisoner in the Tower.

Once the Earl had been in great personal peril. He had ridden forth from London with a following of only a few men-at-arms, when some followers of the King's managed to get possession of the keys of the Southwark gate, and threw them into the river. After this they gathered a number of troops together, and lay in wait for the Earl upon his return, hoping to cut him off and slay him on the spot. Indeed, so great was the peril that De Montfort and his followers gave themselves up for lost, signed themselves with the cross, and prepared to sell their lives as dearly as possible; but the citizens of London, hearing of his danger, rushed out to his defence, broke open the locked gate, and drove back the King's soldiers with much loss. They carried their hero in triumph into the city, and demanded the instant death of the traitors who had planned the deed. The Earl, however, interposed on their behalf, and they were let off with a heavy fine, which was employed in strengthening the defences of the city.

Later on, the Earl returned for a while to Kenilworth, and there set about strengthening that already formidable fortress. He garrisoned it more strongly, and brought thither many warlike engines which he had transported with him from the Continent. For he was beginning to see that there was imminent danger of civil war, although for the present moment he hoped to avoid it.

What gave to him and his followers the keenest anxiety was the attitude taken up by Prince Edward. He had succeeded in escaping from the Tower to Windsor, and was now gathering about him a party of moderate men who had the welfare of the realm at heart, yet who had no desire for any upheaval of existing conditions. He had drawn to himself a number of important personages, one of whom was his cousin, Henry of Almain, son of Richard King of the Romans, the King's brother, who until now had been sworn to the cause of the Barons.

This latter had had the courage to go and tell De Montfort of his defection, though ready then to promise never to take up arms against him ; but the Earl's reply had not been conciliatory. It was one of the things which militated against De Montfort that he could not always command his temper in moments of irritation.

" Lord Henry," he said, " I grieve not for the loss of your sword, but for the inconstancy which I see in you. Go and take arms as you will, for I fear you not at all."

Young Henry had joined his cousin at Windsor with many other good men. All now knew that war must come—unless, indeed, the arbitration talked of by the French King should lead to pacification.

CHAPTER XX.

TURBULENT TIMES.

" SURELY they will not submit!"

"To give up all at the bidding of a King of France! Why, as well might we be slaves at once!"

"I always said no good would come of seeking aid from such an one as he. England is no fief of France. What has Louis to do with her affairs?"

"The brother-in-law of the King!"

"Himself a tyrant, always seeking to curtail the rights of his own nobles and people!"

"A tool of the Pope's and a foe to England!"

"It was shame they should seek to such a man as he! But surely—oh, surely our noble Earl will not be holden back from his righteous work by that Mise of Amiens!"

All Oxford was in a state of intense excitement. The news had just been brought that the French King, whose arbitration had been sought upon the dispute between the King and the Barons of England, had just given his decision.

In every point he sided with Henry. All that the Barons and Commons of the realm had been struggling for

these many years was to be set aside. England was to
be given over to the Pope, and to be governed by aliens;
for the award gave the King full power to choose his own
counsellors, and as all men knew, he had scarce a single
favourite who was not a foreigner. Everything was to be
as before the Provisions of Oxford had been drawn up; and
the French King wound up by counselling both parties to
lay aside rancour, and live at peace, whilst he urged upon
his brother of England to grant an amnesty to his Barons.
It was the kind of award which any discerning man might
have expected from one like Louis of France. He was
a king who desired absolute power in his own realm, and
although he had not abused that power as Henry had, he
would not on that account uphold the subjects of the
neighbouring kingdom against their sovereign. The marvel
is that a man so far-seeing and astute as De Montfort had
ever pledged himself to be bound by the award of France.
He might surely have foreseen, as it seems to us, what the
nature of that award would be.

England was furious—that part of it at least which
followed the fortunes of the Earl. The bulk of the nation
at that time, at any rate in the large and populous districts, was all for the cause of constitutional freedom ; and
the King was hated and distrusted by his subjects, not
without cause. Had his son been on the throne, matters
might have taken a different turn ; but although Edward
was personally beloved, and was becoming a strong power
in the state, he was not yet of sufficient account to change
the aspect of affairs. He was acting with his father, as

was right and natural in the circumstances. He could not form a third party in the state. Had his father abdicated in his favour, the war might perhaps have been averted; but such a thing never entered Henry's head. He was by no means weary of the task of ruling even such a turbulent people as his own was fast becoming.

All Oxford was in commotion. Keen excitement reigned everywhere. The news was three days old, yet the populace was as greatly stirred as at first. For once clerks and citizens were in accord, and denounced in unison the French King and the Mise of Amiens. The greatest eagerness for fresh news prevailed throughout, and every traveller entering the city was besieged for intelligence.

"When Lord Amalric comes back, then we shall know!" was a frequent cry. For Amalric had gone to Kenilworth for Christmas, and had not yet returned. He was said to have been detained there by the accident to his father which had prevented the Earl himself from being present at the Mise of Amiens.

Some thought that had De Montfort been there to urge his cause in person, a different award might have been given; but this seems hardly probable in face of the French King's attitude all the way through. The Earl had, however, intended being present; but just before he would have left the country his horse fell with him, breaking his leg, and he had perforce to remain behind at Kenilworth, and appoint a commission to represent him before the French King.

Amalric, however, would not be likely to remain long

away from Oxford, and his friends awaited his coming with the same eagerness as the whole city. When it was rumoured that he was on his way, and might be expected at any hour, a constant watch was kept for him; and upon his arrival he was received with the greatest enthusiasm, and found himself obliged to halt at Carfax, and respond to the acclamations of the people, whilst his ears were assailed by a thousand questions which he could only partially answer.

Amalric had awaited at Kenilworth the arrival of the news from France, and he was in a position to assure the citizens and clerks of Oxford that his father would not abandon the cause of liberty, despite the award of Amiens.

This statement was received with thunders of applause; hats were waved and weapons brandished, as though every man there was ready to go forth and fight for the liberty of the realm.

What would be the next step, and whether there was any chance of pacification, Amalric could not say. His father, he averred, was very loth to press matters to extremity; but he would sooner draw the sword and die wielding it, than see his country brought a second time under the yoke of papal tyranny and foreign greed. If the King (as was probable) was now resolved to continue in these evil ways, the Barons, with the Earl of Leicester at their head, would stand forth against him. More than that he could not say, but upon that point they might rest assured.

That was enough to raise shouts and cheers of enthusiastic joy. The people crowded about Amalric, blessing him, and calling him by every sort of high-sounding name. To them he represented his father, and the great Earl was at present the idol of the city.

Amalric had some ado to get through the crowd and ride to the Castle, where he was received with great eagerness by his friends there. The whole family, together with Hugh le Barbier, had assembled in one of the lower rooms to meet him, and he had scarcely returned the greetings showered upon him ere he was called upon to tell his news, and to say how his father had received the tidings from Amiens.

At greater length than he had spoken to the crowd, he told the Constable and his friends of the resolve of the Barons to resist to the death. It was no more than Sir Humphrey, and indeed all thinking men, had anticipated. To forego all that had been struggled for during these many years, and to tamely yield up the spoils of hard-fought fights, was altogether foreign to the nature of the English people, and to that of their leader.

"I would they had never asked the King of France," said the Constable, expressing the general sentiment; "I always said no good would come of it. Louis of France may be a saint—of that I know nothing—but he is very much a King, and as such would certainly uphold the royal prerogative on every point."

"And now, will there be war?" asked Hugh, speaking very gravely as he leaned over the back of the chair in which Linda was seated. Dame Margaret and the two maidens had been permitted to come below to welcome Amalric back, and it might be noted how, as he told his tale, his eyes kept seeking ever and anon the face of the fair Alys. Now he came a few steps nearer to make his reply.

"I fear me so. Unless the King hear reason, it can scarce be otherwise; and bolstered up as he now is by his brother-in-law of France, he is little likely to show even the amount of moderation that he has sometimes done."

The faces of all grew grave. War had many times been spoken of, but always as a thing not immediately probable; now it seemed indeed at the very door, and the faces of all betrayed a greater or less amount of anxiety. Amalric looked around him, as though to ask how far his friends would support his party even in extremity; for when once the question came to be settled by force of arms, it was always doubtful how far men would go. There were many who, whilst ardently desiring to see the King advised for his good, would not take up arms against him, regarding him as the anointed servant of God.

This was indeed somewhat the view of Hugh le Barbier, and it was therefore with keen pain that he contemplated the thought of civil war. His sympathies were with the Barons. His personal affection for Amalric inclined him to fight shoulder to shoulder with his comrade. But he had a deeply-seated repugnance to fighting against the lawful sovereign of the realm, and whilst others pressed round Amalric, declaring that they would fight to the death for the cause of liberty, he stood in the same place, behind

Linda's chair, and did not join his voice in promise or protest.

Perhaps Amalric guessed at the struggle going on within him, for he did not seek to draw him into the discussion so eagerly conducted. It was Linda who, presently raising her eyes to her lover's face, asked softly,—

"And thou, beloved, what wilt thou do?"

"I know not," he answered, in a very low voice. "The choice is indeed a grievous one. I would follow Amalric to the world's end in a cause which I knew to be righteous ; but when it comes to raising the standard and taking up arms against the anointed King, I scarce know how I can do it. Would that the choice had not to be made!"

There were not, however, many in the city who seemed troubled with Hugh's scruples. Almost to a man they were eager for the outbreak of war ; and most warlike preparations were set afoot by the clerks and scholars, as though these latter expected to take the field and fight under the banner of De Montfort as soon as ever the collision occurred.

Beaumont meadows were alive from sunrise to sunset with a motley company from the city, the most part of them being members of the University, who spent their time exercising themselves in feats of warlike prowess on foot or on horseback—shooting at targets with bow or catapult, tilting one at the other with the lance, or practising sword-play with such good-will that wounds and bruises were sometimes the result of these encounters. Still, since these were given and taken in good part and for the sake of the cause, no umbrage or ill-will was aroused thereby. The Chancellor himself encouraged these warlike sports, and it was known that he would put no hindrance in the way of students who wished to join the mustering ranks of the Barons' army.

The Chancellor was a warm supporter of De Montfort's cause, and he gave every facility to the clerks for training themselves in the arts of war.

The friars, as has been explained before, were equally in favour of the cause of the people; and Leofric, who after hearing Hugh's scruples had consulted Father Angelus, was quite satisfied by the answers he received, and ready to throw himself heart and soul into the cause of the Barons. The friar admitted that neither party had all the right on its side. Good and evil mingled in both, and personal ambition would be found on both sides, marring the perfection of fruition. But the friars held that a King might lawfully be withheld by his subjects from becoming the slave of evil practices, and that it was better he should be ruled by his own nobles, who had the good of the country at heart, than by foreign hirelings, who cared for nothing but to fill their own pockets, and sell the land to the emissaries of papal tyranny.

Then in the midst of all this seething excitement, when it seemed as though a spark falling might set the city in a blaze, the news was brought that Prince Edward would march through, on his way to the Welsh Marches.

Consternation reigned in the breasts of the authorities when this news was made known. They saw in it a source of real peril to the city. At present public opinion was so entirely in favour of De Montfort, that, in spite of all the excitement and tumult within the walls, the students were in excellent temper with one another, even North and South forgetting their differences for the moment. But if the Prince should appear—the Prince whose personal influence always made itself felt, and who was probably coming this way with a view to enlist the sympathies of some amongst the clerks and scholars on his father's side—it was almost certain that his appearance would result in a demonstration in his favour by a certain number of students, who would then come into instant collision with the bulk of their fellows, and a hideous and indiscriminate battle would be the inevitable result.

> "Read but the records aright, and you'll see,
> When the students in Oxford do once disagree,
> 'Twill be but of months, at the most two or three,
> Ere the conflict in England rage furiously."

This was the common saying of the time, and although not always perhaps borne out by facts, since Oxford was often in a ferment, it was certainly thought advisable to check the possibility of a miniature civil war within the walls of the city; and both Constable and Chancellor sent messengers to the Prince, to request him not to attempt to enter the city walls.

Prince Edward was always reasonable and courteous. He received the messengers with great good temper, and refrained from carrying out his purpose. He could not, however, change his line of march, and he passed close to

Oxford on his way, lodging himself for a few nights outside the walls, in the palace of Beaumont, though keeping his army at some greater distance from the city.

The authorities, of course, could not expect more in reply to their request; but they were still uneasy at the thought of the presence of an army so near to their town, although the students appeared to be unaware of or indifferent to its proximity. To make assurance doubly sure, the city gates were all locked, and the fiat went forth that none should enter or leave the city without special permission from the authorities.

Some amusement and some indignation were felt by the students at this infringement of their liberties. However, for three days they submitted with tolerable grace to the restriction imposed. On the fourth day Prince Edward and his forces resumed their march, and the students saw no reason why they should not resume their pleasures. Beaumont meadows, being beyond the walls, had been closed to them for this period, and now a great band sallied forth to resume interrupted amusements there.

But when they reached Smith Gate, by which they expected to make their exit from the city, they found it still locked and barred, and the watchman told them that he had had orders to keep it shut all day and only open it on the morrow.

"Shame! shame! shame!" cried the crowd, surging round it like a swarm of angry bees, those from behind pushing upon those in front, and adding their voices to the clamour.

It was perhaps rather unwise of the authorities to have been so slow in restoring the liberty of the turbulent clerks. They had behaved better than had been looked for during the time of detention, and it would have been more politic had this detention been ended at the first possible moment. But perhaps they reckoned too much on the temperate spirit showed so far, and thought it more prudent not to be in haste.

Leofric and Jack, coming homewards after morning lecture, were stopped in their approach to their lodging by the presence of this surging crowd, who were all armed, ready for their military pastimes, and who seemed now actuated by an exceedingly warlike spirit.

Jack quickly learned the cause of the commotion, and Leofric exclaimed eagerly,—

"I will to the Chancellor, and get leave from him for the gate to be opened; but I pray you, brother students, make not a disturbance in the city. Wait only one short half-hour, and I will be back with an answer."

Some heard the appeal, and gave a half-hearted assent; but those struggling round the gate neither heard nor heeded.

"Run upon thine errand, good Leofric!" cried Jack, "for they will not have long patience. I will seek to stay them from violence, but methinks they look like storming the city walls!"

Leofric sped away, and Jack remained—sturdy Jack, who must ever be in the heart of the fray. Soon he was more in its heart than he altogether desired; for more and more clerks came flocking up, the birds of the air seemingly having carried the news that mischief was afloat.

"Shall we be pent up in the city, like rats in a trap?"

"Shall we be treated like children, and not suffered abroad save at the pleasure of nurses?"

"Who dares to hem us in like this? Let us show them what free men can do! Let us teach them a lesson! Shall we submit to tyranny, when all the land is astir against it? Never, never, never! Oxford scholars never shall be slaves!"

It needed but words like these to set the whole crowd in a fury. Many of the number had axes in their hands, and all were armed. Flinging themselves upon the gate, they hewed it down with fierce strokes, scoffing at the resistance and remonstrances of the sentries. The woodwork could not long withstand their determined blows. The gate crashed outwards; a fierce yell of triumph arose from the crowd. The victors poured out into the fields beyond, carrying with them the splintered fragments of the strong wooden door.

The spirit of devilry had now got into them. They insisted that the remains must be interred with due formality. They chanted over their burden the office for the dead, and digging a huge trench in Beaumont meadows, they performed mock obsequies in a very irreverent fashion.

But hardly had this been accomplished before the cry was raised,—

"The Provosts! the Provosts! and the worshipful Mayor himself!"

It was true. The city authorities had heard of this out-break, and the Provosts, or Bailiffs, had gathered together a body of bold citizens, and were marching out to quell the disturbance and punish the rioters. Indeed, it was said that they had already made some arrests amongst the clerks, and this news ran like wildfire through the crowd.

In another moment the bell of St. Martin's rang out in the city, and more clerks came flying out to learn what had happened, and where help was needed. Thus the luckless Mayor and Provosts were hemmed in between two furious bodies of clerks, who inflicted grievous wounds upon many of them, tore their banner, and put them to speedy and ignominious flight.

Now the blood of the students was up. They had gone too far to stop without doing worse.

"We will teach the town varlets to interfere with our liberties!" roared the excited and incensed youths, as they rushed back once more into the city, filled with the desire for mischief and destruction which is characteristic of a mob.

"Teach the Bailiffs to mind their manners!" roared the excited students, and dashed upon the houses of their foes. A bowyer's shop was plundered, the house of one Bailiff was set on fire, those of the others were plundered after being broken open, and a store of spicery was scattered in all directions.

"Now for the Mayor! now for the Mayor!" shouted the hot and panting depredators, flushed with victory and carrying all before them.

The Mayor was a vintner by trade, and had a fine cellar stocked with goodly wine. This cellar was on the street level, but was strongly barricaded. Nothing, however, could withstand the fury of the attack made upon it. The mob of unruly clerks rushed in, drew all the taps, drank their fill of intoxicating beverages, and let the rest flow out into the street.

When the Chancellor and the Proctors, who had in the first instance proceeded towards Beaumont meadows through the Bocardo Gate, returned to the city to seek to quell the unseemly riot, it was to find one house in flames in the south part of the city, whilst the drunken mob was clamouring around the vintner's store, singing wild bacchanalian songs, and disporting themselves like veritable demons. The street ran red with good wine, and the Mayor, white-faced and terrified, watched helplessly from an upper window the destruction of his property and the wanton waste of his stock in trade.

The appearance of the Chancellor, however, produced an immediate and extraordinary effect. Clerks upon the outskirts of the crowd took to their heels, flying hither and thither in all directions, uttering cries of warning to their fellows. Of these, some were too drunk and some too wildly possessed with the spirit of devilry to move even for this warning; but most of the men fled as for dear life, the authorities taking note of as many as possible, who felt, as they scudded away under those cold, clear eyes, that they would have to answer for this day's proceedings, probably in a fashion they little liked.

The Chancellor strode up to the nucleus of ringleaders, who alone stood their ground.

"The King shall hear of this!" he said, in calm, cold accents. "It is a case for his Majesty to decide. Go back to your Halls and lodgings, every one of you. You are a disgrace to the city and to the kingdom!"

The abashed clerks obeyed that voice, and retired to their various domiciles; but before three days had passed, Oxford had lost hundreds of her scholars and a considerable number of masters also. An exodus like this not unfrequently followed upon an outbreak of ill-will betwixt "town and gown."

Afraid of what the King's verdict might be, and perhaps with a view to greater liberty upon the outbreak of war, scholars and masters alike vacated their quarters, and made their way to Northampton, where fugitives both from Oxford and Cambridge often assembled, and where there was talk of establishing a third University.

And so ended the "great riot of 1264."

CHAPTER XXI.

KING AND STUDENTS.

OXFORD was all in a ferment. The ordinary life of the University was suspended. Lecture-rooms were deserted alike by masters and scholars, and these were to be seen standing in knots about the streets, talking, gesticulating, arguing—excitement written on every face, and generally wrath and scorn as well. In other quarters clerks were to be seen issuing forth from their lodgings with their worldly goods strapped upon their backs, calling out farewells to their friends, and marching away towards the city gates, generally in parties of six or eight, and singing songs in praise of De Montfort or in despite of the King, but betraying beneath their jauntiness of outward mien an inward secret wrath.

The citizens, too, looked anxious and perturbed, and there was a prevailing unrest throughout the town. The wealthier scholars might be seen talking earnestly together, looking to their arms and accoutrements, and comparing notes as to their horses. It was plain that something very unusual was afoot, and that, too, of a nature disquieting to all.

In point of fact, the King had sent a decree ordering all the students of Oxford to depart to their own homes. The Chancellor had reported to his Majesty on the subject of the recent riot, and it was supposed by a great number of the students that this decree was made as a sort of punishment for their unruly behaviour. But there was another and more personal motive as well.

The King had just summoned a Parliament to Oxford, and it was generally shrewdly supposed that this Parliament would practically annul those famous Provisions of Oxford which had, during the past six years, been the war-cry of the Barons' party. Now the temper of the city was known to be easily aroused, and Oxford was almost unanimous in its support of the cause of the Barons. It would be a bold act on the part of the King to trust himself within the city walls had he come as the confessed foe of De Montfort—at least if the members of the University were assembled there in force; so to get rid of them by some plausible expedient was a wily and politic move.

"He fears us! he fears us!" was a constantly-heard cry as bands of clerks took their way out from the city, some in high dudgeon, others rejoicing in the liberty thus accorded them of openly throwing themselves into the civil war if it should chance to break out, as all men knew must quickly be the case.

The young nobles did not for a moment disguise what they were about to do. Many of them had fathers or friends in the opposing ranks, and they, if expelled from Oxford, intended joining them. Most were on the Barons'

side, but a few leaned towards Prince Edward. Personally he was beloved by many more than hastened to join
him ; for the unpopularity of the King's cause, to which
the son was pledged, held back many a youthful admirer.
It was to De Montfort's banner that the warlike spirits of
Oxford desired to flock, and Amalric was daily besieged
with eager offers from ardent lads to follow him to his
father's camp, if he would only accept their services.

" My father will not fight unless forced to do so," was
the reply he returned to many. " He is not in haste to
plunge the land into the horrors of war. But if the King
will persist in his evil ways, and will refuse all counsel
save from those who advise him to the nation's hurt, then
must swords be drawn, though not till all else has been tried."

And in fact, as the King drew near to Oxford, the
Barons sent representatives to Brackley, with powers to
seek for a reconciliation and agreement before recourse
was had to extreme measures.

Within the Castle was great excitement as the days
passed by. The Constable, by virtue of his office, must
needs stand aloof from any open expression of loyalty
towards the enemies of the King ; and the Chancellor
observed an attitude of grave neutrality. And yet it was
well known that both these functionaries had the cause of
the people at heart, and that they were beloved of De
Montfort and loved him well.

Alys was working a beautiful banner for Amalric ; and
many were the visits he paid to the upper chamber where
she and Linda were to be found plying their skilful

needles. Linda's heart was ofttimes rather heavy within her just now; for Hugh had left Oxford immediately after the King's decree had become known, and she believed that he had departed home, intending, with his father's approval, to join Prince Edward in Wales, or wherever he might have now marched. In times of peril, such as seemed approaching, it was hard to lose sight of a loved one, not knowing when or how the next meeting might be. Sometimes Linda's tears would fall as she worked, and Alys would say gently,—

"Do not grieve so, sweet Linda; the war will not last long, and then he will come back. We shall not love him less—even Lord Amalric says that—because he follows with the Prince. If the Prince were the only leader in the land, we would all follow him too, and this war would be averted."

"War is so terrible, so cruel!" Linda replied. "It goes to my heart to think what may happen when army meets army in the bloody field."

"And yet there is glory in war as well as pain!" cried Alys, with a light in her eyes. "I would think of that were I in thy place, dear Linda."

Linda raised her glance to Alys's face, and asked softly,—

"Thinkest thou that thou wilt be able thus to speak when my Lord Amalric goes forth to fight?"

"Why not?" asked Alys innocently; and then seeming to divine something of her companion's meaning, she added, "The Lord Amalric is a very proper gentleman, but he is no lover of mine."

"And yet methinks he has no eyes for any but thee, sweet Alys ; and has he not said many times that this banner will be his talisman in times of danger and heaviness ? Methinks he worships the very ground upon which thou dost tread."

"Oh no, no," said Alys, with a look of trouble in her eyes. "Lord Amalric has been a kind friend to us all, and we all love him. But it is not so with us—nay, Linda, say, have I ever said or done aught that might seem to speak of this ?"

"Nay ; it is he who has looked this long time at thee as a man looks at his heart's beloved," answered Linda. "And he is such a proper gentleman and such a gallant spirit that I had thought perchance—"

She did not complete her sentence ; but Alys understood, and shook her head. Her cheek glowed, and there was a light in her eyes which looked strangely like that of love. Linda's needle went in and out rapidly, and she bent her head over her task ; but bending towards her companion, she asked in a low whisper,—

"Dearest, tell me, is it Leofric ?"

Alys started, and the crimson flooded her face. She made no reply, only bending lower over her frame, so that even Linda could not see her expression. But somehow from that moment a new bond seemed to establish itself between the two girls ; and when Linda ventured to ask presently, "But what would thy parents say ? he is but a poor clerk, though a bachelor and like to become a doctor in time," Alys made low-toned answer,—

" 1 ofttimes think that the lot of the great ones of the earth is far less happy than that of those less lofty in the eyes of the world. I have even heard my father say the same, and methinks he would deny me nothing that was for my happiness, were his heart but once convinced."

"And truly," added Linda, with a sigh, " these be dangerous and troublous days in which to live. The victor of to-day may be the vanquished of the morrow. In very sooth, a humbler lot is sweeter than one where the cup of prosperity may be dashed from the lips, and adversity follow swiftly on the heels of triumph. All who know him love Leofric, and speak well of him."

Again the cheek of Alys glowed ; her voice faltered as she spoke the next words,—

" Thou hast read mine heart, sweet Linda, but thou must keep its secret locked within thine own. I scarce dare to think of it myself, for never by word or sign has he showed me aught of his heart ; and yet methinks— methinks—"

" Ay, verily, love has a language of its own," said Linda, in sympathetic accents, " and souls may meet when words there be none. He would not dare to lift his eyes to thee, fair Alys, thinking, perchance, that thou art half plighted to my Lord Amalric—as, indeed, others think. Yet, should time pass and he become learned and famous, and shouldst thou remain unwed—ah, well, methinks he will find his tongue ; and thy father will not say him nay when he knows how thine heart inclines."

Alys listened to these welcome words with glowing eyes

and blushing cheeks. Never before had she dared, even to herself, so openly to admit how her childish friendship for Leofric Wyvill was ripening into something deeper and more earnest. Of late she had seen less of him, but he still came and went at the Castle, and was the friend of all. He was thought to be a youth of great promise; and in those days almost any man of learning, however humble his birth, who rose to academic distinction, might hope to win his way to affluence and influence before his beard was grey. There would be no presumption a few years hence in a Regent Master or young Doctor aspiring to the hand of a knight's daughter. The only bar likely to arise would be that imposed by the Church, were the student to desire orders; but Leofric had never showed a leaning towards the religious life, and was the less likely to think of it now——unless, indeed, he believed Alys lost to him as the affianced bride of Amalric, and entered upon the career of an ecclesiastic as a salve for a wounded spirit.

This danger did suggest itself for a moment to Linda, and she resolved to watch earnestly the turn of affairs. The conversation at that moment was interrupted by the entrance of Edmund and Leofric into the room where the girls were sitting. Alys bent over her frame to hide her momentary confusion, but it passed unobserved in the excitement of the moment.

"The King is on his way thither!" cried Edmund; "he is to enter the city to-morrow. The students are pouring out as though the plague were threatening. In a few hours' time, they say, there will be scarce three hundred left, and perhaps not so many. The townsfolks are all agape and disturbed ; for many there be of the clerks who vow they will never return, but will set up their abode in Cambridge or Northampton, and establish a rival University there. The masters have followed their scholars, as is but wise ; and the citizens are crying out that the King has ruined the town. It is but a sorry welcome he will have on the morrow when he makes his entry here."

"Methinks his Majesty will repent him of his mistake," said Alys. "Why did he drive forth the clerks ? My father could surely have kept order in the city."

"Marry, he was afraid," answered Edmund; "and indeed he had some cause, for in his mandate to my father he speaks of his own lords who will attend him as being 'so untamed and fierce' that he dare not trust them so near to an army of turbulent clerks, famous for their unruly conduct."

Alys's lips curved to a smile of some contempt.

"Methinks our monarch is but a poor poltroon," she said. "Small wonder if the realm sink beneath his sway."

"Nevertheless he is about to do a bolder thing than any King has attempted since the days of the Saxons," answered Edmund, laughing; "for he declares that his first action will be, on entering Oxford, to pay a visit to the shrine of St. Frideswyde !"

"And wherefore should he not ?" asked both girls in a breath ; whereupon Leofric was called upon to tell the legend of St. Frideswyde—how she had taken the vow of chastity, but was pestered without ceasing by the King of Mercia, who desired her hand in marriage. She fled from him to Oxford, where he pursued her, laying siege to the town; but in answer to her prayers he was struck with blindness, and returned to his own country, leaving her in peace to found her nunnery and devote herself to the religious life. But since that date no King had ever ventured to intrude himself even to lay offerings upon her shrine, and the resolution of Henry the Third to brave the anger of the virgin saint was regarded as a proof of piety and courage, since he openly declared that he could not believe any ill would be suffered to follow an act of homage to one whom he revered and desired to honour.

Upon the morrow the city was bedecked with banners and costly cloths, and the Constable, together with the Chancellor and all men of importance in the city, went forth to meet the King and his nobles, to bid them welcome to the city, and to conduct them to the church of St. Frideswyde. Here a procession of Canons, with the Abbot at their head, would be waiting to receive the monarch, and to conduct him to the shrine, where miracles were still said to be worked.

Alys and Linda rode forth with the company from the Castle to see the sight, and Edmund, with Leofric and one or two other comrades, formed their bodyguard. It was strange to see the streets of Oxford so empty of their crowds of eager students, who, upon an occasion like this, would naturally have been thronging out with songs and garlands, ready alike for a riot or a reception. But although there were still some scholars who had given no heed to the King's arbitrary decree, they had no intention of showing him any honour, and remained within their own quarters, save a few who, like Edmund and Leofric, had some cause to go forth in one of the processions.

Amalric, of course, would in no case have been one to offer personal reverence to the monarch. He was not, however, in Oxford at the moment, having left to gain news as to the attempt at negotiation which was still to be made, and quite a band of clerks who had arms and horses had accompanied him, eager beyond measure for the coming fray, and, if the truth were to be told, by no means anxious that peace should be restored before the appeal to arms had been made.

"I scarce know the city," said Alys to Leofric, as they rode through the streets, in which the citizens were grouped about, but which were so strangely bereft of their crowds of gowned scholars. "Methinks his Majesty will repent him when he sees what his decree hath done. And methinks he would repent him still more did he know how many stout-hearted soldiers he has dismissed to join his foes. I trow that if the rival armies meet face to face, there will be many an Oxford clerk in the ranks who will deal deadly blows to the King's cherished troops."

Leofric was of the same opinion. He had had some ado in restraining Jack from joining himself to one of the bands sallying forth in search of adventure and warlike pastime. Leofric was of opinion that sooner or later the rupture would come, and they would have to range themselves beside their champion, and perhaps strike a blow in defence of their cause; but he had no desire to anticipate this moment, and still hoped that some good might come of the impending negotiations, although the haughty bearing of King Henry's knights and nobles as they rode into Oxford went far to quench this lingering hope.

The King was haughty in his bearing towards both Constable and Chancellor, whom he knew to be friends of De Montfort. He chided them somewhat roundly in face of all his company for the recent riot, and even threw out a hint of displacing them from office if this sort of thing went on.

He was more gracious in his bearing towards the municipal authorities, but was still very much the triumphant monarch, visiting a turbulent city which had once caused him trouble, but where he meant for the future to be very much the master.

His demeanour did not inspire either respect or confidence in the hearts of those who saw him, and only when he approached the precincts of St. Frideswyde's shrine did he begin to comport himself differently.

When, however, he ceased to have men of the world to deal with, and found himself confronted by those ecclesiastics who had always been the supporters of the royal and papal power, he became another creature altogether. He dismounted from his horse, begged the blessing of the Prior, made costly gifts to the Priory, and finally presented himself at the shrine itself, prostrating himself with every token of outward reverence, and placing there his offerings, which were on a lavish and princely scale.

Only a few of his own followers accompanied him into the church, and the procession which had ridden forth to meet him did not attempt to enter so much as the precincts. It was plain to all that the King had come in no conciliatory mood, but that, puffed up by the award of France, he now intended to rule the realm with a rod of iron, and to listen to neither remonstrance nor condition.

"Pray Heaven the saint may send him a vision that shall change his heart," spoke some one from the crowd, "else the sword will be unsheathed ere many weeks have passed!"

Alys's eyes sought the face of Leofric, and she asked,—

"Does the saint in truth ever send warnings and visions to those who worship at her shrine?"

Leofric looked doubtful; he was not very clear as to the capacities of the saints in this respect.

"In truth, fair lady, I know not. It seems to me that visions and wonders are seldom vouchsafed to those who are puffed up with pride and self-esteem. It is the poor and humble in spirit to whom the Lord reveals His mind—so at least Father Angelus teaches. Yet they say that miracles are worked at the shrine, and I heard that the son of one of the burgesses of the city was raised from the dead not so very long since by being brought hither and laid before the shrine, whilst the monks offered prayers for him. He had died beneath the knife of the surgeons, they say, who had worked upon him some hoped-for cure, which had caused instead his death; but he was restored, they say, by the virgin saint. Would that she could restore to his

Majesty that willingness of spirit towards our noble Earl which in times past he hath been known to show!"

But the saint seemed to have no message or warning for the King. No immediate hurt, however, followed upon his bold act in presenting himself at her shrine. He retired thence puffed up with pride and vainglory, reversed in his assembled Parliament every previous Provision of Oxford, and scornfully dismissed the representatives of the Barons who came to suggest a compromise.

"I will be King, and rule by mine own power!" was the motto he seemed now to have adopted. Men shook their heads and looked gravely at one another, echoing the words Brother Angelus had been heard to speak,—

"Pride goeth before destruction, and an haughty spirit before a fall."

CHAPTER XXII.

IN ARMS.

"FAIR Mistress Alys, we have come to say farewell."

The Constable's daughter, with her banner in her hands, was waiting for this farewell visit from Amalric de Montfort. All knew now that the red flame of war was about to leap forth and devour the land. The King, having scornfully refused all overtures, was already marching upon Northampton, whither so many Oxford students had fled. The Earl of Leicester was in the neighbourhood of London, where Amalric was about to join him; and with him was to march an eager, gallant little band, which included a number of his comrades in this city, and in particular Leofric Wyvill, who for the nonce was acting as his esquire and personal attendant.

The thought of regular study had become impossible even to a studious mind like Leofric's. Confusion reigned at Oxford, and for the time being the students had dispersed in all directions. Masters and pupils had alike caught the infection of excitement. Doubtless the city would return to its normal conditions in time, and the scholars would flock back in great numbers during the course of the ensuing months; but for the immediate present nothing was talked of but the approaching appeal to arms, and books were laid aside for the sword, which was the weapon that must decide this next crisis of the country's history.

Since the King's scornful rejection of the Barons' moderate request, all thoughts of peace had been abandoned. Amalric had got together his eager little band, and now he had come, with a few picked comrades beside him, to say farewell to Mistress Alys, and to receive at her fair hands the silken banner that she and Linda had spent so many long hours in working for him, with his father's coat of arms.

By this time the friends and followers of Amalric had come to regard Alys as his plighted lady-love, albeit in reality no troth-plight had passed between them. It was scarce the right time for proffering love-suits, but yet the Constable and his wife could not be ignorant of the fact that young Lord Amalric had set his affections upon their daughter.

She stood now beside her parents, with the silken banner in her hands, her fair face flushed, her heart beating rather fast, for she had never before taken so public a part as she was to-day called upon to do in the presentation of the banner; and remembering some words spoken to her by Linda not many days before, she wondered whether indeed this act in any way committed her to a step which she had never seriously contemplated, and did not desire to contemplate.

But maidens in those days had little choice of action.

She had been bidden by her parents to appear in the great
hall and give the Lord Amalric the banner. Now she
was holding it out towards him, a blush on her cheek, a
bright light in her eyes; and perhaps it was only Linda,
out of all those standing by, who noted how the timid
glance of the girl's eyes went past the gay and gallant
figure of Amalric and rested upon the graceful form of
Leofric, who in his shining armour, and with his bared
head from which the golden locks floated in a soft cloud,
looked the very image of some pious knight going forth
upon a sacred quest, not in search of gain to himself, but
for love of the good cause.

And this was indeed the feeling which actuated Leofric.
He had small expectation of any personal advantage from
this war. Probably he would have gained more of that
by remaining in Oxford and continuing his studies there,
for he was more of the student than the soldier by nature.
But he was convinced of the righteousness of the cause on
which the Barons were embarked. He had imbibed the
teachings of the Franciscans, and believed that duty and
love of his country demanded this sacrifice and effort.
True, he was sufficiently imbued with martial ardour at
this moment to go forth proudly and eagerly; but the
guiding motive was love for his fellows and for his country,
as distinguished from personal ambition.

The same could not, perhaps, be said so entirely for
Amalric. If this war ended in a victory for the Barons,
his father would be the greatest man in the kingdom, and
his sons must of necessity become men of importance, if

not of wealth. Already he was treated with greater defer-
ence and respect than he had ever been. It was natural
that his heart should swell with pride and joy at thought
of the coming struggle; for with the country so entirely
with them, how could they think of failure?

It was a pretty sight to see the gallant youth come
forward and take the banner from the hands of Alys,
kissing those fair hands at the same time, and vowing that
the very sight and touch of that banner would act as a
talisman and charm.

Alys spoke a few low-toned words of encouragement
and hope which she had conned over beforehand; then
the banner was laid before Brother Angelus, who was
there for the purpose, and he was asked to bless it ere
it went forth to do its appointed work.

The friar performed this office very reverently, and
gave the banner once more into Amalric's hands, charging him to be a true and faithful servant to his hea-
venly as well as to his earthly father; to show mercy
and kindness to his foes in the hour of triumph; to
look for help to God, and not to man; to avoid all
haughtiness of spirit in the time of prosperity, and lack
of faith if adversity should come; always to remember
the poor, and seek to mitigate by every means possible
the inevitable horrors of war: this was the duty of the
soldier who loved the Lord as well as the cause. The
prayers of all good men would follow and aid those
whose hearts were pure and their hands vowed to the
righteous work.

Whilst this charge was being given in one part of the
hall, taking up the attention of the spectators, Alys had
watched her opportunity, and had drawn Leofric towards
her by a little gesture of the hand. It was natural that
she should wish to say farewell to her brother's friend,
and one in whose company she herself had passed so many
happy hours. None noted anything strange in the action,
and few heeded it.

"Thou art going to the war, Leofric?" she asked, in a
voice which faltered a little in spite of herself.

"Yes, truly am I, fair Mistress Alys. I love not war,
and yet methinks I cannot keep away. The Lord Amalric
is my friend, and he and his have shown me great kindness; besides this, I have at heart the cause of the people.
Methinks I would fain strike a blow against the iniquitous
pretensions of the Pope, and the tyranny of false sycophants, who turn his Majesty's heart from his own loyal
subjects."

"But thou wilt come back?" said the maiden, with the
sparkle of tears in her eyes.

"I trow yes," he answered earnestly. "I shall ever look
upon this city as my home. If I come safe through what
lies before us next, I will return when the sword is laid
down, as pray Heaven it soon may be."

"I pray so indeed," answered Alys earnestly; "I shall
pray for thy safety night and day."

For a moment their eyes met, and a flush arose in the
cheek of both. They stood thus for several seconds, as
though no words would come to either.

Alys first recovered herself, and unwinding a scarf of crimson silk which she wore about her waist, she lightly threw it over Leofric's shoulder, saying softly,—

"Wear it as thy sword-belt, and forget me not."

The moment was past. Like one awakening from a dream, Leofric followed the rest from the hall into the courtyard, where their horses were standing. He knotted the scarf across his shining breastplate, and gave one long look at Alys as he passed from the hall. But although she came out to see them all mount and ride away, he did not even seek to catch her eye or to exchange a word with her again. His heart was in a strange glow. He felt like a knight who has received a token from one almost too sacred and high above him to be dreamed of as lady-love; yet in the strength of that token he felt that he could work prodigies of valour. What could he not do for her sweet sake? And yet the idea of asking anything in return never entered his head. Was it not enough that she had shown to him, the poor student and bachelor, that she regarded him with interest, and thought of him as of a friend?

Away rode the cavalcade in the bright sunshine of the early spring, the citizens cheering them to the echo, the friars pausing to bless them and their crusade, their own hearts full of joy and the anticipation of coming triumph.

The King had marched to Northampton, as has already been said, therefore to take a northerly route would be unsafe for the little band. Amalric believed his father to be in or near London, and anyhow the metropolis was known to be favourable to the cause of the Barons. He had therefore made up his mind to proceed thither, and all through the hours of the daylight the little band of horsemen trotted briskly on their way, receiving warm greetings from the inhabitants of the towns and villages through which they passed, and becoming more and more confident as to the feeling of the nation, at least in these regions.

They avoided the road which would take them near Windsor, for there they feared the power of the King was still in the ascendant. They kept a more northerly course, and by the time the daylight waned found themselves close to Watford, where they resolved to encamp for the night. As they approached the place, they were aware of a considerable excitement going on; and when they rode into the streets with the banner of the De Montforts floating before them, the people crowded round them in great excitement, clamouring to know the news.

"They say the war has broken out! They say the people have attacked the King's brother's house at Isleworth, and devastated everything. The Temple is broken open, and the money carried off. The Jews have been pillaged, and their houses burnt. The bell of St. Paul's was ringing all yesterday. They say great things are being done in the city!"

Amalric knew nothing of this; but it sounded like the beginning of war, and he eagerly asked for news of his father.

At the moment none could tell him more than that the Earl was in London, and that this insurrection had been

made in his favour. Amalric would fain have pushed on
through the night to join him, but was restrained by the
unfitness of their horses for a longer journey. The inhabitants of the little place received them most hospitably;
and whilst they were yet at supper after their long day's
travel, a messenger came bursting in full of exciting news.

"The Earl is at St. Albans! The news has just come!
He is on his way to relieve Northampton, which has sent
to him for help against the King. He rests there to-
night, and on the morrow he resumes his march. God
be with him in his undertakings; for we were sick to
death of the exactions of foreigners and the taxes of the
Pope. 'Let us break their bands asunder, and cast away
their cords from us.'"

A great cheer went round, and was taken up by those
without. Now indeed did it seem like the longed-for
liberation, when an army was in pursuit of the tyrannical
monarch to defeat him, and rescue a besieged city.
Amalric could scarce sleep at night for excitement, and
early next day he was astir, visiting his own charger
himself, and assuring himself that a night's rest had put
the gallant creature in trim for his day's work.

All the place was astir. Recruits had joined the little
band. The spirit of enthusiasm and enterprise was working mightily; the consciousness of the near presence of
the Earl acted like new wine on the spirits of the men.

The ride from Watford to St. Albans was but short, and
soon after nine o'clock the little band approached the city
walls. The same air of excitement and animation per-

vaded that locality, and as soon as Amalric's banner was
seen, the people rushed out and gave him eager and joyous
welcome.   Leaving the bulk of his followers drawn up in
the street, and taking with him only Leofric and a couple
of others, Amalric went straight to the quarters of his
father.   All the place was full of soldiers, the clang of
arms was heard everywhere, and the tale of the uprising
of the citizens of London in their hero's favour was passing
from mouth to mouth in the crowd.   Amalric was received
with shouts of welcome when it was known that he was
indeed a son of their chief and idol.   The cheering brought
De Montfort out from his house, and it was touching to see
the eager greeting betwixt father and son.

Amalric was off his horse in a moment, and had bent
his knee to his father; whilst the Earl's eagle face softened at sight of his youngest son, and he embraced him
tenderly, with many tokens of welcome and greeting.

A few words served to explain the mutual position of
father and son.   The Earl was glad of any reinforcements
of trained men at this juncture, and spoke very courteously
to Amalric's gallant little Oxford contingent when he rode
up at his son's side.   Already preparations were afoot for
the moving on towards Northampton, and De Montfort
explained to Amalric that the younger Simon was there,
conducting the defence, and had sent an urgent summons
to his father to march quickly thither to his relief.

"Simon is rash," said the Earl gravely : " he has courage,
but lacks discretion.   I shall not rest till I am there myself.   I would that I could be in a score of places at once !"

It would not be possible to reach Northampton till the morrow; but the army was being marshalled into array for the start, when suddenly there came dashing into the town a mud-bespattered messenger, riding a horse that looked ready to drop, and Amalric suddenly cried out in alarm,—

"My lord father—see! it is my brother Guy!"

Guy de Montfort it was. He had outstripped all his followers in his eagerness when he knew that his father was at hand. His horse reeled in his tracks, and fell panting and exhausted in the streets the moment his task was done; whilst the rider, weary and worn as he was, flung himself upon his father with an eager demonstration of joy, albeit he was the bearer of evil tidings.

"The city is lost to us! Northampton is in the King's hands! It is all the treachery of the foreign foe!" and there and then in the ears of the indignant people he poured out his tale—how the Prior of the monastery of St. Andrew, just outside the walls, had undermined the wall, and so let in a party of the King's soldiers, whilst an attack had been feigned at the opposite end of the town. It was no lack of gallantry on the part of the besieged; for so well had they defended the walls, and in particular so great had been the damage done to the assailants through the slings, the bows, and the catapults of the Oxford clerks, who fought under an independent banner of their own, that the King had vowed he would slay every man of them once he got into the city; so that these had had to fly helter-skelter when the news came that the

town had been taken by strategy, and that the King's
troops were already within.

"And thy brother Simon?" asked De Montfort, who
listened silently to this tale, without breaking into the
lamentations which filled the air from those who stood
round.

"Alack, he is a prisoner in the King's hands!" answered
Guy—"a fate I narrowly escaped myself. For we ordered
a sortie as a last hope, and Simon's horse, terrified by the
noise and confusion, became unmanageable, and carried
him whether he would or no into the camp of our foes.
I was riding after him to seek to aid him, when I was surrounded and carried off, not by enemies, but by friends.
The Oxford clerks having got wind of the King's special
wrath against them, were flying from the city ere they
should be taken, and seeing me in peril, they dashed
round and bore me away with them. I could scarce thank
them at the time; but methinks it is little I could do for
Simon, and liberty with the power to fight is sweet."

Great dismay and anger reigned in the ranks of De
Montfort's soldiers at the news of this disastrous event;
but the Earl himself reminded his followers that it was
but the fortune of war. They could not look for unquali-
fied success in any campaign, but must take the evil with
the good, not being over-elated by the one, nor unduly
cast down by the other.

But the news brought by his son changed the tactics of
the Earl. To march upon Northampton would now be
useless. He was in some ways glad to be spared that task,

and to carry out his former plans of securing Rochester, which had fallen into the hands of the Earl of Warenne and some other nobles, and was now holding out for the King.

But before the army started forth on this counter-march, the heart of Leofric was gladdened and lightened by the sudden appearance of his comrades Jack Dugdale and Gilbert Barbeck, who had been amongst that band of Oxford clerks who had made their way to Northampton, and had narrowly escaped falling into the hands of the enraged monarch.

Now they came riding after Guy de Montfort in straggling fashion, weary and worn with their rapid flight, but full of hope and courage, and eager to join forces with the great Earl, to whose cause they were bound body and soul. It was a gladsome meeting between the comrades, and the Earl himself gave cordial welcome to the gallant little band, and even postponed his march for a few hours, to give them time to rest and refresh themselves, and to obtain fresh horses from the friendly citizens.

"Now, this is like adventure!" cried eager Jack, as they rode forth at last, a gallant company, he and Leofric side by side, to their own infinite content. "I tell thee, good comrade, I have tasted war, and I like the flavour of it mightily. I hewed down with my good sword three fellows who came spurring after us, and from the walls I slew a goodly number. Yes, the King himself stormed at the havoc we clerks of Oxford wrought amongst his followers. I tell thee, Leofric, if he did put slight upon us, we have revenged that slight in baths of blood!"

From his talk, merry Jack seemed almost to have turned into a bloodthirsty soldier; yet he was the good-natured, kindly comrade as of old to those who came across him. He became a favourite with all during that quick march, and even the grave Earl was seen to smile sometimes, either at some of the youth's sallies, or at the mirth they provoked. For Amalric would have him in his company, enlisting him as an esquire, second only to Leofric; so that De Montfort could not but notice him from time to time, and once he called upon him for his account of the fight on the walls of Northampton.

But Jack was destined to distinguish himself in another way ere many days had passed. He was burning with zeal in the cause of the Barons, and intensely eager to avenge the slight put upon that cause by the stratagem of Northampton.

"If they outwitted us once, surely we may outwit them here," he remarked, as he looked at the solid walls of the city of Rochester, and wondered how they were to be captured.

He took counsel with one or two bold spirits, Leofric amongst the number, and presently the vague idea which had suggested itself grew into a definite plan.

Amalric himself led the youth into the presence of his father to tell the thing he had conceived, and Jack spoke out boldly, being a stranger to fear.

"Sir," he said, "I have been used to the water all my days, and yestere'en I took a boat and dropped down with the tide into the city. There is a bridge in the heart

of it, and I thought how that if, whilst we wait without
the walls, we should send a fire-ship up the river's mouth
with the tide, and fire it against the bridge, it would so
affright and disturb the city, drawing all attention to the
centre of the town, that our brave soldiers at the gates
could soon force an entrance, even as at Northampton the
false attack drew off the attention of us all from that spot
where the false foreign Prior had undermined the wall.
If a base foreign traitor can outwit honest Englishmen,
surely it is a game we can pay them back!"

The Earl turned over the idea many times, and it found
favour in his sight. A small fire-ship could be easily
made ready, and the ruse might prove successful.

"And how shall we know that the ship will come to
anchor by the bridge and fire there?" he asked thoughtfully.

"Sir," answered Jack boldly, "if you will accord your
gracious permission, I will guide it thither myself, and
having fired it will dive off, and secrete myself somewhere
amongst the shipping until the tide turn and I can swim
away. Or perchance my comrade, Leofric, will accompany
me in a small boat, and take me aboard when my task is
done."

The idea took hold upon the mind of De Montfort, and
with great dispatch and secrecy the fire-ship was prepared.
The strong walls of Rochester hardly invited assault unless
there were some counter-distraction within the city to
render such assault less perilous to those without.

The warlike Earl was daily weakening the walls by the

resolute action of his engines. He had machines almost unknown as yet in England, and gave the besieged little rest night or day. But for all that the solid walls still defied him, and the idea of assault was too perilous even for the courage of the fearless De Montfort. He must not risk a second repulse, lest the spirit of his soldiers should give way. He must not attempt anything till success was assured.

But Jack's stratagem was destined to prove a complete success. Accompanied only by Leofric, in a light boat towed behind, the bold young soldier guided his phantom craft up the mouth of the river upon a dark, moonless night. By this time he had learned the river by heart, and had no difficulty in quietly grounding the vessel against the bridge. Then silently setting light to her fiery contents, he slipped overboard to Leofric, and the two cast off, and rowed with muffled oars to the appointed landing-place, where their friends awaited them.

Long before they reached it the whole sky was in a glow, and they even caught glimpses of hurrying throngs of people, all hastening to the scene of the conflagration. That the whole town was in an uproar of confusion they could tell even from a long distance. And Jack sang aloud and cheered lustily in the joy and triumph of his heart.

But a greater triumph was in store for the comrades when they finally reached shore, and were brought by their companions into the lines once more.

The stratagem had been completely successful; the

people had all rushed down to the scene of the fire, even the soldiers quitting their posts to assist. De Montfort, with a picked body of men, had made a grand assault where the walls near to the gate had become greatly weakened. Wall and gate had alike given way with a crash, and the besieging army had streamed in in triumph. Rochester had fallen into the hands of the Barons!

CHAPTER XXIII.

ON THE FIELD OF LEWES.

THEY stood looking down upon the green plains and the venerable Priory of Lewes. The cup-like hollow presented a strange appearance, being dotted over with tents, and filled with armed men, moving hither and thither like human ants, intent upon some important task. Within the walls of the Priory the King was lodged, with his brother, his son, and his counsellors.

The little knot of youths, stationed upon the knoll that commanded a view of these things, had their eyes fixed upon a small party of riders who were moving forward towards the Priory, carrying a white flag before them.

A nearer view would have told an observer that two of this party were ecclesiastics in their robes of office, being in fact none other than the Bishops of London and Worcester; but those spectators on the knoll did not need the evidence of eyesight to tell them that. They were well aware of the embassy of the Bishops, and of the import of the message they bore.

"If that fails to bring his Majesty to his senses," said Amalric gravely, "nothing can avert a bloody battle."

" I would we might settle the matter by force of arms ! "
cried Jack, whose blood was up, and who was eager for
the ordeal of battle. "Even if the King doth make
promises, who knows if he will keep them ? I am sick of
parley. I want the sword to be loosed from the scabbard.
The King has wrought desolation and ruin wherever he
has gone. It is time that he tasted that which he has
inflicted."

Jack spoke with eager impetuosity, which seemed
suited to the martial aspect of his strong, well-knit figure.
He had gone up in the world since his escapade with the
fire-ship. He had now a fine charger of his own, and a
suit of mail. He was ranked as one of Amalric's esquires, and was a favourite even with the Earl himself,
who spoke kindly to him whenever they met.

London had of late been the headquarters of the Barons'
army, whilst the royalists had been marching hither and
thither over the country, "accompanied," as the chronicler
of the time described it, " by three comrades—plunder, fire,
and slaughter. There was no peace in the land ; everything
was destroyed by sword, fire, rapine, and robbery ; everywhere was clamour and trembling and woe."

It was a state of things which could not continue, and
the hearts of the nation turned to the Earl as to a deliverer
who alone could save them from such misery. The men
of London were with him heart and soul, and had furnished
him with a contingent fifteen thousand strong, with which
to meet and overcome the tyrant. But still De Montfort
hesitated to draw the sword in open battle against his

sovereign; and even now, at the eleventh hour, when the two armies had mustered about the field of Lewes, he had sent two Bishops of known probity and piety, to endeavour to bring the King to reason before the last appeal to arms was made.

"What said the letter of the Earls?" asked Jack eagerly of Leofric, who as a ready scribe was often employed in such matters as these. "Thou wert closeted long with them last night. What did they say that hath not been said a hundred times ere now?"

Leofric drew from his tunic certain fragments of parchment, closely written, which he scanned several times over, and then made reply to Jack's question.

"The Earls of Leicester and Gloucester did but repeat for themselves and their party what has been said a hundred times before—namely, that they desired peace, and to serve the King faithfully, and only to put down the enemies of the realm, who deceive both his Majesty and the Prince, and do despite to the realm. They offered to pay a large sum as compensation for hurt done to the King's property, if he would make peace and observe the Provisions of Oxford, and submit to the decision of 'certain chosen Churchmen' what statutes ought to be observed, and how far the oaths taken ought to be binding, saying that they wished to keep their faith as Christians, and avoid the stain of perjury."

Long and eagerly did the comrades upon the hillside talk together, wondering whether this embassy of the Bishops would succeed where other things had failed, or

whether the King, blinded by pride and advised by evil
counsellors, would press matters on to the bitter end.
They could observe the signs of commotion below, round
and about the Priory, and finally they watched the great
gates being flung wide open to admit of the exit of the
ambassadors.

"What news will they bring — what news?" cried
Amalric breathlessly, and he turned and hastened towards
his father's quarters, mounting his horse, which stood
tethered a little way off, and galloping away without waiting for his companions.

Leofric had paused when about to follow, for his eye
had been caught by an advancing figure that looked somehow familiar, and which seemed making straight for them
upon the knoll. Just as Amalric rode off, Jack broke into
a quick exclamation,—

"By my troth, here is our quondam companion Hugh!"

The next moment Hugh le Barbier stood beside them,
grasping their hands and looking with eager affection into
their faces.

Although he came from the hostile camp, there was no
hostility in the hearts of the Oxford students as they stood
together once more. Eagerly did Hugh ask of their welfare, eagerly did they question him as to his adventures
during the past months, and, above all, most eagerly did
they ask him if he knew what sort of answer the King
had returned to the messengers just sent, and whether there
was any chance of a cessation of hostilities.

Hugh gravely shook his head.

"His Majesty is greatly incensed against the Barons. He would scarce listen with patience whilst the letter was being read. Had it been brought by others than Bishops, I fear me he would not even have heard it. His brother sat beside him, and in scorn he declared that he alone claimed the full sum offered by the Barons, as indemnity against his own personal losses. He and the Prince were equally indignant with the King; and whilst his Majesty dictated the terms of a wrathful letter in which he defies the Earls, and throws back their allegiance and their oaths of fidelity in their teeth, the Prince and his uncle together wrote another letter even more haughty and insulting than the one composed by the King, calling the Earls of Leicester and Gloucester 'faithless traitors,' and I know not what besides, and hurling defiance at them in a fashion that can but lead to one end. There will be no avoiding a battle now!"

Jack's eyes lighted with triumph, but Hugh spoke sorrowfully. He loved the Prince, and he felt bound to the royal standard by his duty as a subject. But the cause was not dear to his heart. Henry was not a monarch to inspire either confidence or love, and his embracing the cause of his foreign favourites—against whom this movement was really directed—and telling his own English Barons that any opposition to them was opposition to him, and that their quarrel was his, rendered him but a pitiful creature in the eyes even of those who desired to serve him loyally and well. None could stand near the royal presence without being continually galled and chafed by seeing aliens and sycophants preferred to honest and noble subjects of the realm. Hugh had had a fair insight of late into the methods of the King, and his heart was somewhat heavy within him at the thought of what must lie before the kingdom if the issues of the day should be favourable to the royal cause.

"If only the Prince were King!" he breathed. "He is hot and rash now, stirred up to filial emulation in his father's cause; but his heart is true and his judgment sound. Were he to be at the head of the state, we should not have to groan as we are groaning now."

And then turning suddenly away to another subject, he asked news of Linda, where and how his comrades had seen her last, and if she were still safe in the care of the Constable.

"Yes, and like a sister to Mistress Alys," answered Leofric. "I trow she is safe from any threatened peril there. But we have heard and seen naught of her foes since they were driven forth from the city by the Chancellor. I misdoubt me if they will ever seek to return."

"And Lotta—is aught known of her?" asked Hugh.

"She dwells with her parents yet," answered Leofric. "I seldom see her; but Gilbert Barbeck tells me sometimes of her. She refused to visit Linda in the Castle, and spoke fierce words which show that her heart is yet bitter within her. But more than that I know not. She was always a strange creature. Her own mother knows not how to deal with her."

"Some say she hath a familiar spirit, and some that she is mad, which perhaps is one and the same thing," said

Jack. "All I know is that she looks at you with eyes that burn like live coals. Methinks she has been dabbling with Tito's evil books. If she takes not care, she may be ducked or burnt as a witch yet!"

But this was scarce time or place to dwell on private topics. Little doubt could now exist that they were on the eve of a great battle. Hugh looked regretfully into Leofric's eyes as they clasped hands before parting.

"I would we could fight side by side, instead of in hostile camps," he said; "but when this cloud of evil and misery has swept by, I trust that we may be comrades once again, in Oxford or elsewhere."

"To be sure! to be sure!" cried cheery Jack. "Let once the King be brought to reason, and all those vile foreigners sent back to their own country, and our good Earl (foreigner though he be in race, yet not at heart) at the head of his Council, then we shall forget our troubles and feuds, and all will go merry as a marriage-bell."

Yet for the moment there was nothing of merriment in the hearts of men, but a stern nerving of themselves for coming strife.

Leofric and Jack were met by the news that the King had received the embassy with coldness and hostility, and had sent back an answer so insulting and uncompromising that nothing was now thought of but the appeal to arms.

Leofric, going in search of Amalric, found himself in the midst of an earnest gathering of knights and nobles, and heard the clarion voice of De Montfort raised in solemn protest.

"By the arm of St. James, I have done all that man can do to keep the peace of the realm and my oath of allegiance. Be the result of this day's work upon the head of his Majesty! He has brought all upon himself. I would have saved him from it if I could."

The Earl had had a presentiment, of which he had spoken before, that May was to be a fortunate month for him, and an unlucky one for the King. He went about amongst his people now with a look of serene courage upon his face; and whilst stimulating them to do their best in the coming fight, he urged them not to forget that their foes were also their brothers, and that they must show mercy to the vanquished in the day of victory.

A sense of great seriousness and earnestness prevailed in the ranks of the Barons. They trusted their cause to the God of battles, assured of its righteousness, and inspired by a religious as well as a patriotic zeal. Many friars were with them, encouraging them by their presence, and filling their hearts with fervent and pious thoughts. The soldiers regarded their cause as a holy crusade against tyranny and slavery, and in token of this feeling they fastened upon their arms a white cross, as an outward mark of their faith. In a battle with their own countrymen some such sign might be needed to distinguish friend from foe. A stern enthusiasm filled all hearts, and the confidence of the soldiers in their leader was unfaltering.

De Montfort had won great renown as a soldier in Gascony, and his troops had implicit faith in his powers. Moreover he set them an example even in faith and piety;

for upon the eve of the battle he spent the night in prayer, whilst the Bishop of Worcester—one of the emissaries to the King, and himself a notable patriot, Walter de Cantilupe by name—rode through the ranks, and urged the men to confess their sins and receive absolution, that they might ride forth upon the morrow in the full assurance that the power of God was with them.

Early upon the morning of the fourteenth of May, before the sun had risen, the army of the Earl set itself in battle array, and prepared for the march. In sight of all his men De Montfort bestowed the honour of knighthood upon his brother-in-arms and brother Earl the young Earl Gilbert of Gloucester, and two others; after which, with brave hearts and cheery faces, the men marched in capital order towards that very crest of rising ground from which a few days before Leofric and Jack had looked down upon the town and Priory of Lewes, when the Bishops had gone forth with their embassy.

Since his accident in the winter, the Earl of Leicester had not been able to ride as much as formerly, and he had a litter in which he was carried. In that he travelled as far as this halting-place, although he was to mount his charger during the battle. His litter would, however, be kept in readiness upon the field, in the event of his requiring it; and it was to remain beside the standard upon which his arms waved proudly. For the nonce, instead of himself or any of his own followers occupying it, there were placed inside for security those four traitors of London who had once plotted his destruction, and who had been hostages in his hands ever since. These men, bound, were placed in the litter when it was vacated by De Montfort in favour of the charger now led up for him to mount.

But before doing so, the Earl turned to his soldiers, and addressed them in his clear, ringing tones,—

"Beloved comrades and followers, we are about to enter upon battle to-day in behalf of the Government of the kingdom, to the honour of God and of our mother Church, and moreover for the maintenance of our faith. Let us pray for grace and vigour, that we may overpower the malice of our enemy. Since we are His, to Him we commend our bodies and souls." With these words he fell upon the ground, stretching out his arms in the form of a cross, all his soldiers following his example, whilst the Bishops cried aloud,—

"Grant us, O Lord, our desire of a glorious victory, to the honour of Thy name."

Then the battle was set in order, and Leofric and Jack found themselves placed in the right wing, which was to be led by Henry de Montfort, with Guy and Amalric as his assistants. The centre was under the command of the newly-made knight, Gilbert of Gloucester, who was to show his valour to-day. The left wing was composed mainly of the Londoners, many of whom had never seen war. They were commanded by three young nobles of known courage. As for De Montfort himself, he took up a position where he could watch the progress of the fight, and give help to that portion of the army which seemed most to require it.

The situation was a good one, on rising ground; and the tents and baggage were piled on the crest of the hill, where the banner of De Montfort floated by the side of his vacated litter.

They had marched rapidly, in order to surprise the King's party; but warning had reached them, and already there was a great stirring in the hollow, which was alive with bands of soldiers being drafted into position.

Jack looked down with kindling eyes and flushed cheeks, and almost immediately a strange sort of roar began to run through the ranks. The cause of this excitement appeared to be the banner which had just been unfurled in the royalist ranks.

"The red dragon! the red dragon!"

Leofric and Jack looked wonderingly at each other.

"What mean they by that? What is the red dragon?" they asked. And Amalric, looking over his shoulder with a stern, set face, made reply,—

"When the ensign of the red dragon is unfurled in the ranks of the King, it is the sign that no quarter is to be given. We are to be slaughtered like sheep in the shambles if it pleases Heaven to give our foes the victory."

At the sound of these words a strange murmur ran through the ranks. Men gripped their sword-hilts hard, and set their teeth with a sense of iron resolution, and an indignation which would go far to win the day.

The field was in motion. The quick eyes of those posted upon the hillsides saw that the royalists had begun to move. Prince Edward on the right, was bearing vehemently upon their left wing, which consisted of the London levies. The Prince had been bitterly angry with the men of London ever since they had stoned and insulted his mother's barge, as she tried to escape by water from the Tower, but was driven ignominiously back by the citizens, who hated her for her many extortionate charges upon the city. Now he was rushing furiously against his foes, who wavered before the charge of trained horsemen. But no more of that could Leofric and Jack see, for at this moment their own ranks were called upon to move forward, and, behold, the battle had begun!

The King's brother, Richard of Cornwall, King of the Romans, was leading his forces against them. In another moment the rival armies had met with a crash of arms. There was a stifling sense of pressure, and then a recoil; whilst over the heads of their own men came hurtling showers of stones cast from above at their assailants, and soon the closely-serried ranks both of friends and foes were a little broken and scattered, whilst man met man and horse charged horse in the indescribable *mêlée* of a hand-to-hand battle.

Side by side, shoulder to shoulder, rode Amalric, Leofric, and Jack. They felt rather than saw the recoil of their foes, who at first had been pressing upon them with such fiery vehemence. Charging down the hill, they met the answering charge of mail-clad warriors; but the slope of the field was in their favour, and they hewed them down and routed them, despite the fiery resistance they met.

They were down upon the level now, and before them

stood the serried ranks of the centre of their foes' army
behind which floated the red dragon, marking the spot
where the King himself was posted.

But from behind, the ranks of the young De Montforts
had been reinforced by the contingent commanded by the
Earl himself, and the knowledge that their great leader
was with them and amongst them seemed to turn to steel
the muscles of the soldiers, and with shouts and cries of
fury and anticipated triumph they hurled themselves again
and again against these opposing warriors, till at last they
felt the solid wall give way before them, and with a yell
that rent the firmament they dashed into the breach.

" For God and Earl Simon ! for God and Earl Simon !"
was the cry upon the lips and in the hearts of the soldiers
as they felt the breaking up of their royalist foes.

Leofric had been fighting might and main, blindly sometimes, and breathlessly, yet with a skill and fury which
surprised even himself.   Suddenly he began to feel everything swimming around him.   He had been conscious of no
wound, but he saw that his blood was flowing fast.   If he
fell in the midst of this *mêlée*, he must surely be trodden
to death in a moment.   But he was becoming so faint that
he scarce cared what became of him, when he suddenly
felt an arm cast about him, and heard a voice say in his
ear,—

" Hold up, good comrade, hold up ! I will get thee out
of this. The victory is won ! The King is wounded and
in full flight ! We may quit the battlefield with glory
now. The day is ours !"

An hour or two later Leofric opened his eyes to find himself lying in a tent, amid a number of other wounded men, the honest face of Jack bending over him with kindly solicitude and concern.

" How goes the day ? " he asked, as soon as he could find voice ; and Jack's face beamed all over as he replied,—

" Why, right gloriously ! The King's forces are routed. He has taken shelter in the Priory. The King of the Romans has shut himself up in a windmill, whence he has been besieged by our men, who will shortly have him out— treacherous Richard, as all call him, who once called himself the Barons' friend. I trow there be no man in all the kingdom more hated than he ! "

" And the Prince ? " asked Leofric, striving to sit up in his excitement, but finding himself exceeding weak.

" Why, the Prince might have made things worse for us, had he been as wise as he is brave. He routed the London wing, but pursued them so furiously and so far that whilst he was slaying and hacking the fortunes of the day went against his father. Then on his return, ere he knew this, he set his men against the litter which stood beside the standard, and where he thought to find our great Earl seated. His men came furiously up the crest of the hill, and surrounding the litter began to cry out, ' Come forth, come forth, Simon, thou evil one ; come forth from that litter, thou worst of traitors ! ' And at last, getting no response, they broke open the litter, and in the confusion which followed, all the four hostages, men of their own party, were hacked to death by their own friends ! "

"Poor creatures!" said Leofric, with compassion; "that was a gruesome fate. But what did the Prince next?"

"He made a circuit to get to his own side of the plain once more, and only a while back was about to make a sally; but the Earl sent proposals for a truce, and these were accepted: for indeed what could even so brave a Prince do, with a band of men exhausted by fighting and marching, and dispirited to the verge of despair by the knowledge that the cause was lost?"

"Hast thou seen aught of Hugh?" asked Leofric; but Jack shook his head. He had had his hands full in helping first his own wounded comrade, and afterwards those who lay stretched upon the field of victory. He had been working and toiling from dawn till now—marching, fighting, and carrying in the wounded. He had had no thoughts to spare for any but his own side.

A shout of laughter, and the tramp of many feet, announced that something fresh had happened. There was a great tumult of sound, and Jack darted out to see what was happening.

He came back with his face bubbling over with mirth.

"They are bringing in Richard, treacherous Richard, the King of the Romans," he cried—"he who, in his letter but the other day, called himself 'always august.' They are calling him a bad miller, and twitting him with his august windmill! Oh, thou shouldest see his face! He looks like a dozen thunder-clouds all rolled into one!"

A great burst of cheering from some place hard by told that the prisoner had been brought to Earl Simon's tent; and with the failure of the light came the knowledge that the battle was fought and won. The field of Lewes had decided the fate of the country for the present. The Barons had achieved an undoubted victory.

CHAPTER XXIV.

AFTER THE BATTLE.

"Sitteth all still, and hearkeneth to me:
The King of Alemagne, by my loyalty,
Thirty thousand pounds asked he,
For to make the peace in the countree,
    And so he did more.
Richard, though thou be ever trichard [treacherous],
    Tricken [trick us] shalt thou never more.

"The King of Alemagne gathered his host,
Made him a castle of a mill-post,
Went with his pride and his mickle boast,
Brought from Alemagne many a sorry ghost
    To store Windsor.
Richard, though thou be ever trichard,
    Tricken shalt thou never more."

THIS was the song which resounded through the camp of the victors after the battle of Lewes, together with others in praise of De Montfort, too lengthy to be quoted here.

Richard, the King's brother, King of the Romans and Earl of Cornwall, was the especial butt of the popular disfavour, and his recent behaviour had added greatly to his unpopularity.

He had betrayed a very grasping spirit in claiming as his individual due the entire sum of thirty thousand pounds, offered by the Barons as an indemnity to the King; and his haughty note to the Barons afterwards was taken in very bad part, seeing that once he had been their friend and ally. He was looked upon as being both treacherous and vindictive; and this song (which is remarkable as being the earliest specimen of its kind in the English language, nearly all such compositions being in Norman-French or Latin up to this date) was composed in the camp at Lewes, and sung lustily by the soldiers in the very ears of the captive Richard.

Leofric, from his place in the tent where the wounded had been conveyed, could hear the sounds of mirth and mockery as the triumphant soldiers passed to and fro. His friends came in and out with various items of news; and upon the second day a new face looked in upon him as he lay, and eagerly stretching forth his hands, he exclaimed,—

"Hugh, is that truly thou? Right glad am I to see thee. I did fear that thou mightest have been numbered with the slain. But how comest thou hither?"

"I came with the Prince, to give myself up prisoner, even as he hath done. But they desire no captives save a few of the highest in the land. Your great Earl knows how to use nobility and generosity in the hour of triumph. He even spoke a kind word to me, and restored to me my liberty. I heard that thou wert here, and came to visit thee. How goes it with thee, good comrade? I trust thy wounds are not grievous."

"Nay, little more than scratches; only there be many

of them, and I did lose much blood ere I was aware. Tell me of thyself, Hugh, what didst thou do? I see thou hast thine arm slung in thy scarf. Thou hast not come off scot-free."

"A fellow broke the bone of my sword arm with his axe," answered Hugh; "but that matters the less, since there will be no more fighting, they say, these many days. All the talk is now of peace and brotherly accord. There are messengers passing to and fro betwixt the Earl and the King; and already the royalist troops are melting away. I cannot grieve that the fight has ended thus, even though I fought upon the royal side. I love not the crooked dealings of the King; and I hate the minions he surrounds himself with, so that honest subjects cannot get anigh him. It will be well for the land when these are banished. And yet I would that the King should be a King, and not a puppet even in the hands of a worthy man such as your Earl."

Leofric made a sign of assent. He was enough of a student and scholar himself by this time to be well aware that no subject, even though he were the highest in the land, could long rule in the name of a practically captive King. It was against the traditions and instincts of the nation. The people might support a movement for the redress of crying grievances, even at the expense of the King's liberty; but when things had been put upon a better footing, jealousies were certain to awaken, there would come disunion amongst those who had been united in the hour of peril, and he who had been regarded as the

saviour of the nation at this crisis would doubtless come
to be looked upon as a tyrant and even a usurper, if he
succeeded in imposing his will upon the King for any
length of time, and held the reins of government firmly in
his hand. Something of this had been seen already, after
the Provisions of Oxford had made De Montfort so great a
man in the kingdom. It was likely to be seen again more
markedly now, when a great victory had put him in actual
possession of the person of the King.

Nevertheless the news which reached the camp as to
the terms suggested by the Barons showed that these were
characterized by great moderation. "The Mise of Lewes,"
as it was called, provided that all foreigners should be ex-
cluded from office, though aliens should have free entry
into the country for trading and private purposes. The
royal revenues were to be managed with greater economy,
and the abuse of church patronage to be checked. Other
disputed matters were to be referred to arbitrators—some
French and some English nobles.

For the rest, a general amnesty was to be declared, and
a release of prisoners on both sides effected. The King
and the Prince, and a few of their next of kin, would remain hostages in the hands of the Barons; but all men of
lesser account might return to their own homes.

Indeed, it was the Earl's great desire that peace should
be restored to the troubled kingdom, and that the ravages
of the recent campaign should be forgotten.

Jack came bursting into the tent where Leofric lay, his
face alight with excitement.

"Hast heard the news? The Earl has made a proclamation throughout the camp ordering all the clerks and students of Oxford to return to their studies. As a token that he means what he says, his own son is to head a party of returning students. Amalric has said that he will take me in his train, and has sent me to see if thou canst likewise travel. On the morrow Lord Henry sets out along the coast in charge of his cousin, the Prince, who is to be taken for security to Dover Castle. Lord Amalric desires to travel a part of the way with them, and then turn northward and pass through London, which is said to be full of rejoicing and triumph. They say the Earl and the King will go thither in company shortly. I trow it will be a gallant spectacle, and I would be there to see. Hugh will go with us, and Gilbert likewise, and others who have followed the fortunes of the Earl's son. Prithee, say that thou wilt also be of our party!"

Leofric eagerly declared himself quite fit for the saddle. None of his wounds was severe, as he had said; and he was much restored by those few days of rest in the hospital tent. He would greatly have regretted the necessity to remain behind when his comrades moved onwards, and he at once left his bed and proceeded to array himself, and to walk forth leaning on Jack's sturdy arm.

The camp was in all the commotion of breaking up. Numbers of men had already been dismissed to their own homes. Hugh came up to his friends with a beaming face.

"Right glad shall I be to see Oxford again!" he said, "and to resume the peaceful life of study there. Battles

and camps are well enough in their way, and against a
foreign foe would I serve most willingly. But it is ill
work drawing the sword upon a brother Englishman.
Let me rather meet him in disputation and strife of well-
sharpened argument, than in the bloody field of battle!"

Leofric heartily agreed with this sentiment, and even
Jack, who had perhaps enjoyed the excitements of the
campaign more than the others, admitted that he would be
glad enough to see Oxford again, and resume his studies
there.

"It was the King's doing that ever we left at first,"
he said. "I trow his Majesty has had good cause to wish
that he had left the clerks of Oxford to their books and
studies. He has had reason to know that they can wield
other things than the pen, when the blood in them is
stirred up."

The comrades visited their horses and looked well to
them. A few days of rest and feeding upon the green
plains of Sussex had done them much good, and they
looked well able to carry their owners gallantly upon the
proposed journey.

"We shall be too large a company to push on very fast,"
said Hugh. "Moreover there will be interruptions in the
march from our friendly well-wishers, who will desire to
show us honour as we go. And if thou canst not ride
with the party, Leofric, why, thou and I will tarry behind, and send Jack forward to see all, and tell us what
has betided when we meet in Oxford again."

Leofric, however, expressed a hope of being able to ride

the whole way; and upon the morrow a gallant-looking company started forth eastward along the coast.

Prince Edward and his cousin, Henry de Montfort, were the two most noteworthy figures, the Prince being by far the more majestic and dignified, although Lord Henry had an ample dower of good looks and a corresponding amount of self-esteem. He and his brother Simon were already giving their father anxiety by symptoms of that rashness and pride which had a disastrous effect upon the fortunes of their house a little later on; but in private life they were amiable and warm-hearted, and towards their cousin Edward the whole family of the Earl felt a great affection. The young men had been comrades and playfellows in childhood and youth, and the fact that they had met in hostile fight but a few days earlier did not seriously interfere with amicable relations when brought face to face once more.

Nevertheless it was Amalric who was really the greater favourite of the Prince, and his face lighted brightly when he saw that he was to be of their company. Guy and Amalric were far more lovable in disposition than Henry and Simon, their elder brothers, and Edward greeted his younger cousin with affection and pleasure.

"So thou art on thy way back to Oxford? Would that I were going with thee! If I am to be kept in durance awhile, why not as well there as in another place? Had not Providence thought well to make a Prince of me, I would verily be a clerk of Oxford. Tell me some of thy student tales as we ride along, good cousin. I would hear of that great riot which disturbed the peace of the town just after I had been asked to keep away. I trow you clerks and students have other pastimes than the study of your books!"

The Prince laughed heartily at the tale told him of the obsequies of the shattered gates, and of the attack on the property of the hapless Mayor.

"So that is how you clerks learn to handle your weapons so well! I trow your Chancellor must have as hard a task in ruling his city as a monarch in ruling his kingdom."

And then the Prince suddenly grew grave, and fell into thought, perhaps revolving in his mind the events of his father's reign, and the incapacity he had shown in ruling his people in lawful fashion. He sat looking straight out before him with set lips and sombre eyes, and none dared speak to him again till the midday halt was called.

Then he roused himself, and was gracious and friendly of aspect to all. He recognized both Leofric and Hugh, and spoke to them both. Hugh had been with him in his band, and had fought lustily and well. He had won the approval of the martial Prince on more than one occasion since he had been with him, and now he greeted him with a smile.

"So thou art going to exchange sword for pen, and the strife of arms for the war of words? Well, I trust thy studies will not again be broken up by warlike clamour; and yet if it should so betide, I would that I might find myself surrounded by such trusty followers as thou hast proved thyself to be."

"My liege lord," said Hugh, slightly bending the knee, for he desired to show even more reverence to a captive Prince than he might have done to one having his liberty, "I trust that if such a day should ever come again, thou wilt find my poor sword again beneath thy banner. The Prince has but to command, and the soldier must obey."

Edward gave him a slight smile of gratitude and approval, and turned his keen glance towards Leofric.

"Ah, my friend of the boar-hunt! said I not that we should meet again some day? So thou hast been in the fight, and hast gotten some wounds? Well, well, it is but the hap of war. I know that thou canst strike a lusty blow when the fighting mood is on thee."

Leofric bent the knee, but made no answer. He loved the Prince, and found it hard to realize that they had fought in hostile camps. Edward asked no question; but Leofric knew he must be aware of this, and something like remorse filled his heart. War which pitted brother against brother, and subject against Prince, seemed to him a horrible thing, abhorrent in essence both to God and to man. The disease that was eating into the heart of the country might need the remedy of the knife; nevertheless the application of it was painful and terrible, and at that moment Leofric was keenly conscious of it.

Perhaps Edward guessed at the thoughts which were passing through his mind, for his own face softened slightly in expression as he said,—

"Think not that I reproach thee, good youth; I tell thee of a truth that were I in thy place, methinks I should act as thou hast done. These hideous things must needs be for the sake of the realm. But pray Heaven there be brighter and happier days in store for England yet. Leofric Wyvill, I once did promise thee the reward of thy lusty stroke which perchance saved the life of thy Prince. Not yet has come the day for the redemption of that promise. What can a captive Prince do for the recompense of those who have served him? But my word is passed, and I shall not forget. The time may come when I shall redeem that pledge. Till then I have naught but thanks to offer."

Then he passed upon his way into the interior of the inn, and Leofric turned upon Hugh with something almost like bitterness in his voice, as he said,—

"Why, why does such a son league himself to the crooked policy of such a father?"

. Hugh slightly shook his head.

"It is no love for the policy, believe me; it is filial duty towards his sire. How could a son take up arms against his father, without incurring the wrath of God? Or how can a son of the spirit of young Edward stand aloof whilst the sword is drawn against his father and his King? No, no, he can do nothing else than fight for him; but thou canst see for thyself how he feels in his heart. He hates the methods and the crooked ways of the King. Once let him sit upon the throne, and we shall see a different rule indeed."

Leofric was not destined to travel far with the cavalcade which escorted the Prince. That very night he was

attacked by an access of fever, brought on probably by
riding too soon ; and he had perforce to remain behind
when the troop started forth the next morning.

Hugh remained with him of his own accord, bidding
Jack go on with the others, and bring them all the news
when they met in Oxford. Hugh found his broken arm
rather stiff and painful, and was not sorry to be spared
the long days of riding ; whilst his heart was turning ever
more and more impatiently towards Oxford, where Linda
would be waiting for them, and whither they would travel
by easy stages so soon as Leofric was fit for the saddle.

They were detained a week at this place before they
attempted to resume their journey, and then they travelled
very leisurely. They found the country full of rejoicing
at the termination of the war and the success of the
people's party, as they liked to call it. Rumour declared
that there was to be a Parliament in London almost at
once, and that, besides the nobles and knights, "four discreet men" from some of the leading towns were to be
summoned to attend. This was a distinct step in the direction of constitutional government, and the policy of the
great Earl was warmly commended on all sides. Little
feeling at present existed with regard to the captive condition of the King. The nation began openly to say that he
was always the slave and captive of his own favourites.
It was better he should be in the hands of those who
cared for the liberties and rights of the English people than
in the hands of those who sucked the blood of the nation
and reviled its down-trodden sons at the same time.

Everywhere the name of Earl Simon was in all men's mouths. His praises were chanted aloud in rude songs, in which he was described as the saviour of his country, the instrument of God, the upholder of right and justice, the wisest, most valiant, and noblest of men.

Leofric began to wonder whether, indeed, the country would settle down contentedly to what was practically the reign of a subject, and that subject by birth an alien. For the moment they seemed to desire nothing better than that De Montfort should reign in the name of the King; but was it possible that such an anomaly could long continue? And what would be the result of the release of the King? for it was not possible that he should remain a permanent captive in the hands of his Barons.

These, and many like points, were discussed with keen interest by Leofric and Hugh as they pursued their leisurely journey. Hugh had a few stout serving-men in attendance on him, afterwards to make their way northward to his father's house. So the two youths travelled in comfort and safety, and were welcomed everywhere along the route as having been eye-witnesses of and partakers in the battle of Lewes.

But as they neared the familiar town of Oxford, public matters sank into a secondary place in the interest of the anticipated meeting with comrades and friends. Leofric's heart could not but beat with the thought of seeing Alys once more—although to him she was as a bright particular star, far, far above him, whom he loved and worshipped from a distance, with no conscious sense of anything nearer and more personal; whilst Hugh was engrossed by thoughts of Linda, from whom he had been long sundered, although, knowing her to be safe and happy, he had left her with a mind at ease.

Had their approach been seen? Surely it must have been; for as they approached the Castle by the Quaking Bridge, there was a little commotion at the gate, and in another minute Edmund came hastily forth, bare-headed, as if taken by surprise, his face alight with eager welcome.

"Now welcome, welcome, good friends! We have been wearying for news of ye twain. Many of our clerks and students have been flocking back from all parts of the country, some even from the field of Lewes; but none could give us tidings of you. One indeed declared that thou, Leofric, hadst been sorely wounded; but whether for life or death the fellow could not say. Come in, come in, and tell all thy tale.—Come in, good comrade Hugh; right glad are we to see thy face again! Peace and good-will everywhere abound. Oxford has begun to look like herself again. Come in and see my father. We have much to hear and to tell. Come and give us news of young Lord Amalric, for our Alys has been like a drooping flower ever since he departed; albeit, as I kept telling her, we should speedily have heard had any hurt happened to one of the sons of the great De Montfort."

Thus speaking, Edmund led the way into the Castle hall, where already the Constable, his wife and daughter, and Linda had gathered. Rumour had already gone forth that some arrival had taken place, and Sir Humphrey had

a warm greeting for the two young student-soldiers returned with news from the campaign.

But Hugh had no eyes for any save Linda. He
could not speak or think of anything in the happiness
of that meeting. It was Leofric who was forced to be
spokesman, and he was set down in the midst to tell his
tale; whilst Alys, from behind her mother's chair, hung
upon his words with kindling eyes, flushing and paling
cheeks, scarce drawing breath as he spoke of the perils of
the fight, and how he had been brought out of it by trusty
Jack. She did not look like a drooping flower any
longer as at the supper board she took her accustomed
place, Leofric being at her right hand. Father and
mother both noted the sudden change in her; and Sir
Humphrey said to his wife that night,—

"See what the news of Lord Amalric has done for her!
She is a changed being since we have known him to be
well and sound."

But Dame Margaret uttered a slight snorting sound, as
if she were less satisfied with what she had observed.

"If my Lord Amalric desires the hand of our daughter,
he had best lose no more time in the winning of it," she
remarked. "Else may he chance to win the casket when
the jewel it encloses has been stolen thence."

"What mean you, wife?" asked Sir Humphrey in
dismay.

Dame Margaret snorted again.

"Men have no eyes!" she remarked scornfully.

"But what mean you, wife? I would know more of this."

"Marry, then thou shalt. But I say not things are so; I only say what I fear. If the maid's heart be not rather given to Leofric Wyvill, the bachelor, than to the Lord Amalric, the Earl's son, then are mine eyes wofully at fault!"

Sir Humphrey looked first astonished and then scornful.

"Tush, woman!" he said impatiently; "the thing is impossible."

Dame Margaret pursed her lips and said nothing.

"It must not be!" cried the Constable, rather excitedly; "it must not and shall not be! The Earl is now the first man in all the realm. His sons will rise to be nobles themselves. It will be a great match for our little daughter, and she hath always been well disposed towards Lord Amalric."

"True; yet is she not better disposed towards another?"

"It shall not be!" cried the Constable once more. "I will put a stop to it at once. A daughter's hand is disposed of by her father. None shall dispute my right to give that of Alys where I will. The Lord Amalric has shown every disposition to ask it in marriage. And this I say and mean: if he ask it, he shall have it. The maid shall be a great lady yet, and I pray I may live to see the day."

The mother said nothing, only pursed up her lips a little. In her heart she was thinking that a sudden elevation to great power had often been followed by as sudden a fall. What if that should happen to the house of De Montfort?

CHAPTER XXV.

CHRISTMAS AT KENILWORTH.

"ALYS! Alys! Alys!" cried a clear young voice from above. Alys, muffled to the very eyes in her furs, and stiff from the exposure of her long ride, had been almost lifted from her saddle by strong arms, and carried within the hospitable portals of the grim-looking fortress. She was dazed with the change from snowy darkness to the blaze of light, confused by the number of strange voices and faces around her, and not even reassured by the welcome of Amalric, who was seeking to win from her one of the smiles that had become so much to him.

"Alys! Alys! Alys!"

The call was repeated in clear, imperious tones of bell-like sweetness; and Alys, lifting her eyes to see whence they came, saw the laughing face of the Demoiselle looking over at her from the dimness of the gallery above.

"Amalric, bring her hither to me; she is my lawful prey—my prisoner! Don't keep her standing down there in that crowd! I am waiting for her here. Bring her to me; I will warm her and make her happy. You clumsy men never understand how to do that!"

The next minute the two girls had met half-way up the great staircase, and the imperious Demoiselle, who had changed but little from the day on which she and Alys had last seen each other, dragged off her willing captive to the bedchamber which the little lady had insisted that her friend should share with her. It was lighted only by the glow of a roaring fire of pine logs, but it looked so bright and cheery and comfortable that Alys uttered a little exclamation of pleasure, and sank down before the grateful blaze, chafing her numbed hands and smiling up gratefully at Eleanora as she loosed her heavy cloak and hood and smoothed the ruffled hair beneath.

"It has been such a cold, cold journey!" she said. "Right glad am I that our mother and Edmund did not attempt it. Fifty times I was minded to implore my father to turn back; but I misdoubt me if he would have done so."

"Nay, fie upon thee for a coward," cried the Demoiselle, with uplifted finger, "with me, thine own friend, waiting for thee at the other end! To turn back is but the act of a poltroon! Fight and not flight is the motto of the brave. O Alys, what a world of things have happened since we said adieu! Didst ever think that men would say of my noble father that he was the uncrowned King of England?"

The maiden spoke with a great pride in her voice, and with a flash in her eyes that bespoke a sense of keen triumph. Alys shivered a little at the words; for she had heard them spoken with different intonation by others not very long before, and knew that a leaven was working in the country of which this child knew nothing as yet.

"My father leads the Council of Three, who really govern the realm," continued the Demoiselle, talking in her eager, rapid way. "They say that Gilbert of Gloucester will give trouble; he is showing himself unruly and rapacious. But I trow my father can control him. Oh, it is a wonderful power which my father has gained! All men bow down before him. And yet his heart is not puffed up; he is grave and sober in his bearing. Why was he not born the King, instead of Henry of Winchester —poor puppet, who can never stand alone, but must be propped up by the will of those about him? Why, my father is ten times more a King than he!"

"And so is his own son," said Alys gently. "If any ruled in the place of the King, methinks it should surely be the Prince."

"Ah yes," cried the Demoiselle quickly—"my cousin Edward. He is different indeed from his father, but he cannot be set upon the throne. If he could, perchance that would end the troubles. Didst know that he is at Kenilworth now? He has been in gentle captivity in many places these past months, and from the Castle of Wallingford but lately his friends sought to obtain his escape. But he is on parole, so he bid them depart. Nevertheless my father thought it not safe to leave him there longer; and now he is here, sharing our Christmas gaieties. I trow we will have a merry time."

But the little lady had much to ask as well as much to tell. She wanted to know where Leofric was, who had been so faithful an esquire to her brother, and had won her own esteem and good-will.

The colour rose in Alys's face as she made reply,—

"In sooth I have seen less of him of late. He is growing to be much sought after for his lectures, and in the spring he will take his degree as Master in Arts. Since that mandate from the King nigh upon a year ago there have been changes in Oxford. Many of the masters who went forth then to other places have not returned, having found pupils and work elsewhere. This has made it the easier for bachelors with good store of knowledge, like Leofric Wyvill, to gain pupils, and obtain the Chancellor's licence to lecture on many books. Men say that he will be a Regent Master ere long, and likely enough a Doctor in time. But for myself, I have not seen him oft of late. He is busy, and Edmund hath his own tutors and lectures now."

The Demoiselle glanced rather sharply into the face of her friend, and said questioningly,—

"Is that a note of melancholy I hear in thy voice?"

Alys shook her head, and her cheek flamed.

"I know not what thou dost mean by that, Eleanora. Come, let us talk of other things; and I must see to my toilet, if I am to be taken to thy lady mother for her greeting."

The Demoiselle put her arm about Alys as she looked into her face half archly, half pleadingly, and said,—

" Nay, chide me not, sweet Alys; for thou dost know I love thee, and that I would not even desire the happiness of calling thee sister, were it not for thine own happiness too."

At those words Alys caught her breath in a little gasp, and Eleanora tightened the clasp of her loving arms.

" My mother will indeed desire to see thee and to welcome thee, sweet Alys. Thou must know that well. But fear not what may befall. My father—ay, and Amalric too—will never urge thee to any act against which thy heart rebels. We cannot give our love as if it were a toy. Our hearts will speak, and they discourse eloquent music that no man hears save ourselves. I would fain call thee sister, but I will be thy friend. It shall never be said of the house of De Montfort that its sons wooed unwilling brides!"

The Demoiselle threw back her head with a gesture of pride, and then kissed Alys on the mouth. It was no revelation to Alys that she had been brought to Kenilworth with the idea of being shown there as the future bride of the Lord Amalric. Her father had never said as much openly, but she had had an instinct of this, and now these words from Eleanora showed her that she had not been deceived.

But it was not a subject on which she could speak. Her heart and mind were alike in a chaotic state. She revered the house of De Montfort; she had the warmest liking for Amalric, and would hate to give him pain. She might well have loved him, and she knew it, had there been no other image graven on her heart.   And now it was hard to know what to say or do.   Indeed she felt, whatever the Demoiselle might aver, that little option would be given her in the matter.   Her father would decide the question of his daughter's betrothal.   She would be expected simply to obey.   She could not urge any dislike to the chivalrous young lord who had honoured her by his preference, and to confess that she had given her heart to one who had never spoken a word of love to her was not to be dreamed of.

Just now, however, there was little time to think of such matters.   Kenilworth Castle was filled from end to end, and all the wild revelry incident to the Christmas season was in full swing.

Alys had seen nothing like it in all her life, and her whole time and attention was engrossed by watching the brilliant scenes about her.   She was admitted into the immediate family circle at the Castle—ranked as the companion and friend of the Demoiselle, tenderly treated by the Countess, and evidently regarded by the Earl and his sons as the future bride of young Amalric.

His own attentions were unfailing, but so chivalrously and deferentially proffered that she could not repulse him.   Indeed, she had no desire to give him pain, although in her heart of hearts she shrank from any open step which should force the thought of marriage upon her.

Just now, however, there seemed too much on hand for any one to press such a matter to a conclusion.   The Earl had his hands and his thoughts full to overflowing, and

although he went about with a face full of courage and
serenity, it could not be disguised that the clouds were
gathering ominously round him in many quarters.

For one thing, the Pope had excommunicated him; and
that was in itself a serious matter in those days. True, he
had appealed against the interdict, which had been brought
by a legate, and having been lost at sea had never been
delivered. The clergy of the realm had joined with him
in his appeal; and the Pope having died meantime, the
matter was still in suspense, and could not be settled till
a successor was chosen. So that for the present the Earl's
household received the benefits of the church, and were
not cut off from communion; but the cloud of uncertainty
rested over them, and made some even of their friends
look slightly askance upon them.

Nor was it any light matter that they held in their
power the person of the King's son.

Edward showed no resentment against his kinsfolk for
his captivity amongst them. He went about the Castle
and its precincts with a brave face and a light heart. He
played with the Demoiselle in the long corridors, helped
Alys with the intricacies of her embroidery silks, when in
the long evenings the party gathered together in some of
the family apartments. He tilted in the yards with his
cousins, and joined in all the revels which made the walls
of the Castle-fortress ring again. No word of complaint
ever crossed his lips. He never betrayed even a consciousness that he was followed and watched, and that he might
not walk or ride abroad without a goodly retinue.

There was about him, as the girls oftentimes agreed, a nobility and magnanimity which was something remarkable in one so young. He even talked of public matters with his uncle without rancour, and with a certain sympathy in the difficulties of the situation.

Personally, the Prince was greatly beloved by all at Kenilworth, and perhaps this made the position all the more difficult. None knew better than De Montfort that it would be impossible to keep the King and the Prince in permanent captivity, however easy and honourable that captivity might be. Yet, let young Edward once be at large, and so great a following would muster round him that he would have it in his power before long to reverse the success of the Barons, and once more set upon the throne his inglorious father, whose incapacity and powers of mischief-working had been so abundantly tested before.

"And my brothers do nothing to help my father!" once lamented the Demoiselle, with tears of anger in her eyes, coming to Alys to discuss some of the anxieties which from time to time she learned from her mother. "Guy and Amalric are too young to be entrusted with much power, else they might perhaps help. But Henry and Simon do naught but stir up strife and ill-will. As if it were not bad enough to have the Earl Gilbert desert our cause, they must go and challenge him in a tourney they desire to hold at Dunstable—openly showing that they hold him to be a foe. My mother says that my father will forbid the tourney, but that the rash and haughty spirit of Henry and Simon give him much pain and trouble. They are so puffed up they will not heed a word that is said to them. They are not worthy to be called my father's sons ! "

It was no wonder that the brow of the Earl was often lined with care, and that the glance of the eagle eye was often dimmed by clouds of anxiety and presage of coming woe. The old trouble with Richard of Gloucester was being repeated now with Gilbert, the son. Young as he was, he would not brook the control of Leicester's guiding hand. He resented his assumption of power, and was almost openly breaking away. None knew better than De Montfort that if once Prince Edward were at large, the whole Gloucester faction, and doubtless many more with them, would go over to him in a body. Already the nation was forgetting its grievances, and was pitying the royal captives. A spark would suffice in many quarters to cause an explosion of anger against him and his "usurpation" of practical monarchy ; and yet, as matters now stood, there seemed nothing for it but for him, in the name of King and Council, to sway the sceptre of the kingdom.

On New-Year's Eve a great banquet was to be held in the vast hall of Kenilworth. Despite the carking care that was gnawing at the heart of the Earl and Countess, the revelries of the season were kept up in full measure. Nothing was omitted which had ever had place before, and the close of the old year had always been celebrated by a great feast, which was kept up until the new year had been ushered in with shouts and songs and the draining of bumpers.

Alys and the Demoiselle had asked to witness the feast from the gallery above, as upon another occasion now several years distant. And as the Countess had no desire to be present herself, ready permission was given them, and they established themselves there, with Amalric as their companion, he having excused himself from sitting at the feast below.

Prince Edward was, however, there, seated upon the right hand of his uncle. His handsome face wore a rather set expression, and although he smiled and jested as the wine circulated and the huge dishes were brought in one after the other by staggering servants, he continued to wear the look of a man in whose head some great purpose lies.

What that purpose was, was presently revealed when the time came for healths to be drunk and speeches made. It was from time to time needful that De Montfort should remind his followers and retainers of their position, of the things which had been achieved, and of those which still remained to be done. It seemed a fitting time, at the close of this memorable year, to speak of the events which had marked its course, and the successes which it had witnessed. To discourse thus, with the Prince sitting by, was not perhaps the easiest of tasks; but De Montfort had a gift for moderation and tact in speaking when his temper was not ruffled. He played his part well, and elicited bursts of applause; and the Prince himself applauded when he spoke of the rights of the nation and the need for wise government by means of a council of Englishmen rather than a crew of foreign favourites. In the end the Earl looked directly at the Prince, drank to his good health and speedy release, when the arbitrators appealed to should have given their decision, and the coming Parliament have ratified the terms of the Mise of Lewes.

Thus openly brought into notice, the Prince rose to his feet, thanked his uncle and host for many kind marks of good-will, and expressed his recognition of the courtesy and friendliness with which he had been treated. But after having said this much he did not sit down; he stood looking around at the company with a strange intent gaze. Deep silence reigned in the hall, for all felt that there was more to come, and waited breathlessly to hear. De Montfort looked up with a keen, quick glance into the face of the Prince, and then a slight cloud as of anxious thought passed across his thin face.

"My lords and gentlemen," said the Prince, in clear tones that were heard all over the hall, "I have once before addressed you, even as I address you to-night. The sword had not then been unsheathed. My heart inclined to the cause which you have made yours, and which even this day I regard with much of good-will. But I warned you then that my duty to my father would compel me to withdraw from your counsels, should you elect to rise in arms against him. This has now been done. I kept the word I gave you then, and to-day I am a prisoner in your chief's hands. The fortune of the day is so far with you, but it may not always be so. As I made an open declaration upon that occasion, so I make another to-day. I have given my parole for the present not to seek to escape out of this honourable captivity in which I am placed; and I redeemed my word at Wallingford Castle, showing to you that when I say a thing, I mean it; when I make a promise, I keep it. Now, in the presence of all of you, and of you my uncle and cousins, I herewith declare that my parole is for one year, dating from the battle of Lewes, when I gave myself up into your hands. One year I give to you for arbitration, for the assembling of Parliament, for all the reasonable steps which a kingdom must take for the adjustment of difficult questions. After the expiration of that year my parole expires. I will not then be bound by any promise. If my liberty is not then accorded me, I shall seek, by whatever means I may, to attain it. Already the nation is impatient of seeing her King and her Prince in captivity. The thing, if needful for the moment, becomes a monstrous iniquity in time. It will not be suffered to continue. *I* shall not suffer it to continue. Shut me up if you choose in the lowest dungeon—keep all my friends away from me—treat me as you will, I shall find means to escape from your hands; and I shall then fight with every weapon in my power for the liberty of my father, and for the restoration of that monarchy which, even though abused, is yet the prop and the source of England's greatness, and which, purged of its faults, will yet shine with undiminished lustre!"

The Prince sat down amid a breathless silence. Men had not been prepared for any such open declaration, and it took them by complete surprise. The Earl himself felt that thrill of generous admiration which the speech had enkindled in many hearts.

"The father I can dominate; the son will be my undoing," was the thought that came to him at that moment, and he felt it still more so when young Simon sprang to his feet and began one of his ill-considered and haughty speeches, which was listened to with cold displeasure even within the walls of his own home, and which brought a little sarcastic smile to the lips of his cousin Edward.

The Prince turned suddenly to his uncle and said,—

"Uncle, I would that thou and I could rule this realm, and that my father and thy sons could play at holding mimic court and gay tourneys in sunny France. Then, methinks, we should see an end of this confusion. But fate has willed that we shall stand in hostile camps; only believe me that for thee and for thy aims and objects I have both love and reverence; and if the day shall come when I sit upon the throne of this realm, the lore I have learned from thee will be my safeguard when I am tempted to forget the lessons learned in the school of adversity, and to think myself too great a man to need to think of the welfare of my people."

Leicester's eyes suddenly softened; he put out his hand and laid it upon that of the Prince.

"I thank thee for that word, Edward," he said; "and believe me, I love thee as though thou wert mine own son. If it were possible, we would fight side by side; but thou hast chosen thy father's cause, and I am pledged to that of the nation."

"I know it cannot be," said Edward regretfully; "yet let us each preserve the love which one brave and honourable man may feel for another, even though he be a foe. In the days to come, if my star arise, and I in turn be victor, I will not forget the kindness I have received at thine hands. It shall be repaid—I promise it."

"But not to me," said Leicester gravely, "for with this cause I sink or swim—I live or die. If it is the will of Heaven to reverse the victory accorded to us, I shall not live to see the day. There is always a soldier's death left for the man who sees his cause lost."

"Nay," said Edward warmly—for, strange as it may seem, he was full of hope and courage to-day, whilst his victorious uncle seemed weighed down by a load of care— "thou must live to be mine adviser and friend; for the time will come when I shall need both, if indeed I live to sit in my father's place."

The Earl slightly shook his head, but uttered no word. He felt from time to time a strange presage of coming trouble, and to-night the feeling was strong upon him.

The Demoiselle in the gallery, leaning over and listening eagerly to all that passed, now turned back to her companions, almost stamping her foot as she cried,—

"I would I could put a gag in Simon's foolish mouth!

Why will he always seek to give umbrage by his arrogance and pride? He has no talents, no powers, nothing but the reflected glory of our great father's name; and yet, to hear him brag, one might well think that he was the lord of all the realm! Why have such sons been given to my noble father and royal mother? They have greatness, talent, goodness, power! Why are their sons such miserable braggarts? It makes my heart burn to think of it!"

But there was no time for the consideration of this point, for a sudden hush fell upon the hall. It was whispered round that the hour of midnight had all but arrived, and in dead silence the company awaited the stroke of the great bell which would clang overhead when the moment should have actually arrived. Glasses were filled, and the company stood, awaiting in breathless expectancy for the signal.

The Demoiselle pressed up close to Alys, and pointed to a dusky mirror hanging upon the wall of the little gallery in which they stood, which was more of an alcove than a gallery proper.

"Dost see yon mirror?" she whispered. "It was taken from one of the rooms and hung here, because they said it was an uncanny thing. They say that if you look in it as the bell tolls in the new year, you will see therein the face of the man whom you will one day marry. It was moved from the bedchamber, where once it stood, because they say it caused the death of a maiden who looked in it, and saw therein a skeleton form with a scythe over his shoulder. I looked once, but saw nothing. Wilt thou not look to-night?—only one maid may do so each year—and I will turn mine eyes away."

Alys was shivering with a strange sort of tremor. Suppose young Lord Amalric were to move so that his face should be reflected in the glass: would that not seem like an omen to her? But he was leaning over the balustrade and looking down into the hall below, and the Demoiselle linked her arm in his as though to keep him where he was.

The silence was a strange, uncanny thing in a place filled with a multitude of revellers. Alys felt her breath come thick and fast, and the colour ebb from her lips.

"Boom—boom—boom!"

The great bell overhead had begun to toll forth its message. Shivering all over, Alys felt her eyes drawn as if by magnetic attraction to the face of the dusky mirror.

Suddenly a little gasping cry broke from her, drowned by the sudden clamour that rose from below; for in the dim black surface of the ancient mirror she had distinctly seen the face of Leofric Wyvill form itself, and stand out distinct and clear!

CHAPTER XXVI.

PLOTS.

AT the sound of Alys's cry Amalric and his sister turned quickly round, and the next moment a startled exclamation broke from young De Montfort.

"Leofric! is this truly thyself? or do we see thy ghost?"

Trembling in every limb, scarce able to separate the real from the unreal, Alys turned round to see that Amalric was grasping the hands of some person who had just opened the little door in the alcove, which was opposite the dusky mirror, and it dawned upon her that it was no phantom face she had seen, nor yet the freak of a disordered fancy; but that Leofric Wyvill was at Kenilworth, and standing within a few feet of her.

Yet for the moment he appeared not even aware of her presence. He was speaking with Amalric in low, constrained tones.

"Say only that I am not too late. The Earl, thy father, how is it with him?"

"Why, well," answered Amalric, in amaze; "thou canst see him below thine own self. Something aged and worn he is by the cares which press upon him; but for the rest, well. What do thy words portend, good friend?"

"Have any mummers arrived of late at the Castle— mummers from foreign parts?" asked Leofric, still speaking hastily and urgently. "They were to be heard by New-Year's Eve. Has anything been seen of them?"

"I have heard naught," answered Amalric. "There be comers and goers all day long at such a season, and open house is kept for all who ask it at Christmas. But of foreign mummers I have heard no word. Come, speak to us more plainly. What dost thou mean? and what brings thee here in such breathless haste, looking more like a ghost than a man?"

"In sooth I have travelled something hard," answered Leofric, who was travel-stained and pale with weariness and lack of sleep. "But mine errand brooked no delay. There is a plot on hand to poison the Earl, thy father; and they who are the tools are sent hither in the guise of mummers—for all I know they may be mummers and jugglers by trade. But they come hither with fell intent, and are paid by the Queen for their crime."

"The Queen!" cried the Demoiselle in horror—"our kinswoman whose bread we have eaten! Would she plan such wickedness against my father?"

"That is the news that Gilbert Barbeck brought post-haste to Oxford. His father got wind of it through some of his sailors plying 'twixt here and France. You know, perchance, how the Queen and her son Edmund are trying by every means in their power to collect and land an army in England for the rescue of the King. Contrary winds and other troubles have baffled them hitherto, and now they are wellnigh desperate. It is supposed the idea has been proposed to the Queen that to rid the realm of the great Earl would secure her husband's liberty. Or perhaps it is some other person who has conceived it, and gives out that it is by the wish of the Queen. But however that may be, it is said of a certainty that a party of foreign mummers has started for Kenilworth, and that they are armed with a deadly draught, which is to be administered to the Earl ere they leave."

"And thou hast travelled all this way with the news?"

"It seemed the best thing to do," answered Leofric. "I know the way. Gilbert was already worn and weary with his ride from the south. And both secrecy and dispatch were needed. My pupils had many of them dispersed for the time being, and I was able to leave. I could not rest till I knew the rights of the matter, and whether in truth the evil deed had been accomplished."

At that very moment the doors of the great hall were flung wide open, and amid the plaudits of the company there rushed in a motley crew of strange-looking creatures, some disguised as gigantic beasts and birds, some in motley, like fools, with jingling bells, all wearing masks, and all capering about with antics and contortions, exciting outrageous laughter from the already hilarious company.

The leading figure was not bedizened like his troop, but wore a sombre black dress, which flowed round him in ample folds. His mask was black, and nothing of his face could be seen save a pair of shining black eyes. He uttered strange cries and calls, which were responded to by his troop, who varied the figures of their strange dance, and made picturesque groups and combinations as they moved about in the only open space in the hall, where the tables had been hastily thrust aside to give them room for their gambols.

Some of these creatures were jugglers, and performed feats of dexterity and sleight of hand which provoked shouts of wonder and admiration. Meantime, prompted evidently by the black-robed director, some of the servants had brought in a small table covered with a black cloth, and when this cloth was removed, the eager eyes of the onlookers fell upon certain strange-looking objects which caused many of them to exclaim,—

"He is an astrologer, and he will tell our horoscopes!"

At the same moment several of the strange-looking dancers whirled out of the hall, and came in again leading with care and reverence a white-robed, white-veiled figure, who came and stood beside the table, but rigid and still, as though hardly endowed with life.

At sight of that figure Alys gave a sudden start, and exclaimed in a low, frightened voice,—

"Pray Heaven that be not Linda! It is just her figure and her carriage! Oh, surely that magician cannot be Tito, and he have gotten possession of Linda for his evil practices!"

Leofric started, and gazed at the speaker with earnest eyes.

"It cannot be Linda; she was safe in Oxford when I left. But she told me that Lotta had lately disappeared, they knew not whither; only their brother Tito had once been seen lurking near the city, and it was thought he had perhaps come for his books and the instruments by which he wrought his unholy trade. Lotta had had the care of them since his departure, and had grown very strange. It may be that she has cast in her lot with him. But can that in truth be he?"

"He would sell his soul for gold," spoke Amalric between his shut teeth. "But he has put his head into the lion's den at last. If he has designs upon my father's life, we have a gallows on the wall whereon he shall pay the penalty of his sin."

"Methinks these mummers are no part of his real company," said Leofric. "Probably he has joined himself to them, and given them something to win him his entrance hither. But let us watch what he is doing. We must not let any devilry of his go unobserved."

"Nay, we will seek to catch him red-handed in the act!" hissed Amalric; "and methinks I will go below, the better to guard my father from his crafty wiliness."

The wizard, as he now openly declared himself to be, was busy practising the smaller arts of his calling upon the credulous, with results which appeared to them to be marvellous. But not content with that for long, he called upon the great ones of the company to come and hear what the future held for them—to look into the crystal, or into the magic mirror, and to ask of the white-robed vestal such things as they desired to hear.

Each person thus coming forward received from the veiled woman a cup containing water from a sacred well; this cup he drained, placed within it a piece of money, returned it to the vestal with a whispered question, and then, looking in the mirror or crystal, awaited either a reply from her lips or an image forming itself there.

It seemed as though the questioners heard or saw enough to mystify them, if not entirely to satisfy their curiosity, and there was quite a crowd around the recess where the wizard had established himself; whilst from time to time he called aloud on one or another of the company by name to approach and test his magic.

It was thus that the Prince and the Earl presently approached the table, partly from curiosity, partly from a sense of semi-superstitious belief in the power of these so-called magicians to read the future.

"Shall we try our fate?" asked the Prince, and he stretched out his hand for the cup.

It was given into his hands with some whispered words which brought a sudden flush into his face. He drained the cup, spoke a few words, and then came away with a strange expression in his glowing eyes.

"There is a spice of witchcraft about it," he said, with a laugh which was not perhaps quite natural; and he retired to the far end of the hall, grasping tightly in his hand a small fragment of paper which had been slipped into it, he scarce knew how or by whom.

The Earl had followed the example of his illustrious prisoner, his son Amalric keeping close at his side. He, too, took the cup from the hand of the maid; but ere he could lift it to his lips, Amalric cried out,—

"Have a care, sir; that cup is poisoned! Let the magician be seized till this thing has been inquired into!"

In a moment all was confusion and affright. The magician made a bound, as though to flee before hands could be laid upon him; but he was held by a dozen pairs of strong arms. He broke then into frantic pleadings and excuses; but no word was addressed to him until the draught intended for the Earl had been forced down the throat of a dog, which almost immediately was racked with violent convulsions, and died within fifteen minutes.

Sternly and with black brow did the Earl and his attendants look on. It was so easy to see what had been planned. The inquirer would have asked some question as to the future, would have received some terrible prophecy, and when this attack took him, those who stood by would think it an access of fear at what he had heard; and in the confusion the magician and his accomplices would effect an escape, even if suspicion did light upon them.

"How didst thou know this thing?" asked the Earl of his son; and Leofric was brought forward to tell his tale. A cry of rage and execration went up from the crowd as they listened. The terrified mummers, who knew nothing of the plot, slunk away and hid themselves in any dark corners they could find. No one heeded them, all eyes being fixed upon the magician himself; and when his mask was plucked from his face, it revealed the white, scared countenance of Tito Balzani.

In vain he pleaded his innocence, and implored mercy. There was no mercy in the stern faces around him. Even Prince Edward, in whose favour the intended crime was supposed to have been planned, came forward with wrath in his eyes, and desired the death of the miscreant.

"He dares to say that my mother was the instigator of the crime!" he cried. "Let him hang from the highest battlements for that foul lie! Some evil-disposed person, thinking to do us service, may have planned this hideous deed; but my mother—never! Let him die the death of a perjured traitor!"

"But my sister—who will care for my sister? She at least must not suffer for my sin!" wailed the hapless man. "It is Roger de Horn who ought to hang. It was he who showed me the gold, and tempted me to my ruin. But he ever escapes, and leaves me to bear the punishment. Let the woods be scoured for him, and I refuse not to die if he die too. But let him not escape. And, I beseech you, save my sister; for if she knew—the deed was none of hers."

"The maid shall not suffer; her sex shall be her safe-guard," answered De Montfort sternly. "And as for that miscreant, whose name I have heard before now, search shall be made for him, and he shall suffer the fate he merits. Assassins and their accomplices find no mercy at Kenilworth.—Guard him well, men, and with the first of the daylight let him die!"

Thus upon the morn of the new year, Tito Balzani met his death upon the battlements of Kenilworth Castle; but though the woods were scoured and the Castle hunted from end to end, no trace of the veiled maiden nor of Roger de Horn could be found. It seemed as if in the confusion the girl had slipped away, perhaps to give warning to their comrade without. None had seen her from the moment when Amalric had denounced the wizard in the hearing of the whole assembly. She must have taken instant alarm, and have made good a clever escape, leaving her hapless brother to his well-earned fate.

The mummers, who soon explained their innocence and ignorance, were permitted to depart unhurt; but from that day when he knew that his life had been attempted, a darker cloud rested upon the stern, worn face of De Montfort, and sometimes he would break into passionate speech when alone with his wife or his sons.

" If the realm has done with me and wants me no more, by the arm of St. James let them say so, and I will be content to return to France, and live a peaceful life there, away from all this stress and strife. Yet if I do, all will cry shame upon me for deserting the cause to which I am pledged; whilst if I stay, I am reviled alike by friend and foe, called tyrant and usurper, and charged with all manner of crimes, of which not one can be proven against me ! "

In truth, the Earl's position at this time was a very trying one. The Earl of Gloucester openly charged him with self-seeking and striving after personal aggrandizement, in order to cover his own defection from the cause of the Barons. De Montfort's sons fomented the dissensions by their haughty and overbearing conduct, so that all manner of charges were raised against them by their foes. True, the conditions imposed upon the captive King and Prince by the Parliament which met at Westminster early in the year placed almost regal powers in the hands of De Montfort; yet he himself knew that his tenure of power was most precarious. In that very Parliament the Barons' party had been most meagrely represented, so many nobles having declined to appear. Jealousy and party strife were doing their disintegrating work amongst the victors of Lewes, and the nation was beginning to murmur at the detention of King and Prince.

Plots of all sorts were being hatched for the deliverance of the latter (the King himself being personally useless to head any national movement), and the Earl, his uncle, was compelled by policy, as well as by his own sense of right and justice, to make his captivity as light and easy as possible.

So his friends were permitted access to him at Kenilworth—even such pronounced loyalists as Mortimer, Clifford, and Leiburn, who had declined to lay down their arms at the close of the campaign, but had retired into Wales in sullen displeasure, there to await the turning of the tide. A safe-conduct was granted to these and to other friends of the Prince to visit him in his captivity, albeit the Earl could not but be aware that in all probability the end of the matter would be that the Prince would escape from his prison, and immediately appear in arms against the foes of his father.

De Montfort was not, however, at Kenilworth in person now. He was in Westminster, directing the deliberations of Parliament; and Henry was left as the companion of the Prince, together with Thomas de Clare, brother of the Earl of Gloucester, and other knights congenial to the royal captive. The breach between Gloucester and Leicester had not yet been openly proclaimed, and no actual rupture had occurred between the members of the two houses.

Amalric had, together with Leofric and the De Kynastons, returned to Oxford. No formal betrothal had taken place between him and Alys. The affairs of the Earl had taken up so much time and thought, that there had scarce been space for the consideration of other matters. Moreover the father had once said to Amalric,—

"Press not the matter home too soon, my son. It may be that we are a falling, not a rising house. Link not the fate of an innocent maid with thine till we see whether this rising cloud will disperse again, or whether it will gather into a tempest that will overthrow us."

Nevertheless it was well understood by the two fathers, ere the Constable took his departure, that the betrothal of Amalric and Alys would, if all went well, take place very shortly. Both Earl and Countess bestowed upon her many rich gifts, and Amalric begged her acceptance of a costly ring, which she could not refuse, the eyes of her elders being upon her, although her heart misgave her that this would be regarded as a pledge when the time came for the settlement of the question of her marriage.

"It may be thou wilt learn to love him yet," whispered

the Demoiselle, who took a keen interest in the matter, greatly desiring to have Alys for a sister, and earnestly desiring her brother's happiness, yet feeling a keen sympathy with the unconfessed romance which she guessed at, and regarding Leofric as, after her own brother, a very proper mate for her friend. "Amalric is more like our father than any of them, and I trow he would be a gallant lover and a loyal husband. But thou shalt never be forced to do a thing at which thy heart rebels. I will myself tell him all sooner than thou shalt be made unhappy, sweet Alys."

But at that Alys shrank as though touched upon a wound, and made almost hasty answer,—

"Speak not so, dearest Eleanora; thou dost not know what thou sayest. I shall seek in all things to do right; I only wish that my poor heart were worth the winning of so gallant a gentleman as thy brother. I am sore ashamed oftentimes to think what a paltry thing he seeks after."

"It is not paltry to him, so it be all his own," answered Eleanora; but at that word Alys winced again.

However, the party for Oxford rode off from Kenilworth in due course, in good spirits—Amalric willing to wait for his betrothal till his father's affairs should be more fully arranged, yet full of confidence that the day would come when he could call Alys his own.

Meantime Prince Edward remained behind, the playmate of his little cousin Eleanora at Kenilworth, a pleasant guest and kinsman, never showing the least spark of resentment at his prolonged captivity, yet bearing

himself with a princely air to those about him, as though
he would have them remember that, if a prisoner, he was
a King's son and the heir of the realm. He received his
friends with pleasure, and held various consultations with
them at different times. Henry de Montfort looked with
some suspicion upon these meetings, and wrote once to his
father cautioning him to put a stop to them. But the
Earl would not do this. He felt keenly the difficulties
attending holding in captivity his monarch and that
monarch's son, and he was resolved to give as small
reason as possible for complaint.

The talk of arbitration was still going on, but few
believed in any important results, save perhaps the release
of King and Prince. Meantime weeks and months slipped
by in quick succession, and the affairs of the state so
engrossed De Montfort that he knew little of what went
on within the walls of his home, save what was reported
by his wife and son.

With the approach of summer, outdoor exercise and
amusements were taken up with zest. The Demoiselle
was a fearless rider, and loved to fly a falcon, or to gallop
side by side with her cousin over the green meadows and
golden moors. The Prince delighted in every sort of
manly exercise, and though always attended by a sufficient
escort, was permitted to indulge himself in these pleasures
round and about the Castle of Kenilworth.

Presents were from time to time sent to him by his
friends, and one day there arrived at the Castle a fine
horse, which had come from the Earl of Gloucester. The

Demoiselle was greatly pleased with the creature, and eager for her cousin to try it.

Upon the next morning, therefore, the party rode forth to a green meadow about two miles distant, bounded on one side by a wood ; and here Prince Edward laughingly challenged his escort to a series of contests of fleetness and strength. All entered with zest into the spirit of the thing. The horses were drawn up, and the Demoiselle was called upon to give judgment.

"Six times round shall be the course," cried the Prince, "and whosoever comes in first shall be victor."

"Agreed !" cried the other young men, all well mounted, as was needful when they had so great a prize as the King's son in their custody ; and forthwith the race began.

Six times round that great expanse of turf, six times round at the reckless speed which young knights strove to attain when engrossed in feats of skill and daring, was no small strain upon a horse's powers, and would be an excellent test for the stranger.

Breathlessly did Eleanora watch the gallant creatures sweeping round and round the course, sometimes one forging ahead, then another making a gallant dash and passing his comrade, but all the field keeping near together; for it was a point of honour with his escort not to let the Prince get far out of reach, and perhaps it occurred to Henry de Montfort that this might be a ruse on Edward's part to make some desperate effort at escape.

His year of parole had now expired. He was no longer bound by his plighted word. Perhaps that detail had

escaped the memory of the Earl; at any rate no request
or command had reached the captive for a renewal of the
promise, or for any stricter rule of captivity.

Eleanora, however, thought of nothing but the excitement
of the race; and when upon the sixth round the field
came sweeping up towards the spot where she had placed
herself, just within the friendly shade of the adjacent
forest, her face was flushed with excitement, and she cried
gaily,—

"Edward wins—the Prince wins!" just as he brought
his panting and foam-stained horse to a halt beside her.

Edward leaped from the saddle, and made his cousin a
graceful bow. There was a slight rustle in the thicket
close behind.

"Farewell, sweet cousin," he cried; "we shall meet again
ere long, I trow!" and before any of those about him had
taken in the sense of these words, the Prince had vaulted
upon the back of a strong young horse, led forth that
moment by an unseen hand.

With a shout and an oath Henry de Montfort sprang
forward, but was forcibly held back by young De Clare.
The next minute the Prince was galloping off at a pace
which rendered it impossible for any of the jaded horses
to strive to emulate.

"Farewell, gentlemen," cried Edward, waving his hand;
"I thank you for your. courtesy and good company these
many days. And tell my royal father that I shall soon
see him out of ward! A merry meeting to us all another
day!"

The last words were inaudible. Already the receding figure was disappearing from their view.

De Clare burst into a loud laugh, and turning fiercely upon Henry de Montfort he cried,—

" Ride after him and welcome if thou wilt, young fool ! He is by this time with Roger Mortimer and a goodly following, who will hack thee in pieces with a right good will ! I go to join them and my noble brother. Neither Gloucester nor England will long be content to be ruled by King Simon the usurper !"

NOTE.—The escape of Prince Edward really took place from Hereford, though in the same fashion as that described above.

CHAPTER XXVII.

THE CAPTIVE A CONQUEROR.

"WE shall meet again!" the Prince had said as he rode off from Kenilworth upon that bright summer's morning.

The time was drawing near when that promise was about to be fulfilled—when Edward, the King's son, was to come to Kenilworth once more, not as captive, but as conqueror.

All England was up in arms, watching with a sense of breathless expectancy the result of the collision, when the armies of Prince and Earl should stand face to face and meet in mortal conflict.

De Montfort was still the idol of the people, and many a notable fortress and city was in his hands, declaring for him and his cause. But the anomaly of a captive King ruling through and by the will of a conquering subject was becoming intolerable to knights and nobles. It was a state of affairs which could last only so long as King and Prince remained captives. The moment young Edward was free, ready to head a party that was already gathering enthusiastically about him, De Montfort knew that a great and grave peril threatened him and his cause. They had the King in their hands, and the King was induced to disclaim and denounce his son as "a son of rebellion;" nevertheless all the world knew that, were Henry himself free, he would not lose a moment in joining young Edward, and in crushing by every means in his power the strong opposition of his Barons.

And now the Barons' party was split and rent. Gloucester and all his following had gone over to the Prince. He was master of all the line of the Severn, and his own county of Chester had unanimously declared for him.

London and the Cinque Ports were all in the Earl's interest, and the Welsh had joined with him against their English foe. The struggle was plainly to take place out here in the west, where the Prince seemed to be gathering power and the Earl losing it, unless indeed the ·vild Welsh kerns could be regarded as a set off against the desertion of English knights and nobles.

The heart of the Prince beat high with anticipation of coming triumph. He was at Worcester, and his position was not without elements of peril; for Leicester was at Hereford, and was looking for reinforcements from his son Simon, whom he had summoned from the south to meet him. It was rumoured that Simon was returning by way of Kenilworth, and it was the purpose of the Earl to hem in the army of the Prince between his own lines and the advancing forces of his son. If he could achieve this purpose, all might yet be saved; but Simon had already delayed too long, and even now no certain tidings of his whereabouts had reached the Earl's camp.

The household of Kenilworth was broken up. Almost immediately after the escape of the Prince, De Montfort had sent his son Amalric to fetch his mother and sister away to some safer place, nearer to the coast, where they would be farther removed from the scene of conflict, and ready to leave the country should the day go against them. The Countess with her daughter was now at Dover, eagerly seeking to gather and send reinforcements to her lord in the west.

Some of these things were known to Edward as he lay in his quarters at Worcester; and yet his soul was in no wise dismayed, for he was surrounded by brave hearts and willing hands, and had a premonition within him that the tide of fortune had turned, and that the days of his adversity were drawing to a close.

He was walking to and fro in meditation in the precincts of the Cathedral, where he had heard mass earlier in the day, when the sound of rapid approaching steps caused him to turn, and he saw Hugh le Barbier hastening towards him.

"Comest thou with tidings?" asked the Prince eagerly.

"I have been told that a woman has arrived at the city, desiring speech with the Prince," answered Hugh. "She will not answer questions, nor unveil her face, but says that she comes from Kenilworth, and that she brings tidings for the ears of the Prince. Since she would not say more whatever was asked of her, I came forth to find you. Will it please you to grant her an audience? If she comes indeed from Kenilworth, she may bring news worth hear-

ing, for men say that young Simon de Montfort is collect-
ing reinforcements there."

"I will see her at once," answered the Prince. "Go,
have her brought to my quarters, and come thou thither
thyself. It may well be that she brings tidings. I will
hear what she has to say."

Hugh hastened away, the Prince returned to his lodgings, and before long there was brought before him a
veiled figure that seemed strangely familiar, albeit for the
moment he could not recollect where or in what circumstances he had seen it before.

"Who art thou?" he asked courteously; "and whence
dost thou come? and what is thy message?"

"I come from the forests surrounding the Castle of
Kenilworth," answered the veiled woman in a low voice.
"I have come with news for thee, O Prince. I have sworn
to be avenged upon the house of De Montfort for the death
of my brother. I come now to sell one scion of that
bloody house into thine hands!"

As she spoke the woman threw back her veil, and Hugh
gave a great start of surprise. For standing before him,
wan and wild, haggard and dishevelled, was the once
beautiful Lotta Balzani, the woman who had once madly
loved himself—or feigned to do so—the twin sister of his
own wife!

For Hugh was married now. He had wedded Linda
shortly after the battle of Lewes, with the full consent of
his parents. His wife was not far away, for Hugh's home
lay not any great distance from this town, and he had but

lately parted from her to join the standard of the Prince. With a great astonishment in his eyes he gazed at the changed face of Lotta. There was in her look something of wildness akin to madness, and when her eyes met his she gave no sign of recognition. It seemed as though the present had completely blotted out the past.

The Prince was eyeing her intently, almost sternly.

"Art thou the veiled woman who whispered strange words to me at Kenilworth on New-Year's Eve, and brought to me a word in writing from my mother?"

"The same," answered Lotta, in her still, low-toned fashion.

"The sister of him who did strive to do to death mine uncle, the Earl of Leicester, in his own house? Was it, in sooth, thine hand which placed the fatal chalice in his?"

"It was!" answered Lotta, flinging back her head in a superb gesture of scorn; "and would that he had drained it on the spot! I knew not then what it contained, though I would have given it to him even had I known; for why should I pity or spare? none has ever showed pity upon me! But when he did to death my brother—when I saw that lifeless form swinging from the battlements of the Castle in the dim light of dawn—then, then I lifted my hand to heaven, and vowed vengeance upon Earl Simon and his house! I have bided my time—I have waited and watched—and now the hour for vengeance is at hand. I will sell him into the hand of his foes, even as Jael sold Sisera. Would that I could with these very hands drive a nail into his temples, that he should no more lift up that proud head!"

There was something so wild and strange in the manner of the woman that the Prince recoiled a little, and glanced at Hugh with questioning eyes.

"I know her well," he replied in a whisper to the Prince. "She is that strange creature of whom we have told you, the twin sister of my wife—the one of whom we heard that she had been dabbling in black magic and forbidden arts, and that she had disappeared from her home, no one knew whither."

Edward, who had the proverbial memory of royalty, bent his head. He remembered the strange story told him of the twin sisters, and the adventures which had befallen Hugh during his courtship of the one. Little likeness now existed between the gentle Linda and this gaunt, haggard sister; but the Prince's eyes rested with interest upon the once beautiful face, and he spoke more gently as he put the next question,—

"But the Earl of Leicester is at Hereford; what canst thou do against him?"

"Simon the elder may be there, but Simon the younger is at Kenilworth—feasting, drinking, idling his time away; whilst his men lie not within the strong walls of the Castle, but in the village—unprotected, careless, secure! They spend their days in drinking confusion to the Prince and his army, and laugh to scorn all thought of fear. Instead of pressing on to join his father, the foolish youth delights himself in his present pleasant quarters, and sends forth

wine and all good stores from the Castle, to refresh and
strengthen the men after their march, as he says, but
rather that they may enjoy themselves and sing songs to
his honour and glory. He is so puffed up that none may
speak a word of warning to him. Fall then upon him.
Cut his army in pieces. There will be none to resist, none
to give battle. All are sunk in the security of the fool;
the Lord will give them a prey into thine hand."

Edward's face lighted up with a strange expression. If
this news were indeed true, it was a great thing for him to
know. He had been aware of his own peril should father
and son effect a junction, and he had marched thus far to
seek to avert it. If he could fall upon young Simon's
army in this state of demoralization, and effectually rout it
or cut it to pieces, why then he could give battle fearlessly
to the Earl, with at least equal chances of success.

But if this should be a trap?

He looked earnestly into the woman's face. The eyes
were wild, but there was no shiftiness in them. Rather it
seemed as though a fire of fury burned within her—as
though she were inspired with a prophetic fire. Suddenly
she raised her arms and called aloud in tragic tones,—

"Fall upon them! fall upon them! do unto them as
they have done! The Lord has given them an easy prey
into thine hand. Let not one of them escape thee! Slay
them without mercy, even as Elijah slew the prophets of
Baal at the brook Kishon. Let the river which washes
the walls of Kenilworth be dyed red by the blood of those
that serve the bloodthirsty Earl, who slew my brother!"

The Prince turned to Hugh and said in a low voice,—

"Methinks she speaks truth. These may be the words of madness, but not of falsehood. I will forthwith summon the men, and to-night we will make a rapid march and seek to surprise this sluggard captain. But what shall we do for this poor creature? She is not fit to be left to wander in the woods as she speaks of doing. She should be cared for somewhere, and brought if possible to her right mind."

"I will take care of her," answered Hugh quickly; "I will take her home to my wife, her sister. If any one can do her good, it will be my gentle Linda. Methinks that the old fire of malice and jealousy is burnt out. She seems not to know my face or voice. Let me have the charge of her, and I will join your highness's forces at Kenilworth as soon as may be."

"Yes, that will be best," answered the Prince. "Take her to thy home and thy wife, and leave her not till thou dost see all well betwixt them. Then follow me if thou canst; for methinks the tide of battle is about to turn, and that soon I may have the power as well as the will to reward those faithful and loyal servants who have followed me in the days of adversity."

Hugh approached Lotta, who with trembling hands was drawing the veil over her face once again, and he noted that she seemed to sway like a broken reed.

"Lotta," he said, in a very gentle tone, "come with me, my sister. I will take thee to Linda."

A little shiver ran through her frame, and suddenly she spoke in wild, eager tones,—

"Linda! Linda! Linda! O sister, sister, have pity, have mercy upon me!" and then she burst into wild weeping, and sank senseless to the ground at his feet.

A litter was quickly prepared, Lotta was placed in it, and before nightfall Hugh had arrived with his charge at the door of his own home.

Already the stir of arrival had aroused the inmates, and Linda came running forth from the parlour, uttering a cry of joy as she flung herself upon her husband's neck. Then Hugh, holding her close to him, whispered in her ear the strange story he had to tell, and Linda approached the litter with a face full of awe, affection, and eagerness.

"Lotta!" she said softly, "dear, dear Lotta! Thou hast come back to me—at last!"

With a strange strangled cry Lotta sprang forward, clasped her sister wildly in her arms, and then once more fell senseless to the ground.

Late that night, as Hugh sat over the fire after having told all his tale to his parents, who had then gone to bed, the door opened, and Linda stole in, a strange expression upon her pale face. She made straight for the shelter of her husband's arms, and lay there, the tears coursing quietly down her face.

"How is it with Lotta, sweetheart?" he asked.

"Hugh," answered Linda, "I think she will die; but she has no desire to live. I think she has bitterly repented of the past; and if she can but lay aside her thoughts of hatred, and learn to forgive even her enemies, methinks death would perhaps be the happiest thing for her.   Oh, she has had a strange and terrible life! Heaven grant that she has not lost her soul, seeking after unhallowed things! But that was Tito's fault.   Surely God will not visit it upon her!"

Then Linda told to her husband the tale that she had heard in fragments from her sister's fevered lips.

After the failure of the second attempt upon Hugh's life and liberty, when Lotta had been forced to the conclusion that she would never win him against his will, and when Tito and Roger, who had been the authors of both plots, had been forced to fly, the unhappy girl had turned her attention to the study of those black arts of magic and mystery which had so fascinated Tito, and of which he possessed a certain amount of knowledge, gleaned from books in his possession.   Lotta now studied these, with the result that a morbid and unhealthy curiosity arose within her, and she believed herself gifted by some occult powers which she might develop, did she but know how.

Thus it was that when, after a considerable interval, Roger and Tito ventured once more to return to England, and Tito desired to obtain possession of his books and other things, he found that Lotta was eager and willing to join them; and in their travels she proved a valuable ally, her gifts of thought-reading and her mesmeric powers, which rapidly developed with practice, making her a useful medium.

They travelled both in England and in France, and after

a time she married Roger de Horn, who appeared to have transferred to her the fierce affection he had once shown for Linda. It did not appear, however, that her heart was greatly drawn towards her husband. It was more of Tito that she talked, and his untimely and tragic death was plainly graven upon her heart in characters of fire.

Of the poisoning plot itself Lotta had small knowledge. She could not say at whose instigation it had been planned, though she knew that a large sum had been paid to her husband and brother for the death of the Earl, which they had sworn to compass. Part of the reward was paid beforehand, but the bulk was to be given if the matter were brought to a successful issue. When all was lost, Lotta had rushed out to seek to rouse Roger to some desperate attempt at the rescue of the hapless Tito. But not only did Roger refuse to move hand or foot; he also forcibly withheld her from seeking to save him or to die with him, as she desired. Since then there had been burning within the sister's heart a fierce flame of hatred against the Earl who had condemned her brother, and against the man who refused to try to aid his comrade in the hour of extremity.

She had refused to leave the neighbourhood of Kenilworth, and Roger had seemed afraid to leave her there alone. They had led a strange life in caves and fastnesses of the forest, living upon such game as they could snare and shoot, and upon the wild berries and herbs of the woods. They had money, and occasionally bought from the peasants, but feared to show themselves openly; for it was said that there was a price set upon the heads of the accomplices of the wizard, and they were afraid of being recognized.

Now, however, in the confusion and excitement of Lord Simon's arrival with his disorderly host, and their ill-advised stay at and about the Castle of Kenilworth, Lotta felt that her day of vengeance had come. Without a word to her husband—who was drinking with the soldiers, secure now from recognition in so great a company—she had started forth to find the army of the Prince, and having delivered her foe into the hands of the enemy, it seemed as though all wish for life had expired within her. To be avenged for the fate of Tito had been her one desire; if that were accomplished, she seemed to have nothing else for which to live. But she had turned with all the affection of childhood towards her sister, and Linda's tears flowed as she spoke of this. Lotta appeared to have no real recollection of the episodes of her life in which Hugh had a part. When Linda had spoken of them, she had assented with something of perplexity in her face, but without seeming to recollect fully what it was all about. She appeared to know that her sister was married, and showed no emotion at the sound of her husband's name. To hold Linda's hand, to feel her near, to feel her kisses on her cheek, appeared all she wanted. She was so tired, she kept saying, she wanted to rest— to rest. And presently when she sank to sleep, Linda had gone to find her husband to tell him all.

"I must forth to join the Prince to-morrow," he said;

"but I am right glad to leave Lotta so well cared for. Perchance she will live to be our sister and friend yet; and I will seek news of that evil man her husband, and we will hope that he may yet come to repent of his sins. Keep her safe, and let her rest. Whether she live or die, we shall always be glad that we have seen her again, and that she has returned to her better self."

Hugh rode forth at break of day, after a few hours of rest, and in due course found himself drawing near to Kenilworth. The sun was sinking by that time, and he was aware of a great tumult and excitement as he approached. All the country folks were in a state of the greatest agitation and alarm, and from them Hugh first learned the nature of the engagement in which he had not partaken, but which had occurred early that very morning.

It had been as Lotta had described. In fancied security, in the heart of his own county, where all were loyal to the cause, the younger Simon had neglected all precautions, had left his soldiers outside the Castle walls, and had not even posted sentries to watch the roads.

At dawn upon that fatal first of August, the sleeping soldiers had been awakened by the clash and crash of arms, and by loud, fierce cries.

"Come forth, traitors; come out of your holes, ye dogs! Ye shall all be slain. Ye have betrayed your King. His vengeance be upon you!"

Then had followed a scene of indescribable confusion. The wretched men, thus awakened from sleep, their enemies actually upon them, sprang from their beds, and rushed half naked to their death. Some fought gallantly for their lives, and fighting fell. Some fled across the moat, and found a temporary asylum in the Castle with Lord Simon himself, who, paralyzed by terror, could do nothing but hide behind his strong walls, with a few of his own immediate knights and gentlemen about him, whilst his army melted like snow before this vigorous attack, and the waters of the moat were dyed red with the blood of the slain.

This was the tale that Hugh heard from the terrified peasants as he rode onwards, and indeed soon enough he saw for himself abundant signs of carnage. But the slaughter, if sudden, had been brief; for the Prince had given quarter to all who asked, and had been content to permit the escape of great numbers of raw youths, who, having been hastily levied during Simon's march, were ready to disperse in the extremity of terror, and could be trusted, once they reached the safe shelter of their own homes, not to tempt their fate by taking up arms again.

As for the plunder, that was something to boast of. Simon had made requisition all along the route from the friendly towns, and his mother had collected and furnished him with ample supplies. The horses taken were so numerous that the very pages and foot-boys of Edward's army could ride the steeds of knights, and the weary chargers which had brought the victors all those miles from Worcester could take their ease in the wake of the army, whilst the Prince, with fresh horses, rode forward as fast as he would.

For he had no desire to tarry here, nor to attempt to storm the fortress itself, with its small garrison and Lord Simon at the head. The Prince's great aim and object now was to meet the Earl in person on the battle-field, and to try conclusions with him once and for all, before he had had time to recover from the heavy blow struck him to-day, of which he could not yet be aware.

Hugh found him giving personal orders for a rapid march on Gloucester, with prisoners and booty, from which place he would next march against De Montfort's army, and overthrow it in open battle. The light of victory was already in Edward's eyes, and his cheerful confidence seemed to have communicated itself to all his host.

A touch upon his arm made Hugh look suddenly round, and he found himself face to face with his quondam comrade Gilbert Barbeck. Gilbert was not a man of war, but had fallen in with the Prince's army as he was taking a journey upon business. He had seen the battle and its result, and now spoke a word in Hugh's ear.

"Come," he said ; "I have somewhat to show thee."

And when Hugh followed him wonderingly, he added,—

"Dost remember how we fruitlessly pursued Roger de Horn into the forest long ago, and how he once and again escaped the fate he deserved ? Well, he has not escaped it to-day. He has been eating and drinking and sleeping with the soldiers of young De Montfort since they came here. And now he lies in the trench with the slain, and will trouble the earth no more. He has met the fate his deeds deserve, albeit not as we once desired."

Hugh started at the sound of these words, and followed Gilbert quickly to the spot where the soldiers of Edward were burying the slain. If indeed this thing were so, he ought to know it for a certainty.

"See there," said Gilbert, pointing downwards; "methinks there is no mistaking that face!"

Hugh looked, and a slight shiver took hold upon him.

"True enough," he answered briefly, as he turned away; "that is the dead face of him who was Roger de Horn."

So Lotta was a widow!

CHAPTER XXVIII.

THE FATAL FIGHT.

THE mellow light of an August evening was falling upon the cloistered walls of the Abbey of Evesham, and in deep thought a martial figure was pacing the smooth sward of the quadrangle formed by the various buildings.

The face of the Earl of Leicester was lined by care; but the light in the eyes was not quenched, and the old eagle look was even more marked than before, now that the features were more sharp and chiselled.

One of the monks approached the Earl, and waited till he should pause in his walk. Then he delivered his message.

"A party of riders has just arrived, asking for the Earl of Leicester, and one of them calls himself your son."

De Montfort started, and looked round him eagerly.

"My son? Then bid him come to me at once;" and as the monk retired, the Earl repeated slowly, "My son, my son—which son? Henry and Guy are with me. It can scarce be Simon. He will come with banners flying and the sound of martial triumph. Sure it must be Amalric, with news from my dear ones in the south. He comes in good time, I trust and hope, to witness another gallant victory."

At that moment there was a little stir, and a few figures appeared in the archway which divided the grassy quadrangle from the outer world. Over the Earl's face there flashed a look of welcome and pleasure.

" Amalric it is," he cried ; " come in a good hour, and with good tidings, I trust and hope," and he tenderly embraced his son as he spoke.

Amalric knew nothing of the misfortune which had overtaken his brother. His heart was full of hope, and he eagerly made answer,— —

" The hearts of the people are very warm in our cause. I have met with kindness and good-will wherever I have been. I have left my mother at Dover, where all men are her very loyal and true servants ; whilst at Oxford all hearts are with us, and I have even brought thence a few comrades, eager to serve 'neath our banner once again."

And with a wave of his hand he indicated some half-dozen youths, clustered together in the gateway, amid whom were numbered Leofric Wyvill and Jack Dugdale.

The Earl looked at them with a softening of his glance, and came and spoke them kindly words.

" I trust we shall again achieve a victory," he said. " If I can but join forces with my son, methinks all will be well. Yet he hath tarried overlong, and delay at such times is fraught with danger. The issue of the struggle is yet undetermined, and let none join with us who will not stand beside us in the moment of disaster. Faint-hearted soldiers never yet won battle."

But Amalric's little band were not faint-hearted, and none of them moved at this word, save to toss their caps in the air, and cry,—

"God save the Earl of Leicester, the saviour of the kingdom! Confusion to his enemies! Success to the noble Earl!"

De Montfort gave them thanks for their good-will, and after charging his friendly hosts to look to their bodily wants, he linked his arm within that of his son, and began discoursing with him of many things.

Amalric had good news to give of his mother and sister, and of the loyalty to the cause displayed by the governors of the Cinque Ports, who had refused to give up their fortresses at the demand of the King's son. Simon had been to Dover, and obtained supplies lately; Amalric was astonished that he had not already joined his father, and the Earl's face looked careworn and grave.

"My heart misgives me about Simon," he said. "He was always rash and headstrong. I summoned him a long while since to meet me, and join forces; and had he obeyed without question, we might perchance this day be standing victors once again. But instead of coming to me, he has been marching through the country gathering re-inforcements. These may serve us well, I do not doubt; yet sooner would I have had his help with a smaller band at an earlier date, than have waited all this while, with our enemies gathering strength daily. The Prince is nigh at hand, and he is no mean soldier, for all his rashness at the battle of Lewes. That blunder he is not likely to repeat, and I myself have trained him in the art of war on the Gascon plains. I trow he will not forget my lesson a second time!"

"And the King—where is he?" asked Amalric.

The Earl pointed to the chapel of the monastery.

"He is with us. He professes to call his son a rebel. Yet in his heart I know that he longs to see that rebellion crowned with success. Edward will place him once more on the throne, if he succeed; and he will again surround himself with foreign flatterers and sycophants. For ere that day dawn, the hearts of those who have beat high with love for their country's best weal will lie cold and still in death."

"Nay, father, say not so!" cried Amalric, with sudden pain in his voice, for it was not like the Earl thus to speak of impending disaster; his was rather a nature that looked forward to triumph and success.

"God grant it may not be so!" he answered; "but my heart is heavy within me this evening. I have a premonition that ere the sun set once more some great event will have befallen this land, but whether for weal or woe who can say?"

When Amalric that night joined Leofric in their quarters —a clean, bare cell, which they were to share together— he related to him all that his father had said.

"Dost think, good comrade, that a man, upon the eve of some great crisis in his life, can foresee what lies before him?"

Leofric shook his head doubtfully.

"Nay, I know not how that may be. Yet didst not thou thyself, Amalric, in bidding farewell to sweet Mistress Alys, speak as though thou didst portend misfortune to thy cause?"

"I trow I did," answered the youth, thoughtfully. "I know not how or why, but there came upon me the feeling that I was looking my last upon that sweet face, and I could have wept aloud had not my manhood cried shame upon such weakness. Yet methinks she saw somewhat of the trouble in my face, for ere we parted she did give me the ring from her hand, and never before had she given me token of her own to wear—nothing beyond that silken banner, which, if I fall to-morrow, Leofric, must be my shroud. Let it not fall into the hands of the foe. I would go down to my grave wrapped in its martial folds."

Leofric made no response, his heart was too full for words; and long after Amalric was sleeping quietly he lay broad awake, turning many things over in his mind, and wondering if this presage of evil, felt by both father and son, was a foreboding of some misfortune soon to fall upon them.

Leofric had had no intention a short time back of meddling more in wars. He was now a Master in Oxford, with a career before him there, and the profession of arms had no real charm for him. Yet when Amalric had suddenly appeared there, to take leave of Alys and of his old friends and comrades, and had told all he knew of the position of parties, and of the peril which threatened the cause dear to many through the action of the escaped Prince, Leofric's heart had burned within him, and it had seemed impossible to him to let his friend and once master ride forth perhaps to his death without his esquire at his side.

So Leofric had resolved once more to leave Oxford, once more to face the perils and uncertainties of war. There were others who were of like mind with him, and Amalric had gathered together a compact little body-guard, who had accompanied him upon the slightly circuitous route he had decided to take, and were with him now at Evesham Abbey, where he had joined his father.

Next morning, with the first dawn of the day, the little community was astir. Mass was said in the chapel, and the King and Earl, and all the more devout of the leaders and men, attended with pious devotion. Then they repaired to the refectory to breakfast, but had not been long seated before Nicholas, the Earl's barber and personal attendant, came running hastily in.

"Good news, my lord and gentlemen!" he cried, "good news, indeed! The banners of Lord Simon are approaching us from the direction of Kenilworth. He will be with us ere another hour has passed."

The Earl sprang to his feet in great excitement.

"Art sure they are the De Montfort banners, and not those of the Prince?" he asked; and Nicholas, who combined a knowledge of heraldry with other miscellaneous accomplishments usual in one of his craft, declared that he was absolutely certain of this, and described the banners he had seen, and their blazonry.

"These are without doubt the banners of my son," said the Earl; "I will myself mount the Abbey tower, and mark the order in which they advance."

The King calmly remained seated at table, and the Prior and many of the others remained with him; but the Earl and his son, and two or three others amongst whom was Leofric, ascended the tower, and gazed long and earnestly at the advancing host, which could plainly now be seen coming toward them.

The banners of De Montfort floated in the front ranks; but even as the Earl looked with sparkling eyes upon them, a sudden change was made. These banners were halted and sent to the rear, whilst the leopards of young Edward were now brought forward and placed in the van.

The Earl understood in a moment what had happened, and his face took a strange grey pallor.

"Simon has been overcome," he said; "his banners have been wrested from him. It is our foes, our victorious foes, who are marching to meet us—not our friends."

A moment of dead silence ensued, and then Amalric said with an air of cheerful confidence,—

"Let them come. We are here to meet them. We will show them battle without fear."

At this moment he felt his arm touched, and glancing round saw that Leofric was standing beside them with a white, troubled face. He did not speak, but only pointed in two directions different from that in which they had all been gazing. The Earl and his son looked too, and from Amalric's lips there broke a startled exclamation.

The Prince was advancing upon them from one point, but he was not the only assailant. Upon two other sides there now appeared the banners of Gloucester and Mortimer, hemming in the devoted little army of De Montfort upon flank and rear. The only unmenaced side was where the Avon with its flowing waters cut him off from all hope of retreat.

Truly the Prince had learned his lesson. This simultaneous advance showed a masterly generalship that was wholly unlike the headstrong recklessness which had characterized his actions only the previous year.

"By the arm of St. James," cried the Earl, "they come on right skilfully; they approach in admirable order. They have learned this style from me, not from themselves." Then turning towards his sons, who stood looking on in amaze, he said: "Let us commend our souls unto God; as for our bodies, they are our enemies'."

"Nay, father, do not despair!" cried Amalric passionately.

"I will not," answered the Earl sadly; "yet I fear me that the pride and rashness of my sons has been mine undoing. Our friends have been turned to foes by their haughtiness, and when peril threatened they have proved disobedient and unready."

Henry hung his head. He knew how often his father had had good cause to chide him for these very faults; and now throwing himself almost on his knees before his sire, he cried,—

"Father, if the fault be ours, let us bear the brunt of

the battle. Do thou fly whilst there be yet time, to be the prop and stay of the country another day. We will do our best to die like brave soldiers, and thou wilt avenge our fall when thou shalt return once more victorious."

Amalric would have joined his brother's plea, but the Earl spoke with almost stern decision.

"Far be it from me, my sons, to turn my back in the hour of peril. I have grown old in wars, and my life hastens to an end. There is that in my blood which will not let me flee before danger, for never, methinks, did our forefathers so fly. But you, my sons, do you retire, lest you perish in the flower of your youth—you who are to succeed me (God grant it) and prolong our race, illustrious in the glories of war."

But not one of the young men would consent to move. They would conquer or die, fighting at their father's side beneath the banner of De Montfort.

No time was to be lost in mustering the men and putting them in battle array. The situation was a desperate one. They were hemmed in on all sides. There was but one hope, and that a forlorn one--the chance of cutting their way through Edward's ranks before those of Gloucester and Mortimer could close up.

It was but little that Leofric saw of that desperate and fatal fight at Evesham. Soon after the impact of the deadly struggle, when foe met foe in unexampled fury, Amalric received a deadly wound, and falling upon his horse's neck, would have slipped to the ground and been trampled underfoot, had not Leofric and Jack, with the

energy and determination of despair, got him between
them, and by fighting every inch of the way with a
resolute valour which overcame all obstacles, bore him
at last into the precincts of the Priory, where they were
safe. Nor did Leofric omit to carry with him the precious
banner, which he knew his comrade was certain to ask for
if his eyes ever unclosed in this world again.

The good monks tended the dying youth with care and
skill, but knew from the first that the case was hopeless.
Leofric knelt beside him, striving to win one glance of recognition or one farewell word; and Jack hurried to and
fro between them and the tower, bringing news of the
battle, which was grimly fought, but which had been from
almost the first moment a hopeless struggle.

"The traitorous Welsh are flying! They will be our
undoing!" he cried. "They are fleeing away like smoke before the wind, causing confusion and dismay in our ranks!"

Amalric's eyes suddenly opened, as though something in
the urgency of Jack's tones had penetrated to his senses.

"The battle—how goes it?" he faintly asked.

"I fear me badly—for us," answered Leofric gently.

"My father?" questioned Amalric, with wistful eyes.

Leofric looked at Jack, who answered quickly,—

"I saw him fighting as though the strength of ten were
in him. I trow had we but fifty such as he, not all the
Princes and nobles in the land would turn the tide of fight
against us!"

Amalric's eyes opened more widely, and fixed themselves
upon Jack's face.

"Go, and bring me back word of him, good comrade," he said. "Ye should not have borne me hence. I would I might have fallen fighting by my noble father's side."

"It was his will that thou shouldst be taken out of the press," answered Leofric gently, and for a while the wounded man said no more; but presently he roused himself to ask, "Is there any hope for my life?"

Perhaps what he saw in Leofric's face was answer enough, for he said, as though he had received a reply,—

"Methought not. I feel my life ebbing away. I would seek the help and counsel of one of our good monks. But first, I have a charge to thee, my trusty friend and comrade. Thou hast the banner safe; thou wilt see that it is my shroud when they lay me in the dust. But take now this ring from my finger; I have somewhat to say to thee anent it."

Leofric obeyed, and gently took Alys's ring from the pulseless hand of his friend.

"Let me kiss it once," he said; "and then keep it for her, and give it back to her, telling her how I fell, and that I loved her to the last. But, Leofric, she hath never loved me, save with the love which a sister bears a brother, or as friend bears to friend. I have sought the other love, but I have found it not. Sweet she was, and gentle and tender, and her father approved my suit. But in my heart of hearts I knew that her love was never mine. Tell her I am well content now that it should be so. I die the easier for knowing that her heart will not be widowed. I doubt not that one day she will make another happy with that love which I trusted once myself to win."

This was not all spoken at once, but bit by bit as the dying man could gather strength. Leofric listened with a beating heart, holding the ring to the lips of his companion.

"Yet she gave you this token," he said.

"Yes, but only in that sort of pity and love with which a maid will always regard the departure, perhaps to his death, of one who has truly loved her. Methinks perhaps her heart, too, told her that we should meet no more. Sweet Alys, farewell, farewell. Now methinks I have done with life. It is after all but a battlefield to fit us for the haven of peace beyond. Pray God be with my father in his hour of extremity, and give to us a meeting on the other side!"

Leofric bent his head and spoke a low-toned Amen; then one of the monks approached to administer the last rites of the Church, and hear the faint confession breathed by those white lips.

How went the battle? Leofric was rent in twain by the desire to fling himself into that fight and die for the cause he had embraced, and by reluctance to leave his comrade whilst the spark of life still lingered.

Suddenly Jack came rushing back, his breastplate covered with blood, his sword recking, his whole aspect distraught. He had no horse under him, and he staggered slightly as he pressed onwards; but when Leofric sprang to his side, he said,—

"I am not wounded—would that I were—I am but choked with dust and reek. Undo my vizor and give me air. Leofric, the battle is ended. The great Earl is dead!"

"Dead!" cried Leofric, startled in spite of himself, and the look upon Jack's face as it was exposed to view corroborated his words.

"I could not get near him, though I fought like a fury. Methinks my right arm has slain a score of men this day. I cared not how soon they hewed me down, and yet I escaped. But I was near; I heard and saw, and I heard what they said of him. They brought him news that Lord Henry had fallen, whereat he grasped his sword in both hands and cried, 'By the arm of St. James, then is it time that I died also!' With that he laid about him right and left with such fury that men fell like thistles around him. But others pressed on from behind, and all called aloud upon him to surrender—to surrender—" and Jack drew his breath hard in rage and scorn.

"But he did not?"

"Didst think he would? Nay, his was no coward blood that would surrender to caitiff churls. I, even I, heard that clarion voice ring out once more amid the din of battle. 'Never will I surrender to dogs and perjurers!' it cried. 'To God alone will I yield. To Him I give up my spirit.' And even so saying he fell, pierced by a hundred wounds;" and there Jack suddenly broke off, with a look upon his face of concentrated fury which for the moment Leofric did not understand.

"And Lord Henry is dead, thou dost say? What of Lord Guy?"

"Wounded and made prisoner. Some say he too will die; but the Prince has given orders that he is to have every care. The Prince is a noble victor; but for those dogs that he allies himself with—"

Jack set his teeth as though he could say no more.

"What have they done?" asked Leofric breathlessly.

"Wellnigh hacked his body in pieces," cried Jack, with quivering lips. "Roger Mortimer claims one hand to send to his wife as a trophy. Another they vow shall be sent to the Countess of Leicester at Dover—his own wife, Leofric, his own loving wife! I trow if the Prior had not come forth from the gates, with his monks after him, and carried away the headless trunk, that it would have been truly hacked to pieces by the savages who surrounded it. They are even now carrying it devoutly into the chapel, to lay it beneath the altar. But the head, the hands, the feet— they cannot prevail to save those. Our great and noble Earl—to think that it should come to this with him!"

Jack turned away to hide the tears which bodily exhaustion and mental distress forced from his eyes. Leofric, with a shocked face, returned to the side of Amalric, where the monk still retained a place, although the rites were all concluded.

Amalric's eyes flashed open once more.

"My father?" he asked.

"Thou wilt see him soon; he has gone before thee," answered Leofric gently; and Amalric understood at once.

He closed his eyes with a faint smile. To him the strife
of arms, the clash of wills, the storm and stress of life,
meant nothing. He was drifting out upon an ocean where
such things had neither part nor lot. Perhaps in that
hour it soothed his spirit to know that his father had
passed thither before him. The things of time had no
concern for one who was launching forth upon the tide of
eternity.

"Is he dead too?" asked Jack, with a break in his
voice.

"It is better sometimes to die than to live," answered
Leofric softly in his ear. Then both knelt down by the
side of their comrade, and the monk commended the de-
parting soul into the hands of God. When they arose,
Amalric lay still with a smile upon his lips, and the monk,
folding the hands upon the mailed breast, said reverently,
"*Requiescat in pace.*"

Jack's sobs could not be controlled; Leofric's tears were
on his cheek, but he commanded himself, and whispered
a word in the ear first of the monk and then of his companion.

Together they lifted the inanimate form and reverently
carried it to the chapel, where before the altar, beneath a
velvet pall, lay the mutilated body of Simon de Montfort,
Earl of Leicester.

They laid Amalric down beside his father, and Leofric
spread over him the silken banner which had been worked
by the fingers of Alys and Linda.

It mattered not in the eyes of the monks that De

Montfort and his sons lay under the ban of papal excommunication. England had never altogether submitted to the tyranny of the Pope, and at a moment like this nothing was remembered by those pious men save that the Earl had fought a good fight, had been their friend and the friend of the people, and had died a hero's death upon the field of battle.

For long was it reported that marvellous miracles were performed by the remains of the slaughtered warrior, and he was regarded by a large portion of the nation as both saint and martyr. Many were the songs composed to his memory, most of them being in Norman-French, of which this may be cited as a specimen, showing how greatly the hearts of the people were wrapped up in him :—

> " I needs must sing, my heart so bids, although my words be drear ;
> With tearful eyes was made this song of England's barons dear,
> Who for the peace made long ago went down unto the grave,
> Their bodies maimed and mangled sore, our English land to save.
>   Now here lies low the flower of price,
>   Who knew so much of war,
>   Brave Montfort knight, his woful plight
>   The land shall long deplore.
>
> " But by his death the Earl Montfort the victory has won ;
> Like holy martyr Thomas, he to cruel death was done ;
> Like Thomas, would not that aught ill should holy Church betide ;
> Like Thomas, fought, and showing naught of flinching, like him died.
>   Now here lies low the flower of price,
>   Who knew so much of war,
>   Brave Montfort knight, his woful plight
>   The land shall long deplore."

NOTE.—Amalric de Montfort, though wounded and made prisoner, did not really perish upon the field of Evesham.

CHAPTER XXIX.

LEOFRIC'S REWARD.

STRANGE as it may appear, it was with tears in his
eyes that Edward, the victorious Prince, attended
the obsequies of his two cousins, Henry and Amalric de
Montfort, after the fatal fight of Evesham. He and
Henry had been playfellows in childhood and comrades
in youth. The tie between them had not been broken
even when one was a captive and the other his jailer.
Warmly as he had espoused his father's cause when it
came to a question of arms, Edward had always felt a
deep respect for the policy of his uncle, and would have
kept the peace between the rival factions had he had
power to do so. It was with sorrow of heart that he
looked on whilst the grave closed over two such brave
young warriors. He had already given orders that every
attention should be bestowed upon the wounded Guy, and
had even expressed a hope that he might be permitted to
join his mother as soon as his wounds were sufficiently
healed for it to be safe for him to travel.

Although elated by his victory, and the object of an
immense amount of praise and laudation, Edward was not

puffed up by his success, and strove to influence his father
to act with moderation and liberal-mindedness. He had
not been able to save the corpse of the Earl from dishonour and despite; but he was resolved to let all the
world know that he was not ashamed to show affection
and respect for the sons of the great noble, or disposed
to put on one side his own near relationship to them.

He would not be dissuaded from attending in person
the obsequies of his cousins, and it was when standing at
their grave that his glance suddenly rested upon the bowed
head and pale face of Leofric.

"I would speak with that youth," said he to Hugh,
who chanced to be near at hand; "bid him come presently
to my tent."

So later in the day Leofric once more stood face to
face with the King's son.

Leofric had never attempted to fly from the scene of
the battle. He scarce knew whether he was ranked as a
prisoner or not. No one had spoken to him or molested
him. It seemed as though the common bond of brother-
hood had now asserted itself amidst the ranks of the rival
hosts. The leaders of the rebellion (as it would soon be
termed) would doubtless receive punishment in the form
of fines and confiscations when there was time to consider
their cases; but the Prince was in favour of a general
amnesty to rank and file; and though the adherents of
the Barons were melting away like snow in a thaw, no
attempt was made to keep them. They were, for the
most part, suffered to depart to their own homes. Num-

bers had laid down their lives in the slaughter of the battle day; the rest were free to return whence they had come. Leofric was meditating a journey to Oxford as soon as he should be fit for the long ride: but both he and Jack had had little heart to think of their own affairs, their distress at the loss of the cause and of so many true friends and comrades having for the time being driven all else from their minds. They had, however, the previous evening decided that there was nothing left for them to do here after the morrow, and had settled that upon the following day they would set forth for Oxford, taking with them a few mementos of their fallen hero, and carrying to Mistress Alys the last message and token of her whilom lover Amalric de Montfort.

This summons from the Prince, however, might possibly cause a change in their plan. Jack looked a little apprehensive as he heard it; but Leofric had no fear. He had faith in the good-will of Edward.

"Thou canst come too, good Jack," said Hugh, who had brought the message from the King's son. "He has some words to speak to many of those who have served under the De Montfort banner. Be in nowise afraid. He is a right noble Prince, and meaneth well to all."

When Jack and Leofric reached the tent where Prince Edward had preferred to establish himself—leaving the quarters in the Abbey for his father and the older nobles—they found awaiting them, just without, several of the Oxford students who had joined Amalric at the last, and had been present at the fatal fight of Evesham. Together

they all entered the presence of the Prince, conducted by
Hugh le Barbier and Gilbert Barbeck, who seemed to have
the oversight of this matter.   Gilbert had joined the Prince
shortly before the march on Kenilworth, bringing him supplies of money which had been entrusted to him by his
father.   It was reassuring to the students to see these comrades of theirs at such a moment, and to feel that there
was no ill meant them.

Within the tent stood Prince Edward, his face grave
and thoughtful, but wearing a look of friendliness also.
He returned with courtesy the salutations made to him,
and then began to address the youths who stood silently
before him.

" My friends," he said, " I have desired to see you and
to speak with you face to face, and therefore have I had
you brought thus privately to my quarters here.   England
has just been through a time of terrible trial, and I hope
and believe that the benefits of this great struggle will not
quickly pass away.   War is a fearful thing at all times,
but tenfold worse when waged betwixt brethren.   I trust
that the sword sheathed to-day will not be again drawn
in such a fashion.   Brethren should live together in unity
and peace.   Is it not so ? "

He looked around him as he spoke, and only Leofric
dared to make reply.

" Yes truly, sire, if peace can walk hand in hand with
honour and freedom."

Edward gave him a piercing glance.

" I know what thou wouldst say Leofric Wyvill, and

in part thou art right.--I stand before you here this day
to testify to the love and reverence I bear to a great man
who has passed away from this world, who has died the
death of a hero. Though I be the King's son, and though
I myself bore arms against the great Earl mine uncle, yet
here I stand before you, and boldly avow that the cause in
which he laid down his life was a noble one, and that I
bear no enmity towards those who fought at his side,
even though they fought against me. Can you understand
this, my friends ? "

A murmur of assent went up from the wondering group.
They had little expected such an avowal from Prince
Edward ; and yet, to those who knew him and his history,
there was nothing incompatible in his words and actions.
Duty to his father and to his own position had forced him
to rise against the usurper of the royal prerogative and
the custodians of his own and his father's person ; nevertheless he fully and candidly recognized the justice of the
cause in which his foes had embarked, and even gave it
in no small measure his sympathy.

" You will ask why I say all this to you," he said ; " but
I will soon explain myself. You come from a city which
has been forward in the cause of the Barons, a seat of
learning, whose voice must ever weigh with the people.
For the moment the cause you have at heart is, or seems
to be, lost. Its leader is dead, its army cut to pieces, its
fugitives straggling back to their own homes. Yet the
feelings which gave rise to the movement are not dead.
They live immortal in the hearts of a free people ; and if

the teachers and leaders of that people's thought preach once more a national crusade, doubtless leaders could be found to bring an army again into the field."

The youths looked at one another with a covert surprise. It was strange to hear their Prince speaking to them thus.

Edward noted their glances, and a slight smile crossed his handsome face. He looked earnestly upon his listeners.

" My friends," he said, " I speak to you thus freely because I have somewhat to ask of you. I pray you use all the influence you possess with your comrades and townsmen, and preach to them the doctrine of patience. If they will but be patient a few years, I trow that the causes of complaint will speedily be removed. Listen, and I will further explain. My father grows old. Twice has he been wounded; his powers are failing him somewhat. It may be that his life will not be greatly prolonged; or that if it is, he will take his son, mine unworthy self, more fully into his counsels. I cannot honestly believe that he himself will greatly change his methods or his habits. Change comes easily enough to the young, but not to the old. I fear that many abuses will be revived, but I trust and hope that it will not be for long. I am growing of an age to claim my share in the government, and to speak openly to my father. The people, I think, have some love for me, and I desire their welfare with my whole heart. In all things I shall seek to counsel my father to wise measures, and to a policy akin to that which the Barons have so long and vehemently urged upon him. If

in course of time I should sit upon England's throne, I
will strive to profit by the lessons learned in these days
of struggle and adversity, and to rule wisely and well. I
have never loved my father's foreign favourites. I would
surround myself with native-born counsellors; I would
withstand the unlawful tyranny of the Pope; I would
have England to be a free and prosperous country—prosperous at home and respected abroad. That is what I
shall seek to attain to if ever I sit upon her throne.
Wherefore, my friends, preach patience to those from
whom ye have come, if they speak bitterly of those
things which have been done. Seek not to raise up
another leader, but wait till your Prince can with honour
be the leader and head of his people. Believe me, I love
the English nation, and will never patiently see the poor
trampled under foot, or the charters of the nation set
aside. Only have patience, only wait awhile, and all will
be well."

These sincere and politic words were eagerly listened to
by the Oxford students, and received with a buzz of
applause. It was indeed a hopeful sign that the heir to
the throne should thus address them. They knew well
that for the present it would be hopeless to renew the
struggle; and yet that the nation, having begun to assert
her rights, even at the sword's point and in the teeth of
royal oppression, would not easily be content to forego the
ground once won. But if she could be taught to regard
the coming King as her best champion, how much misery
and wretchedness might be spared! Leofric's face kindled

at the thought, and there was an eager look in the eyes of all which told the Prince that his words had been understood and appreciated, and that he had won himself friends and advocates in the heart of one of the most important cities of the kingdom.

Then Prince Edward dismissed the greater part of his guests with words of courteous thanks and good-will; but he signed to Leofric to remain behind, and Jack remained with him.

"And now, my good friend," he said, very graciously, "I have long desired to redeem my pledge, and to reward thee for the service thou once didst render to me. Hitherto I have had small chance of keeping my promise, but for all that it has never been forgotten."

Leofric spoke a few words disclaiming any service; but the Prince cut him short.

"Twice hast thou rendered to me notable service," he said: "once when thou didst risk thy life in the forest of Kenilworth to save me from the furious assault of the boar; and again when thou didst bring timely notice to Kenilworth of the attempt to be made upon mine uncle's life, which attempt, if successful, would have been laid, however unjustly, at the door of my mother, or perhaps even at mine own, seeing that I was a captive guest within those walls, having intercourse with friends from without. I have owed thee this debt of gratitude for long. But the time has come when thou shalt receive thy reward;" and the smile in the Prince's eyes was frank, and pleasant to see.

"I have taken counsel, therefore, with our good friend and thy comrade Hugh as to what may be done for thee. I would have bestowed upon thee a fair manor, where thou couldst have lived at ease; but he has told me that thine heart is inclined to learning, and that at Oxford, perchance, a career of honour lies before thee. I would have placed thee in some vacant benefice if thine heart did incline to the Church; but as it is not so, I must wait till thou art something older ere I can place thee in some office which thy talents will adorn."

Leofric made a grateful bow. To have the favour of the heir to the throne was no small matter in those days. He might well look forward to a career of great success and honour if he were marked out by the royal favour.

"Meantime," added the Prince, "I have instructed the steward of Beaumont Palace to pay to thee one hundred marks year by year; and when thou hast become a notable disputer, lecturer, doctor, perhaps, and when thou art ready for a change, there will be promotion and honour awaiting thee elsewhere. I shall not forget one who was so faithful in his friendship to a losing cause, and who was so well beloved by those whom I loved well."

A sudden quiver in the Prince's voice betokened a wave of unwonted emotion. He had been deeply attached to the De Montfort family, despite political differences, and he knew how Leofric had followed Amalric, and had been with him at the moment of his death. This formed a strong link between them now, and as Leofric would have stammered out his thanks for this great and wonderful gift, the Prince held out his hand suddenly, and said,—

"Farewell, good Leofric; we shall meet again. Be thou as true and faithful as thou hast ever been, and happiness and success will surely attend thee."

Leofric bent the knee, pressed his lips to the hand of the Prince, and then, making a deep obeisance, he retired from the tent, Jack following him open-mouthed with amazement.

He broke into loud exclamations of delight.

"One hundred marks a year! Why, good comrade, thou wilt be rich for life!" he cried. "Thou canst take a Hall of thine own, and become rich and prosperous. Or thou canst wed Mistress Alys—"

But there Jack was brought to a sudden standstill by the look upon his comrade's face. Leofric flushed crimson, and then turned pale, and said almost sternly,—

"Jack, Jack, thy tongue doth run away with thee. Dost thou not know by whom the Mistress Alys was beloved?"

Jack grew red in his turn, but he muttered beneath his breath, half afraid that Leofric might hear,—

"Marry, I know well enough who loved her, but maidens do not always return the love of their finest suitors."

Leofric's cheek was rather flushed; Jack could not say whether he had heard these words or not. He returned to his first theme.

"At least thou canst hire a Hall, and scholars will flock

to thee. Thou wilt be renowned for thy lectures, and
wilt become a Regent Master, if thou dost not 'incept' in
theology or law, and wear the Doctor's gown. Thy fortune
is secure now, and some day, doubtless, when the Prince
has ascended the throne (which pray Heaven may be
soon), he will raise thee to great honour and dignity; for
methinks he hath a princely heart, and hath taken a
mighty liking for thee."

"But thou shalt not leave me, Jack," cried Leofric,
"even though we have a grander lodging than we have
known before. Thou wert my first friend. Thou hast
stood at my side in many an hour of peril. If I have
won the crown of success, thou hast merited a share in it.
Thou art a bachelor thyself, and thou shalt assist me in
my lectures, and use my school for thine own. We will
not part company. We have travelled too long the same
road. Thou hast throughout been my faithful friend.
Thou wilt not desert me now?"

Jack gripped his friend's hand hard, and there was a
huskiness in his voice as he declared that he desired
nothing better than to remain always by his comrade's side.

A few days later the camp broke up; but Hugh had
declared that Leofric and Jack must pay a visit to his
house before they journeyed to Oxford, and Jack was
desirous to travel by way of his own home and see his
relatives ere he took up his abode once again at the seat
of learning.

So first they journeyed to Worcester, eager to hear
news of Lotta, whose strange history had been related to

them, and whose tidings, brought to Prince Edward so promptly, had been the immediate cause of the defeat of De Montfort.

Already the country had begun to assume a more peaceful aspect. Traces of war's ravages were everywhere only too visible, but it was plain that the overthrow and death of the Earl of Leicester had for the moment crushed in the hearts of the people any idea of further fighting. They revered his memory, they mourned and wept for him, they regarded him as a martyr and a hero; but there was no one upon whom his mantle could fall, and the hopes of the nation gradually began to centre in Prince Edward; for the King's life had already lasted beyond the ordinary limits attained in those days, and it might well be that before long his son would succeed him upon the throne.

The news of the victory at Evesham had preceded Hugh to his home, but not that of his personal safety, so that his arrival sound and whole was the signal for great demonstrations of delight throughout the household.

Hardly had the little cavalcade ridden into the courtyard before Linda was at her husband's side, welcoming him with tears of joy; and she had a very gracious and joyful greeting to give to Leofric and Jack, both of whom seemed so closely linked with her past life.

The board was quickly laid, the hungry travellers sat down, and breathlessly did father, mother, and wife listen to the story of the bloody fight at Evesham, and the death of the great Earl and his sons.

Linda's tears fell as she heard of Amalric's death. She

had known him well in old days, and there was something
about him which always won the hearts of those with
whom he came in contact.

"I can be thankful now," she said in a low voice to
Leofric, "that sweet Alys never truly yielded him her heart.
She loved him as friend and brother, but she never gave
him the treasure he longed to possess. There have been
moments when I have been almost sad at heart to see this,
but now I can rejoice."

Leofric's face changed colour a little.

"My Lord Amalric said somewhat of this to me as he
lay dying," he answered, in a low voice; "yet I had
thought that he and the maiden were very much one to
the other, and that their betrothal was nigh at hand."

"In truth they might, had things gone otherwise, have
been betrothed by the act of their elders; but the heart
of Alys was not truly his. I have not lived with her as
sister and friend all those years without knowing that much."

Leofric said no more. A thoughtful look settled upon
his face, and into his eyes there began to creep a new
look. He did not care to ask himself what the hope was
which suddenly awakened in his heart, but it seemed in
some strange way to change and glorify his whole life.

Hugh now claimed his wife's attention. He asked news
of Lotta, and heard that she was recovering strength slowly,
but that her mind seemed strangely affected. She appeared
to be losing hold upon recent events, and was going back
more and more to their childhood's days. She spoke constantly of their mother, and asked for her, and wondered

when she should "go home!" Linda did not think she now remembered that she was the wife of Roger de Horn, and heard the news of his death with feelings of great relief.

"I trust it is not wicked, but I cannot grieve for him. I do not think Lotta would even understand if told: from that night when you brought her here and went away, everything seems to have been gradually fading from her mind that belongs to the stormy and unhappy part of her life. I believe now that if I were to take her to mother and Aunt Bridget at Eynsham, where I lived so peacefully and happily myself, she would be perfectly happy there; and that mother would be the happier for having a daughter to love and tend."

For Linda had recently heard that her mother was a widow, and had retired to live with her sister at Eynsham. Balzani had never really recovered from the shock of hearing the manner of his son's death, and had shortly afterwards taken a fever and died. It would no doubt be a comfort to the widow to have one of her children back again with her, especially if she needed motherly care and tendance.

So it was quickly arranged that as soon as Lotta could bear the fatigues of a journey, she should be carried by easy stages to Eynsham; whilst Linda should take this opportunity of paying a visit to Alys, who had earnestly prayed her at parting not to be too long without coming to see them.

Leofric and Jack would visit their old homes—the farm and the monks of St. Michael—and join the other party as they approached Oxford. Leofric had the messages and the token to deliver to Alys from Amalric, and greatly would he have feared this part of his task had it not been for Linda's words.

They often talked of Alys as they paced the alleys of the garden together during the few days that Leofric remained the guest of Hugh, recalling the past days of their student life in Oxford, and how strangely fortune had dealt with them, throwing them together, and into the company of the Constable's daughter.

Now Linda was the wife of a prosperous gentleman, who by the favour of the Prince had good prospects of rising to knighthood ; and Leofric, from being a poor clerk, almost of the begging class, was a Master, a man of some substance, as riches went in those days, and could, as Linda once softly suggested, " mate with any maiden, even of a noble house, for his learning and the prospect held out to him of princely favour."

Then a red flush crept into Leofric's cheek, and he made answer,—

" There is only one maiden in all the world for me ; and how can I dare to hope that she will have thought to spare for so humble a suppliant as myself ? "

" Thou hadst better ask her what she thinks of the suppliant," said Linda softly. " Methinks a faint heart beseems not an earnest wooer."

Leofric gave her a searching look.

" Mistress Linda, what dost thou mean ? " he questioned.

She looked at him with a smile in her eyes.

" Thou hadst better ask Alys what I mean."

CHAPTER XXX.

ON THE STILL ISIS.

THE breath of spring was in the air. The verdant meadows had put on their rich new dress, and the flowers were springing up as if to welcome the returning strength and heat of the sun. The fritillaries gemmed the river-banks, and the stretches of woodland were blue with the carpet of fragrant wild hyacinth. The song of the cuckoo was in the air, and on north slopes the star-like primrose lingered yet. The chill east winds were changed to soft, summer-like zephyrs from the south, and everything in nature spoke of joy and hope and coming summer-tide.

Between its green banks, fringed sometimes by stately forest trees; meandering sometimes through wide stretches of green pasture, where cattle fattened upon the rich herbage or stood knee-deep in the shallow tide, the silent Isis slipped leisurely along.

Passing the Abbey of Eynsham, it widened out to a considerable breadth as it pursued its leisurely course towards the city of Oxford, seeming to linger lovingly in these pleasant reaches, far from the tumult and stir which surrounds the abodes of man.

The sun shone lovingly down upon the green world, and upon the shining, silver river, on this bright day in May. A boat was drifting slowly along the tide, propelled sometimes by the strong arms of the rower, at others idly lying upon the bosom of the stream, gently floating downwards with the slow, still current. Half-way betwixt Oxford and Eynsham two fishermen on the banks awaited the return of the tardy boat; but engrossed by their occupation, and soothed by the soft stillness of the afternoon, they were in no haste for its arrival. They had met with considerable success in pursuit of their craft, and a number of shining fish lay upon the bank beside them.

Edmund de Kynaston and Jack Dugdale were the fishermen; the fair Alys and Leofric Wyvill were the occupants of the boat.

They had all started forth together, with the intention of paying a visit to Lotta and her mother; but in the end the temptations of the river had proved too much for the anglers. Instead of waiting till they reached the pool near Eynsham, they had been landed some miles lower down; and whilst Alys and Leofric pursued the original plan, they remained engrossed by their sport, in no hurry at all for the return of their companions.

Nor did those companions appear in any haste to rejoin them.

Eight years had passed away since Leofric, an almost penniless lad, had first entered Oxford, uncertain whether or not he should ever succeed in maintaining himself there. Now, although not yet five-and-twenty, he had achieved many successes and distinctions, and was regarded by the authorities of the place as a promising young Master, secure of honours and rewards. He had become the recipient of royal bounty, and was in a position of modest affluence, which seemed to him almost like riches.

Already he had in part carried out the plan suggested by Jack when first the knowledge of the Prince's generosity had been made known to them. One hundred marks represented something like sixty pounds, and sixty pounds in those days was equivalent to several hundreds in our times. It was positive wealth to Leofric, and enabled him to enter at once upon a new phase of his career.

Since the exodus of students from Oxford a couple of years before, the Halls and houses had not filled up to quite their former strength, and there were still buildings to be had at moderate rentals. Leofric found a couple of houses in Cat Street, which their owner was glad enough to rent to a man of substance. One of these Leofric retained for a dwelling-house for himself and his friend and assistant Jack, turning the lower floor into a commodious lecture-hall, and repairing and furnishing the upper story for his own use, although it was larger than he required at present.

The second house was speedily furnished as a Hall for clerks and students, and already was full to overflowing. The personal popularity of the young Master was great, and his determination to accept as his pupils only men who really desired to study, and who would refrain from joining in the tumults and riots of the city, made something of a new departure amongst the keepers of Halls, and attracted at once the better sort of student, to whom a quiet place of abode, where study was the rule, was regarded in the light of a boon and a blessing. The Chancellor had expressed great approval of the rules boldly laid down by Leofric for the regulation of his house, and Jack was invaluable to him in assisting him to carry out his plan.

Leofric had recognized the fact that in order to keep his pupils within reasonable bounds he must make their quarters comfortable. How could they be expected to remain at home after dark if lights and fires were denied them, and if the rooms they lived in were kept foul, ill-smelling, and wretched? So simple were the ideas as to plenishing and furnishing in those days, that Leofric found it easy to provide for his pupils comfort sufficient to render his Hall the favourite throughout Oxford. He insisted on cleanliness, and by doing his own share to ensure it, stimulated the lads to second his efforts. They paid him rather more than some Hall Masters asked (save those who were really poor yet honestly studious, to whom he showed himself liberal and generous); but they received a liberal diet, comforts undreamed of in other places, good fires in cold weather, lights after dark, liberty to play reasonably quiet games in the lecture-room if desired, and a well-aired and cleanly dormitory to sleep in.

Already many nobles and prelates had sent their sons to Leofric, and he had been obliged to refuse applications from some of the most notable men of the day. The

Chancellor was urging him to open another Hall; and already it was being whispered that if the schemes already being discussed for the foundation of regular colleges should be carried out, Leofric Wyvill would be the man to place over such an institution.

Leofric was keenly interested in these proposed schemes, and had held many discussions with those in authority upon that very subject. It was evident to all that the present condition of Oxford must be reformed; that the massing together in one place of hundreds and thousands of lads and men, under no regular discipline and control, was likely to lead to grave evils, and had been the cause of an infinite amount of bloodshed and confusion.

Walter de Merton and John Balliol had already given endowments, and the question of the establishment of colleges, where students should reside beneath sufficient oversight and control, was being earnestly discussed. Probably other benefactors would come forward when once a start had been made; and there seemed little doubt that in the near future Leofric would obtain a high place as Master or Dean of one of these proposed buildings.

Leofric's personal popularity was great, and his position rather unique. He was the favourite of the Prince, from whom he received an annual bounty; so that all those who supported the royal cause regarded him with favour. But he was also known as the friend of the De Montforts, as one who had fought side by side with young Amalric at the battles of Lewes and Evesham. A halo of glory therefore surrounded him in the eyes of those who

favoured the popular cause, and all men listened to him
with respect and enthusiasm, as to a man who had seen
great things, had shared in the most notable movement of
the day, and had covered himself with glory and renown.
For all sorts of stories were afloat about his prowess and
valour, many of which he had combated in vain. He was
fain to submit at last to be regarded in the light of a
hero, though marvelling not a little at having won such
a reputation.

His position, however, was assured. Although a layman,
and resolved to remain one, he saw before him a career full
of possibilities. He knew that his advancement would be
more rapid if he consented to take orders, but he had
never wavered in his resolve against so doing. A man
might now advance to high distinction even in the University, and yet remain a layman, and Leofric had never been
tempted for a moment to the clerical vocation. Perhaps
some amongst his closer friends knew the reason why.

He had been admitted to the Castle for long as the
friend both of Edmund and his father. The Constable
liked and respected him, and his successes had made him
rather a notable man. The death of Amalric had taken
some hold upon the minds and hearts of the De Kynastons,
who had loved him well, and regarded him almost in the
light of Alys's betrothed husband.

She herself had been much affected by the story of his
death, and had looked pale and pensive for some time.
But to-day her cheek had regained its bloom, her eyes
were bright and soft, and her voice and laugh showed a

heart where happiness had made its home, and from which sorrow and pain had been banished.

A journey by water to Eynsham was always a treat to Alys. Linda and she corresponded as regularly as the uncertainty of messengers would permit; and when she heard from her former companion, she always sought to take news of her to the mother and sister dwelling beneath the Priory walls.

Lotta had never recovered from the effects of her strange illness. Her mind remained a blank as to the events of her stormy girlhood. She was like a gentle child, living in the present, or in the more remote past, happy with her mother, and always eager for news of her sister, yet without any real comprehension or memory of the events which had transpired during the past eight years.

The news to-day was of an exceptionally happy nature. Linda was the mother of a fair son, and Hugh had received knighthood and the gift of a goodly Manor at the hands of the Prince. There had been extensive confiscations of the estates of the supporters of the De Montforts, and the Prince had not forgotten Hugh when he came to distribute this spoil amongst those who had served him at the critical time of his career.

Having brought tidings of these good things to Lotta and her mother, Leofric and Alys were on their way to rejoin their companions; but the beauty of the day, and the warmth of the sunshine upon the flowing river, tempted them to idleness. They were talking of past days, and of how the friendship between them had grown and grown.

"The first time I saw you," said Alys, " was when you lifted me from my palfrey, that day when he was frightened and nearly threw me to the ground. How little we thought then of all that would happen later!"

"Indeed yes," he answered earnestly. " Looking back to those days, it all seems like a dream ; and yet, Alys, I think I loved thee from that very day. Dost know that thou hast always been to me a bright particular star, set high above me in the sky, yet leading me ever onwards. Alys, sweetheart, I have waited long, but tell me I have not waited in vain. Hope has sprung up in my heart of late. Sweet Alys, dost thou love me ?"

· A beautiful light leaped into her eyes. She put out a hand and laid it upon his.

"I think I have loved thee always, Leofric," she said.

THE END.